Minority Rights in Central and Eastern Europe

Minority rights is an important issue in all modern states, but for those countries hoping to join the European Union, the protection of minorities is a key condition for success in the accession process. This book provides a comprehensive assessment of minority rights in Central and Eastern Europe, covering all the countries that have joined the EU since 2004, including Poland, Czech Republic, Hungary, Slovenia, Estonia, Lithuania, Latvia, Slovakia, Romania and Bulgaria. For each country it outlines the major developments since 1989, highlights the salient issues in minority rights politics, assesses the actual implementation of policies and legislation, explores the roles that domestic and international factors have played – including the impact of the EU accession process – and discusses whether there have been any major changes once EU accession was secured. Overall, this book is important for all those interested in European integration and minority rights politics, as well as for specialists on Central and Eastern Europe.

Bernd Rechel is Postdoctoral Research Fellow at the Centre for Russian and East European Studies at Birmingham University, UK. He has published widely on minority rights in Central and Eastern Europe and is author of *The Long Way Back to Europe: Minority Protection in Bulgaria.*

BASEES/Routledge series on Russian and East European studies

Series editor: Richard Sakwa
Department of Politics and International Relations, University of Kent

Editorial Committee:
Julian Cooper, Centre for Russian and East European Studies, University of Birmingham
Terry Cox, Department of Central and East European Studies, University of Glasgow
Rosalind Marsh, Department of European Studies and Modern Languages, University of Bath
David Moon, Department of History, University of Durham
Hilary Pilkington, Department of Sociology, University of Warwick
Stephen White, Department of Politics, University of Glasgow

Founding Editorial Committee Member:
George Blazyca, Centre for Contemporary European Studies, University of Paisley

This series is published on behalf of BASEES (the British Association for Slavonic and East European Studies). The series comprises original, high-quality, research-level work by both new and established scholars on all aspects of Russian, Soviet, post-Soviet and East European Studies in humanities and social science subjects.

1 **Ukraine's Foreign and Security Policy, 1991–2000**
   Roman Wolczuk

2 **Political Parties in the Russian Regions**
   Derek S. Hutcheson

3 **Local Communities and Post-Communist Transformation**
   Edited by Simon Smith

4 **Repression and Resistance in Communist Europe**
   J.C. Sharman

5 **Political Elites and the New Russia**
   Anton Steen

6 **Dostoevsky and the Idea of Russianness**
   Sarah Hudspith

Minority Rights in Central and Eastern Europe

Edited by Bernd Rechel

Routledge
Taylor & Francis Group

LONDON AND NEW YORK

Transferred to digital printing 2010
First published 2009
by Routledge
2 Park Square, Milton Park, Abingdon, Oxon, OX14 4RN

Simultaneously published in the USA and Canada
by Routledge
270 Madison Ave, New York, NY 10016

Routledge is an imprint of the Taylor & Francis Group, an informa business

Typeset in Times New Roman by Wearset Ltd, Tyne and Wear

British Library Cataloguing in Publication Data
A catalogue record for this book is available from the British Library

Library of Congress Cataloging in Publication Data
Minority rights in Central and Eastern Europe / edited by Bernd Rechel.
p. cm. – (BASEES/Routledge series on Russian and East European
studies; 54)
Includes bibliographical references and index.
1. Minorities–Civil rights–Europe, Eastern. 2. Minorities–Civil rights–
Europe, Western. 3. Europe, Eastern—Ethnic relations. 4. Europe,
Central–Ethnic relations. I. Rechel, Bernd, 1970–
JC599.E92M56 2009
323.143–dc22   2008030176

ISBN10: 0-415-45185-X (hbk)
ISBN10: 0-415-59031-0 (pbk)
ISBN10: 0-203-88365-9 (ebk)

ISBN13: 978-0-415-45185-7 (hbk)
ISBN13: 978-0-415-59031-0 (pbk)
ISBN13: 978-0-203-88365-5 (ebk)

Contents

Illustrations

Figures

Maps

Tables

Contributors

Stefan Auer is Senior Lecturer in History and Politics at La Trobe University in Melbourne. He is the author of *Liberal Nationalism in Central Europe* (Routledge, 2004) which investigates nationalism and democracy in the Czech Republic, Poland and Slovakia.

Dovile Budryte is Associate Professor of International Studies at Georgia Gwinnett College. Her research interests include democratization and nationalism. She has published a book and several articles on ethnic politics and the role of historical memory in the Baltic states.

David J. Galbreath is Lecturer in the Department of Politics and International Relations at Aberdeen University. He has written a number of publications about minority rights in the Baltic states, including the book *Nation-Building and Minority Politics in Post-Socialist States: Interests, Influence and Identities in Estonia and Latvia* (2005).

Rainer Hofmann is Professor in Public, International and European Law at the Johann Wolfgang Goethe University in Frankfurt. He has written extensively about international minority rights and their application to national contexts and was President of the Advisory Committee for the Council of Europe Framework Convention for the Protection of National Minorities between 1998 and 2004.

Kristina Kallas is Lecturer at the Department of Political Science, University of Tartu. Her main research interests are nationalism and citizenship issues and integration policies. She is currently consulting for the Estonian government in developing a new national integration programme.

Nils Muižnieks is Director of the Advanced Social and Political Research Institute at the University of Latvia, former Latvian Minister for Social Integration, and Member of the European Commission against Racism and Intolerance.

Vello Pettai is Professor of Comparative Politics at the University of Tartu. He has published on ethnopolitics in the Baltic states in *Nations and Nationalism*, *Post-Soviet Affairs*, *Nationalities Papers* and *Journal of Baltic Studies*. From 1997 to 1999 he was advisor on minority affairs to the President of Estonia.

Vilana Pilinkaite-Sotirovic is Lecturer at the European Humanities University and project coordinator at the Centre for Equality Advancement, Vilnius, Lithuania. In 2001–03 she worked as a senior officer at the Department of National Minorities under the Government of Lithuania. Currently she is actively involved in the activities of European Network Against Racism. Her research interests include human rights, equality and non-discrimination policies in Lithuania and the EU.

Melanie H. Ram is Assistant Professor of Political Science at California State University, Fresno and Research Associate at the Institute for European, Russian and Eurasian Studies at The George Washington University. Her research over the last decade has focused on European Union enlargement and Central and East European reform, with a particular focus on minority rights, the Roma, Romania, and the Czech Republic.

Bernd Rechel is Postdoctoral Research Fellow at the Centre for Russian and East European Studies at Birmingham University (UK). He has published widely on minority rights in Central and Eastern Europe and is the author of the book *The long way back to Europe: minority protection in Bulgaria* (2008).

Gwendolyn Sasse is Professorial Fellow at Nuffield College, University of Oxford. She has written many publications on minority protection in Central and Eastern Europe and is the author of *Europeanization and Regionalization in EU's Enlargement to Central and Eastern Europe. The Myth of Conditionality* (Palgrave, 2004).

Guido Schwellnus is Researcher at the Centre for Comparative and International Studies at ETH Zurich. He has published widely on minority rights in Europe and the Eastern enlargement of the EU.

Eva Sobotka is working as Human Rights Officer at the EU Agency for International Rights in Vienna. She is author of several articles on Roma, national minorities, and human rights. Her research has focused on EU enlargement, influence of international norms on policy making at national level, multilevel governance of fundamental rights, and conflict resolution.

Peter Vermeersch is Associate Professor in East European Politics at the University of Leuven and Postdoctoral Research Fellow of the Belgian National Fund for Scientific Research. He is the author of several journal articles on minority politics and ethnic mobilization in Central Europe and has recently published the book *The Romani Movement: Minority Politics and Ethnic Mobilization in Contemporary Central Europe* (Berghahn Books, 2006).

Balázs Vizi is Research Fellow at the Research Institute of Ethnic and National Minorities at the Hungarian Academy of Sciences and Lecturer at the Department of International Law at Budapest Corvinus University. He has published several articles on minority rights in Europe and his research interest is focused on minority protection in the context of European integration.

Jelka Zorn is Lecturer at the Faculty of Social Work at the University of Ljubljana. Her areas of research and teaching include asylum, immigration and citizenship issues in Slovenia. She is active in NoBorder networks and in advocacy campaigns for the rights of the Erased.

Acknowledgements

I would like to express my gratitude to all the authors for their hard work and enthusiasm in this project. Financial support for the work of the editor was provided by the Economic and Social Research Council of the United Kingdom. The original idea for this book emerged out of discussions with Peter Sowden. I am especially grateful for the helpful comments by the two reviewers, Will Kymlicka and Tim Haughton, and for the support by the series editor, Richard Sakwa. Finally, I would like to thank Peter Sowden and Tom Bates at Routledge for their support and efficient publication of the book.

Abbreviations

AC	Advisory Committee
CDP	Civil Democratic Party (Czech Republic)
CERD	Committee on the Elimination of Racial Discrimination
CSCE	Conference on Security and Co-operation in Europe (until 1994)
DAHR	Democratic Alliance of Hungarians in Romania
DG	Directorate General
ECMI	European Centre for Minority Issues
ECRI	European Commission against Racism and Intolerance
ECRML	European Charter for Regional or Minority Languages
EU	European Union
FCNM	Framework Convention for the Protection of National Minorities
FIDESZ	Federation of Young Democrats (Hungary)
GDP	Gross domestic product
GR-H	Rapporteur Group on Human Rights
HCNM	High Commissioner on National Minorities
IMF	International Monetary Fund
MEP	Member of European Parliament
MP	Member of Parliament
NATO	North Atlantic Treaty Organization
NCCD	National Council for Combating Discrimination (Romania)
NGO	Non-governmental organization
NHRO	National Human Rights Office (Latvia)
OSCE	Organization for Security and Co-operation in Europe (from 1994)
PACE	Parliamentary Assembly of the Council of Europe
PHARE	Poland and Hungary: Assistance for Restructuring their Economies
PPP	Purchasing power parity
RCI	Roma Civil Initiative (Czech Republic)
UN	United Nations
UNDP	United Nations Development Programme
UNESCO	United Nations Educational, Scientific and Cultural Organization
UNICEF	United Nations Children's Fund
US	United States

Abbreviations

Part I
Setting the scene

1 Introduction

Bernd Rechel

In the last two decades, the protection of minorities has received unprecedented attention.[1] For those countries hoping to join the European Union (EU), minority protection has become a key criterion in the accession process. But how has this political criterion been translated into practice? And what is the current state of minority rights in Central and Eastern Europe after EU accession?

While there is little doubt that the EU had in many cases a far-reaching impact on domestic policies and politics in accession countries, the initial enthusiasm is gradually giving way to a more sober reflection on where and when the EU really mattered (Haughton 2007). This is also the case in the area of minority protection, a policy area that has been largely ignored in the literature on EU accession. Furthermore, the contributors to this volume critically examine how far often declaratory policies or legislation have been implemented in practice, an issue often neglected in the minority rights literature. By providing a comprehensive assessment of minority rights in Central and Eastern Europe, covering all countries of the region that have joined the EU in 2004 and 2007 (Bulgaria, the Czech Republic, Estonia, Hungary, Latvia, Lithuania, Poland, Romania, Slovakia, and Slovenia), this book aims to start filling these research gaps.

EU conditionality

Conditionality is a contested concept, in particular with regard to how it works and when it is effective. According to Schimmelfennig, conditionality was not a clear causal relationship, but rather a 'reactive reinforcement' (Schimmelfennig *et al.* 2002) of democratization. In similar vein, Hughes *et al.* (2004: 8) have argued that there is only a weak 'clear-cut causal relationship between conditionality and policy or institutional outcomes' (please see also the contribution of Gwendolyn Sasse in this volume).

A principal theoretical divide in discussion of conditionality runs between rational choice and constructivist approaches (Schimmelfennig 1999). According to a rational choice approach, actors are rational, goal-oriented and purposeful and conditionality only works when it brings benefits to national governments (Schimmelfennig *et al.* 2002: 36). A constructivist approach, on the other hand, emphasizes processes of persuasion and socialization and the sharing of norms and values (Börzel and Risse 2000; Vachudová 2005). A similar distinction is made in the literature on Europeanization, which differentiates between prescriptive and discursive modes of Europeanization (Faist and Ette 2007). In practice, these different forms of external influence were to some degree complementary. Moreover, socialization-based efforts of the Council of Europe and the Organization for Security and Co-operation in Europe (OSCE) were sometimes tied to EU accession, providing these organizations with additional leverage. In the area of minority rights, EU conditionality often motivated a change of policies, but the Council of Europe and the OSCE often shaped the substance of policy solutions (Kelley 2004a; 2004b).

The leverage of the EU on the domestic policies of candidate states can be usefully divided into 'active' and 'passive' leverage (Vachudová 2005). While 'passive leverage' results from the attraction of EU membership and is not linked to any deliberate policies of the EU, 'active leverage' results from the deliberate use of EU rules and conditionality (Vachudová 2005). The EU's active leverage was mainly based on the political conditions of membership and the *acquis communautaire*, the body of EU legislation which candidate states were required to transpose into domestic law.

The most important step towards the EU's political conditionality was taken at the European Council in Copenhagen in June 1993, which set out the 'Copenhagen criteria' for membership, which required, inter alia, 'that the candidate country has achieved stability of institutions guaranteeing [. . .] respect for and protection of minorities' (EU 1993: 1). The political Copenhagen criteria for membership were of particular relevance for the protection of minorities, as this policy area was, until the 2000 Race Equality Directive, not covered by the *acquis*. The Copenhagen criterion of minority protection has been subsequently elaborated in the monitoring of candidate states. In July 1997, the European Commission published Agenda 2000, which included Opinions on membership applications. Beginning in 1998, the Commission published annual reports on the progress of candidate countries, which became one of the key instruments for monitoring progress towards accession. However, despite the continuing monitoring procedure, starting in 1999 all candidate countries were deemed to fulfil the political criteria of membership.

EU conditionality was further affected by the absence of a single EU policy template in the area of minority rights, as practices in EU member states vary widely. The 'old' EU member states France and Greece, for example, have not even recognized the existence of ethnic minorities on their territories. This meant that there were no 'easily transferable models to emulate' (Ram 2003: 48). Furthermore, many Roma in Western Europe face severe discrimination and racism, while Roma migrants from Central and Eastern Europe have often been turned away or even summarily deported to their countries of origin.

Assessing the impact of the EU

Assessing the impact of the EU faces problems of attribution. Both national governments and the EU have tended to overstate the impact of EU pressure.

Furthermore, the demands of intergovernmental organizations have been conflated and it is at times difficult to ascertain whether a policy change was due to the influence of, for example, the EU, Council of Europe or the OSCE.

Furthermore, minority rights policies and politics are the result of a complex set of domestic and international factors. At the domestic level, these factors include the historical legacy and pattern of transition from communism, domestic political constellations, the process of state nation-building, state capacity, public attitudes towards minorities and minority rights, and the political organization and representation of minorities. At the international level, the conditionality, interest and pressure of Western organizations, and minority 'kin-states' and international non-governmental organizations (NGOs) have an impact on minority rights policies and politics in the region (Figure 1.1).

Figure 1.1 shows in a schematic way the numerous and often interrelated factors that have an impact on domestic minority rights policies. The figure illustrates that international factors do not result directly in any domestic policy changes, but are mediated and filtered by domestic politics, which themselves can be influenced by international factors. As Jacoby observed, the 'constraints

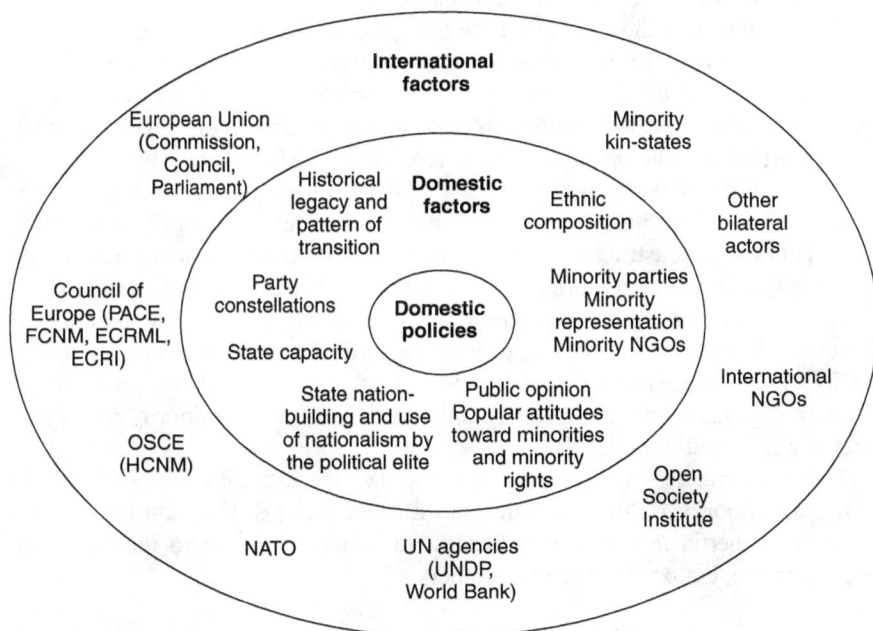

Figure 1.1 Factors influencing domestic minority rights policies.

Notes
ECRI: European Commission against Racism and Intolerance.
ECRML: European Charter for Regional or Minority Languages.
FENH: Framework Convention for the Protection of National Minorities.
HCNM: High Commissioner on National Minorities.
PACE: Parliamentary Assembly of the Council of Europe.
UNDP: United Nations Development Programme.

of historical structures and conservative actors often deflected the reform course charted by elites' (Jacoby 2004: 21). In a number of countries in Central and Eastern Europe, a change of the political party in power led to important improvements in minority rights. In other countries, in particular where ethnic nationalism gained prominence, such as in Romania and Slovakia, domestic politics acted as a brake on external influence on minority protection. Slovakia under the Mečiar government between 1994 and 1998 is an often-cited example in which domestic power considerations outweighed EU rewards, and Western conditionality had no major impact on governmental policies, although ultimately the opposition was strengthened by the increased international isolation of Mečiar's regime.

Figure 1.1 further indicates that actors shaping minority policies are often not monolithic. Within the Council of Europe, for example, the Parliamentary Assembly, the monitoring mechanism of the Framework Convention for the Protection of National Minorities (FCNM), the monitoring procedure of the European Charter for Regional or Minority Languages, the European Commission against Racism and Intolerance, or the European Court of Human Rights sometimes send conflicting messages to EU candidate states. What is even more, some of these institutions may find the backing of the European Commission, while others may not. In the case of Bulgaria, for example, the European Commission ignored relevant court cases of the European Court of Human Rights, as well as the country reports of the European Commission against Racism and Intolerance. This may have contributed to the rather dismissive reaction of the Bulgarian authorities.

Finally, it has to be recognized it is not the actor positions themselves that are decisive, but rather the perceptions of these positions by others (Pettai 2006: 132). This social construction of actor positions is probably most apparent in the way that the actions of minority kin-states, such as Hungary and Russia, are perceived by countries with Hungarian or Russian minorities. The policies of minority kin-states may often appear to be more threatening than they are in reality. These processes of social construction also apply to the positions of Western organizations and further complicate the analysis of minority rights policies and EU conditionality.

The contributors to this volume recognize the complexities involved in analysing minority rights in Central and Eastern Europe. They attribute policy changes or inertia to a range of factors, of which accession to the EU is an important one, but one among many others.

Main results

Convergence

Over the last two decades, an array of policy and legislative initiatives related to minorities has been initiated in the countries of Central and Eastern Europe. It is possible to identify areas where there were converging trends, as well as areas in which there is strong variation across countries. A convergence in terms of minority protection can be observed in the adoption of anti-discrimination legislation, the ratification of the Council of Europe FCNM, the adoption of programmes for the integration of Roma, and the establishment of governmental bodies for minority issues. All of these policy changes can be directly related to pressure from the EU.

The impact of the EU on minority protection in candidate countries is perhaps most evident in the area of anti-discrimination legislation. Directives on non-discrimination were adopted in 2000 and candidate states were required to transpose them into national legislation. The Council Directive 2000/43, also referred to as 'Race Directive', 'Racial Equality Directive' or 'Race Equality Directive', prohibits direct and indirect discrimination on the grounds of race or ethnicity in the areas of employment, training, social protection, education, and access to public goods and services. The directive further provides for the reversal of the burden of proof on the alleged perpetrator and the establishment of enforcement bodies for the promotion of equal treatment (European Commission 2000a). All ten new EU member states from Central and Eastern Europe have made legislative changes to transpose this part of the *acquis*, although with varying degrees of speed and comprehensiveness.

Another point of convergence is that all ten countries have acceded to the FCNM. Instead of setting up its own standards in the area of minority rights, the EU has encouraged candidate countries to adopt the Framework Convention and to follow the recommendations of the OSCE High Commissioner on National Minorities, boosting the leverage of these two mechanisms for the protection of minorities. In contrast to the Framework Convention, the European Charter for Regional or Minority Languages, which has not been promoted by the European Commission in the accession process, had, by the end of 2007, only been ratified by four of the ten new EU member states from Central and Eastern Europe. The Framework Convention has been described as the European Commission's 'primary instrument for translating the minority criterion into practice' (Sasse 2005: 13). However, it seems that this criterion has not been consistently or strictly applied, as Latvia had not ratified the Convention by the time it became a member of the EU in 2004, but only acceded to the Convention in 2005.

Furthermore, all ten countries (except Estonia) have adopted programmes for the integration of the Roma minority. While it is somehow surprising for the countries with significant Roma populations that it took until the second half of the 1990s before they embarked on Roma-specific integration programmes, it is testament to the power of the EU to set the political agenda in the accession process, that even countries with very small Roma minorities (Estonia, Latvia, Lithuania and Poland) have adopted Roma integration programmes. Despite these numerous initiatives, however, changes on the ground have remained remarkably limited.

Finally, all countries have established governmental bodies dealing with minority questions. This has helped to raise the political profile of minority issues, but these new institutions tended to remain consultative bodies without sufficient authority to implement minority programmes.

Divergence

In contrast to these points of convergence, trends with regard to positive minority rights are far less clear. A major reason for this variety is that the EU was not interested in minority rights per se. It paid particular attention to the socio-economic integration of the Roma minority, but this was an area that fell outside the scope of cultural or linguistic rights. Furthermore, a major weight of EU conditionality fell on the 'technical' requirement to adopt the 80,000 pages of the *acquis* (Grabbe 2003; Hughes *et al.* 2004: 25). As the European Commission itself noted, 'incorporation of the acquis by the candidate States in their legislation, and adaptation of their capacity effectively to implement and enforce it, remain the key conditions for progressing in the negotiations' (European Commission 2000b: 31–32). The *acquis*, however, has covered different policy areas to very different degrees (Jacoby 2004: 16–17). Although providing a detailed regulation of some policy areas, others, including the area of minority protection, have not been covered in any detail. The 'thinness' of the *acquis* in these areas resulted in a 'conditionality gap' (Hughes *et al.* 2004: 174) where *acquis* leverage was weak, increasing the scope of action for candidate countries (Hughes *et al.* 2004: 27). Where the *acquis* density was low, candidate states were 'free to pick and choose (or ignore) prevailing Western models' (Jacoby 2004: 16). In these policy areas, policy changes were 'more strongly affected by path-dependent factors in the domestic political settings' (Hughes *et al.* 2004: 169). This was also the case in the sphere of minority rights. In general, minority rights regimes were more strongly shaped by specific historical legacies, dominant national narratives, and the size and status of minorities, whereas the impact of the EU was muted.

Generally, there are various ways in which the state can respond to minority rights claims, or, more broadly, to ethnic diversity. Policies that accommodate diversity and grant members of minorities certain rights can be classified as minority rights regimes. Broadly based on the taxonomy of macro-political methods of national and ethnic conflict regulation developed by McGarry and O'Leary (McGarry and O'Leary 1994) and the different minority rights regimes identified by Kymlicka (Kymlicka 2001), it is possible to establish a taxonomy of state responses to ethnic diversity (Figure 1.2). The taxonomy of minority rights regimes is structured according to the scope of rights granted and the impact on territorial integrity. It serves mainly as a heuristic device and does not imply a judgement on which minority rights regime is most appropriate in a specific domestic context. It should also be noted that, by focusing on the distinction between non-territorial cultural rights and territorial self-government, the taxonomy leaves out the dimension of minority rights related to political participation. Ideas of effective political participation have been incorporated into the FCNM and the Lund Recommendations on Effective Participation of National Minorities, adopted by the OSCE in 1999 (Kymlicka 2006: 55–60, 2007: 239–44).

Although necessarily schematic, Figure 1.2 illustrates several key features of how the countries of Central and Eastern Europe were moving since 1989 in

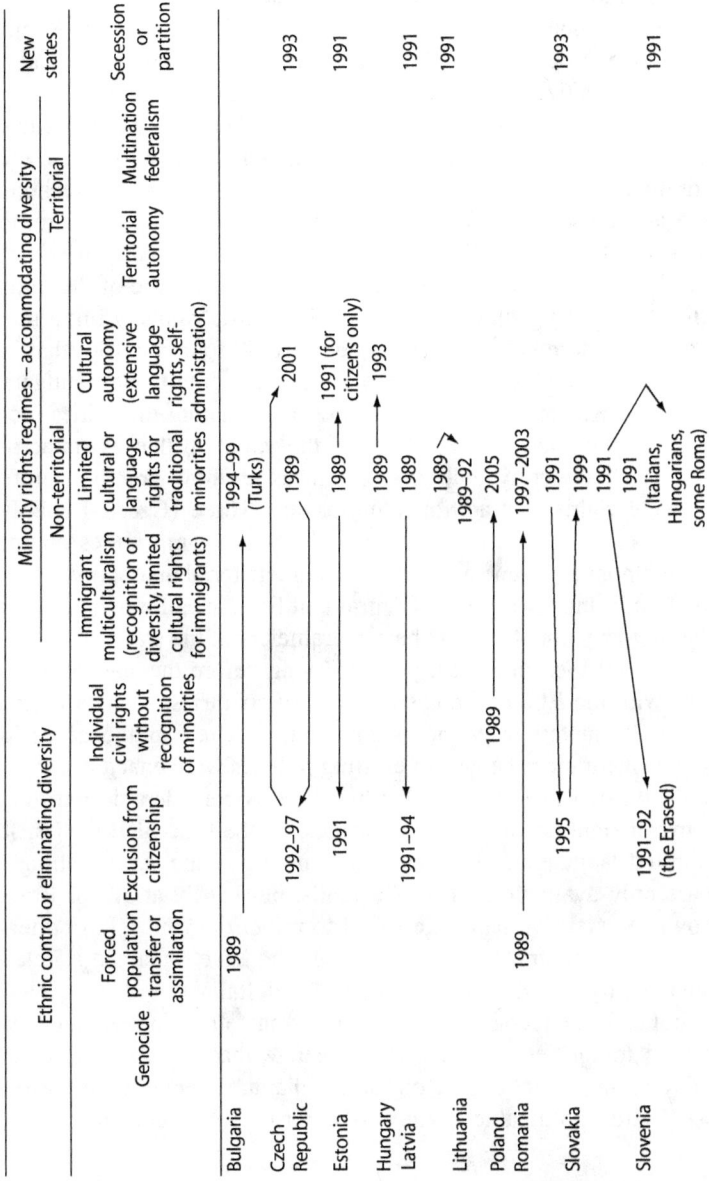

| | Ethnic control or eliminating diversity | | | | Minority rights regimes – accommodating diversity | | | | | New states |
| | | | | | Non-territorial | | | Territorial | | |
	Genocide	Forced population transfer or assimilation	Exclusion from citizenship	Individual civil rights without recognition of minorities	Immigrant multiculturalism (recognition of diversity, limited cultural rights for immigrants)	Limited cultural or language rights for traditional minorities	Cultural autonomy (extensive language rights, self-administration)	Territorial autonomy	Multination federalism	Secession or partition
Bulgaria		1989				1994–99 (Turks)				
Czech Republic			1992–97			1989	2001			1993
Estonia			1991			1989	1991 (for citizens only)			1991
Hungary			1991–94			1989	1993			
Latvia						1989				1991
Lithuania						1989 / 1989–92				1991
Poland				1989		2005				
Romania		1989				1997–2003				
Slovakia			1995			1991 / 1999				1993
Slovenia			1991–92 (the Erased)			1991 (Italians, Hungarians, some Roma)				1991

Figure 1.2 Macro-political responses to ethnic diversity in Central and Eastern Europe, 1989–2007 (source: author's compilation).

Note
Dates refer to the starting points of the different countries and to key policy or legislative changes.

terms of minority protection. Contrary to what could have been expected in the context of EU accession, there does not seem to have been a general trend towards improved protection of minorities. Of the ten countries under consideration, six either restored statehood or gained independence with the dissolution of the Soviet Union (Estonia, Latvia, Lithuania), Czechoslovakia (Czech Republic and Slovakia) and Yugoslavia (Slovenia). All of these countries had to address the question of citizenship and four of them (Czech Republic, Estonia, Latvia, and Slovenia) opted for solutions which excluded certain minorities from becoming citizens in the new states. The 1992 Citizenship Law of the Czech Republic was drafted in such a way as to exclude many Roma from Czech citizenship. Estonia and Latvia both followed a restorationist logic, which turned the large Russian-speaking minorities into an illegal settler population without any automatic right to citizenship. Slovenia, finally, stripped some of the immigrants from other former Yugoslav republics of their basic rights, turning them into illegal migrants. It is remarkable that, in contrast, all four countries that did not face any changes to their statehood since the end of communism (Bulgaria, Hungary, Poland, and Romania) have moved towards granting minorities more extensive rights than they had in 1989. Despite the variation that exists across the region, it is also noteworthy that most countries are now granting limited cultural or language rights to traditional minorities. Three (Czech Republic, Estonia, and Hungary) have even moved towards granting minorities cultural autonomy, although none has gone as far as offering territorial autonomy.

Another feature of minority rights in Central and Eastern Europe indicated in Figure 1.2 is that in many countries, the basic parameters of the status of minorities were already established in the early 1990s, long before the start of accession negotiations with the EU. In the case of several countries, such as Estonia and Latvia, these parameters were not significantly altered in the accession process, although some minor changes to existing policies were enacted.

A final point indicated in Figure 1.2 is that there is considerable intra-case variation in terms of rights of different minorities. In the case of Bulgaria, for example, the limited language rights that exist (minority language teaching in state schools) are only available to Turkish pupils, but hardly at all for Roma. Estonia has provided extensive language rights to minorities, but it has done so only for citizens of the country, leaving out those who have remained stateless. Slovenia granted minority rights to Hungarians and Italians and, to a lesser degree, Roma, but did not recognize immigrants from other former Yugoslav republics as ethnic minorities. These cases illustrate that minority protection systems depend to an important degree on factors that are specific to minorities, such as their size, status, political leverage and minority rights demands.

Conditionality

According to the contributions to this volume, the EU has played a paramount role among the international actors influencing domestic minority rights policies. More often than not, recommendations of the High Commissioner on National

Minorities (HCNM) of the OSCE, as well as international treaty obligations, remained without consequences, until the EU added its weight to the recommendations of the OSCE or the Council of Europe. For several countries, the 1997 Opinions of the Commission on the applications for membership proved a key turning point, as the governments realized that they have to embark on policy reforms if they do not want to jeopardize their membership aspirations. The threat to withdraw the offer of EU membership proved to be the most effective mechanism available to the EU. Once the countries had become EU members, the power of conditionality had vanished.

A major reason why the EU did not have a greater impact on minority rights in Central and Eastern Europe is that it was not concerned with minority rights as such, either for lack of interest or lack of capacity. One of the main concerns for the EU was the potentially destabilizing role the large Roma population could play for the enlarged EU and it aimed to put their integration onto the agendas of candidate countries. However, this was mainly conceived as socio-economic integration and traditional minority rights were deemed to be of secondary importance in this context. Even in the case of Estonia and Latvia, which excluded a significant part of their populations from citizenship, the EU accepted the basic parameters of statehood and citizenship and only exerted considerable pressure with regard to specific policy details, such as stateless children or language requirements for political candidates or private business.

While the direct impact of the EU on minority rights was limited by its neglect of positive minority rights, in several countries, the accession process empowered domestic actors with a minority rights agenda. This was for example the case in Slovakia, where the Hungarian Coalition Party participated in coalition governments in 1998–2006, or in Romania, where the Democratic Alliance of Hungarians in Romania became part of the government coalition in 1996–2000. In both cases, the political participation of minority parties facilitated by EU accession led to a number of policy changes in the sphere of minority protection.

With accession, the power of the EU has dramatically declined in the sphere of minority protection that is left outside of the *acquis*. However, there were no major changes in minority policies in the countries under investigation, once they had acceded to the EU. Legislative frameworks for minority protection remained largely unchanged and the countries continued on their trajectories, no matter to what degree they had (or had not) previously granted rights to minorities.

Implementation

The contributors to this volume paint a critical picture of the status of implementation of the various legislative and policy changes adopted in the sphere of minority rights. Where policy changes were adopted, they were often confined to the level of legislation or policy formulation, without being followed by implementation. The EU may have contributed to this trend by equating the adoption of policies or legislation with a successful outcome of conditionality (Rechel

2008). Obstacles to implementation often included a lack of institutional capacity, low levels of budgetary funding, and resistance from local authorities.

One of the main hurdles for adopting and implementing policy changes in the sphere of minority protection are public attitudes towards minorities. In Slovenia, for example, a referendum was held in 2004 on reversing the 1992 erasure of long-term residents from the Register of Permanent Residents. In a highly symbolic vote, 94.7 per cent voted against the Law that would have redressed the erasure. Negative attitudes are particularly worrying with regard to the Roma, and anti-Roma racism does not seem to have significantly declined during the EU accession process.

Structure of the book

The book is organized in three parts. The chapters of the first part following this introduction examine cross-cutting issues that apply to all or most of the ten new EU member states from Central and Eastern Europe.

In Chapter 2, Gwen Sasse assesses the impact of EU conditionality at the domestic level of accession countries. She argues that the minority condition is best understood as a political construct and as a contributing factor rather than the single or predominant cause of minority rights policies. She points out that the monitoring process of the European Commission was characterized by a hierarchy of minority issues, ad hocery, and inconsistencies. Sasse identifies two dynamics that have shaped the outcomes of EU conditionality: international involvement and the presence of ethnopolitical parties.

In Chapter 3, Guido Schwellnus explores how the EU Race Equality Directive was transposed into the domestic legislation of the ten countries under discussion and what its status of implementation is. He finds that all countries have moved towards transposition of the anti-discrimination directives, but that those countries facing strong political conditionality due to large Roma populations (Bulgaria, Czech Republic, Hungary, Romania, and Slovakia) were quicker in adopting relevant legislation and were more likely to adopt comprehensive and unified anti-discrimination acts. Schwellnus identifies major obstacles to the implementation of the adopted legislation, including societal prejudice and the lack of awareness-raising.

In Chapter 4, Rainer Hofmann examines the accession of the countries of Central and Eastern Europe to the FCNM and explores whether adoption of the Convention has led to noticeable changes at the domestic level. While it is too early to assess Latvia's compliance, as it ratified the Convention only in 2005, all other nine countries have undergone at least one monitoring cycle. Hofmann concludes that all nine countries with the exception of Bulgaria have a good or very good compliance record both with the formal and the substantive aspects of the Convention.

In Chapter 5, Peter Vermeersch and Melanie H. Ram describe the particular situation of the Roma minority. In many countries of the region, the Roma face the greatest challenges in realizing their human rights, let alone securing special minority rights. This chapter describes the domestic policies adopted towards the Roma in Central and Eastern Europe and how the Roma themselves have aimed for political participation. It argues that the EU has been successful in putting the Roma on governmental agendas, but that no major change can be felt on the ground. While the leverage of the EU has now largely disappeared, the newly enacted anti-discrimination legislation, EU structural funds, and the participation of Roma in EU institutions might offer new avenues for addressing the situation of the Roma.

The second part of this volume consists of case studies of the ten countries from Central and Eastern Europe that have joined the EU in 2004 and 2007. As far as all countries under consideration have shared the challenges of transition from communism and belong to the region of Central and Eastern Europe, the case studies can be said to follow a most similar research design (see Landman 2006: 66). However, it is important to recognize that there is considerable cross-case variation, as not only the ethnic make-up of the countries differs considerably, but also the role of kin-states and Western organizations and the outcome in terms of minority rights. There is also substantial intra-case variation, as different minorities are exposed to differing pressures and opportunities. The advantage of this variation is that there was no selection bias with regard to the dependent variable (Geddes 1990).

All of the country case studies cover the major developments since 1989, highlight the salient issues in minority rights politics, try to decipher the role domestic and international factors have played in shaping minority rights, discuss whether there have been any major changes once EU accession was secured, and examine the actual implementation of relevant policies and legislation.

In Chapter 6 on Bulgaria, Bernd Rechel describes how minority rights in this country have remained remarkably restricted. Basic parameters of the minority situation were set in the early 1990s, when the reversal of communist assimilation campaigns was met with nationalist protests. In subsequent years, the EU largely ignored the question of positive minority rights and negative public attitudes continue to be a major impediment for minority protection in Bulgaria.

In Chapter 7 on the Czech Republic, Eva Sobotka argues that, between 1992 and 1997, policies towards minorities were shaped by the notion of Czech exceptionality, which was at odds with minority rights norms. The 1992 Czech Citizenship Law and a number of local government initiatives were specifically directed against the Roma minority. EU conditionality resulted in significant policy changes, but challenges remain with regard to positive minority rights and the integration of the Roma.

In Chapter 8 on Estonia, Vello Pettai and Kristina Kallas show how the doctrine of legal restorianism pre-determined the minority situation in the country already in 1989–91, long before conditionality could be applied. After the EU added its pressure to recommendations of the High Commissioner on National Minorities of the OSCE, some details of minority policies were amended during the EU accession process. Furthermore, Estonia has embarked on an integration programme and the number of stateless Russian-speakers is declining.

In Chapter 9 on Hungary, Balázs Vizi describes how, largely driven by its concern for Hungarians living in neighbouring countries, the country adopted a comprehensive system of minority protection in 1990–93. This system is based on minority self-governments and offers minorities cultural autonomy. Despite a broad range of minority rights, problems emerged in the practical implementation of the system, especially with regard to the financing of minority self-governments, ethnic self-identifications, and the parliamentary representation of minorities. Furthermore, the legislative framework for minority protection did little to address the problems of the Roma minority and this became a major focus of policy initiatives in the context of EU accession.

In Chapter 10 on Latvia, David J. Galbreath and Nils Muižnieks explore how the country, in claiming that it had been illegally occupied by the Soviet Union, followed the same restorationist logic as Estonia. Latvia reinstalled the 1922 constitution and non-Latvian residents had to pass language and civic history exams before becoming citizens, excluding a large proportion of Russian-speakers from citizenship. These regulations were somewhat liberalized when the country strived for membership in the Council of Europe and the EU. Challenges that remain are the implementation of the recently ratified FCNM, the transposition of the Race Equality Directive, and the naturalization of non-citizens.

In Chapter 11 on Lithuania, Dovile Budryte and Vilana Pilinkaite-Sotirovic explain how the country, with a much smaller share of Russian-speakers than Estonia and Latvia, extended citizenship to those residing in Lithuania in 1990 and how it developed a minority rights regime in the late 1980s and early 1990s that offered cultural rights to the country's minorities. However, the authors argue that intolerant public attitudes impede the implementation of minority rights, such as the EU anti-discrimination directives which have so far only incompletely been transposed.

In Chapter 12 on Poland, Peter Vermeersch explores the case of minority policies in a country without a significant proportion of minorities. Despite the relative absence of minorities, the granting of minority rights has been highly contested. Majority-minority relations continue to be shaped by historical legacies of genocide and forced population transfers and a dominant narrative of the Polish nation as a victim of history.

In Chapter 13 on Romania, Melanie H. Ram demonstrates how the country moved from one of the most oppressive communist regimes to one that, in 1996, included a party of ethnic Hungarians in its government coalition and, in 1997–2003, granted far-reaching rights to its Hungarian minority. The EU has put the integration of the Roma high on the political agenda, but major challenges remain in the implementation of Roma programmes.

In Chapter 14 on Slovakia, Stefan Auer argues that the power of the EU in the sphere of minority rights depended on the political influence of domestic actors. Between 1992 and 1998, the country was led by the nationalist Mečiar government and constitutional provisions for minority protection were not translated into practice. The situation changed markedly, when the Hungarian Coalition Party participated in the coalition governments between 1998 and 2006. In 2006, the populist government of Robert Fico brought back to power the extremist Slovak Nationalist Party, but so far the legislative framework for the protection of minorities has remained unchanged.

In Chapter 15 on Slovenia, Jelka Zorn shows how the newly independent country granted wide-ranging rights to the small Hungarian and Italian minorities, but failed to recognize immigrants from other former Yugoslav republics as ethnic minorities deserving protection. Furthermore, almost 1 per cent of the population was removed from the Register of Permanent Residents, leaving these 'Erased' without citizenship and resident status. Despite these shortcomings and ambiguous government policies towards the country's Roma, the country was deemed to fulfil the EU's conditions of membership.

The final part of the book contains a concluding chapter, which brings together the main findings, draws lessons for the EU accession process, and discusses perspectives for the future. It makes the case for challenging public attitudes through awareness-raising measures and explores possibilities for expanding the *acquis* in the area of minority protection.

Note

1 I would like to thank Will Kymlicka and my fellow contributors to this book for very helpful comments.

References

Börzel, T. A. and Risse, T. (2000) 'When Europe Hits Home: Europeanization and Domestic Change', San Domenico, European University Institute, Working Paper, RSC, No. 2000/56.

European Commission (2000a) 'Council Directive 2000/43/EC of 29 June 2000 implementing the principle of equal treatment between persons irrespective of racial or ethnic origin ("Race Equality Directive")'. Online, available at: www.europa.eu.int/infonet/library/m/200043ce/en.htm (accessed 5 August 2002).

—— (2000b) *Enlargement strategy paper. Report on progress towards accession by each of the candidate countries*, Brussels: European Commission.

EU (1993) *Presidency Conclusions, Copenhagen European Council – 21–22 June 1993*, Brussels: European Union.

Faist, T. and Ette, A. (eds) (2007) *The Europeanization of National Policies and Politics of Immigration*, Houndmills, New York: Palgrave Macmillan.

Geddes, B. (1990) 'How the Cases You Choose Affect the Answers You Get: Selection Bias in Comparative Politics', *Political Analysis*, 2: 131–150.

Grabbe, H. (2003) 'Europeanization goes East: power and uncertainty in the EU accession process', in K. Featherstone and C. Radaelli (eds) *The politics of Europeanization*, Oxford: Oxford University Press, 303–327.

Haughton, T. (2007) 'When Does the EU Make a Difference? Conditionality and the Accession Process in Central and Eastern Europe', *Political Studies Review*, 5: 233–246.

Hughes, J., Sasse, G. and Gordon, C. (2004) *Europeanization and Regionalization in the*

EU's Enlargement to Central and Eastern Europe. The Myth of Conditionality, Hound-mills and New York: Palgrave Macmillan.

Jacoby, W. (2004) *The Enlargement of the European Union and NATO. Ordering from the Menu in Central Europe*, Cambridge: Cambridge University Press.

Kelley, J. (2004a) 'International Actors on the Domestic Scene: Membership Conditionality and Socialization by International Institutions', *International Organization*, 58: 425–457.

—— (2004b) *Ethnic Politics in Europe: The Power of Norms and Incentives*, Princeton: Princeton University Press.

Kymlicka, W. (2001) 'Western Political Theory and Ethnic Relations in Eastern Europe', in W. Kymlicka and M. Opalski (eds) *Can Liberal Pluralism be Exported? Western Political Theory and Ethnic Relations in Eastern Europe*, Oxford: Oxford University Press, 13–105.

—— (2006) 'The evolving basis of European norms of minority rights: Rights to culture, participation and autonomy', in J. McGarry and M. Keating (eds) *European Integration and the Nationalities Question*, London and New York: Routledge, 35–63.

—— (2007) *Multicultural Odysseys: Navigating the New International Politics of Diversity*, Oxford: Oxford University Press.

Landman, T. (2006) *Studying Human Rights*, London and New York: Routledge.

McGarry, J. and O'Leary, B. (1994) 'The Political Regulation of National and Ethnic Conflict', *Parliamentary Affairs*, 47 (1): 94–115.

Pettai, V. (2006) 'Explaining Ethnic Politics in the Baltic States: Reviewing the Triadic Nexus Model', *Journal of Baltic Studies*, 37 (1): 124–136.

Ram, M. H. (2003) 'Democratization through European Integration: The Case of Minority Rights in the Czech Republic and Romania', *Studies in Comparative International Development*, 38 (2): 28–56.

Rechel, B. (2008) 'What Has Limited the EU's Impact on Minority Rights in Accession Countries?', *East European Politics and Societies*, 22 (1): 171–191.

Sasse, G. (2005) 'Democracy Promotion in CEE: The Political Rights of National Minorities', paper presented at VII ICCEES World Congress, Humboldt University, Berlin, 25–30 July 2005.

Schimmelfennig, F. (1999) 'The Double Puzzle of EU Enlargement: Liberal Norms, Rhetorical Action, and the Decision to Expand to the East', ARENA Working Papers, WP 99/15.

Schimmelfennig, F., Engert, S. and Knobel, H. (2002) 'The Conditions of Conditionality. The Impact of the EU on Democracy and Human Rights in European Non-Member States', paper prepared at Workshop 4, 'Enlargement and European Governance', ECPR Joint Session of Workshops, Turin, 22–27 March 2002.

Vachudová, M. A. (2005) *Europe Undivided. Democracy, Leverage, and Integration after Communism*, Oxford: Oxford University Press.

2 Tracing the construction and effects of EU conditionality

Gwendolyn Sasse

The European Union (EU)'s inclusion of 'the respect for and the protection of minorities' in its Copenhagen criteria for accession gave rise to discussions about the EU's double standards (see for example: De Witte 2000, Hughes and Sasse 2003; Schwellnus 2006). The EU has tried to promote a norm which remains contested in its member states and still lacks a firm foundation in EU law – Article 6 (1) of the 1992 Maastricht Treaty on the European Union lists the values of the political accession criterion with the notable exception of the reference to minorities. The ambiguous minority condition is best understood as a political and social construct. Concerns about security and democratization led to the EU's formulation of the norm of minority protection in the early 1990s, but the lack of a legal base, a policy consensus and political will inside the EU made its translation into a policy tool and, in particular, the definition of benchmarks for the implementation of the norm difficult. Nevertheless, the EU's role in shaping and stabilizing minority issues is often singled out as a key example of its transformative effect on the candidate countries in Central and Eastern Europe. By focusing on Central and Eastern Europe, this chapter analyses the evolution of the EU's minority condition and its short- and medium-term effects. The inclusion of the post-accession period moves the debate about the effects of EU conditionality beyond the documentation of legal and institutional changes to an emphasis on implementation and behavioural change.

Rather than taking the EU's minority condition as a clear-cut phenomenon, the effect of which can be conceptualized as an independent or intervening variable, this chapter traces the actual construction of the EU minority condition, its evolution and application over time. Thus, it emphasizes the politics surrounding EU conditionality and points to direct and indirect and intended and unintended consequences. The EU's impact is seen as an important contributing factor rather than the single or predominant cause of the diverging and in parts counterintuitive trends highlighted in this chapter. The type and intensity of international involvement in the area of minority protection and the presence of an ethnopolitical party in the candidate countries' domestic political scene are the empirical constellations this chapter explores. The effects discussed range from gradual legal changes and ethnopolitical participation in government and opposition to a deepening of structural segregation and an increase in political polarization.

Conceptualizing conditionality

Any discussion about the impact of EU conditionality struggles with the difficulty of isolating the effect of international factors from the domestic incentives for legal, institutional or behavioural change. As a result, many studies tend to assume or overestimate the effects of EU conditionality vis-à-vis domestic factors. The increasingly empirically grounded discussion of concrete policy areas and countries has demonstrated that the record of conditionality is mixed and highly dependent on domestic conditions and actors. The EU is increasingly being given less credit for the democratization process in Central and Eastern Europe – with the exception of the minority condition, the effect of which is widely assumed. Different conceptualizations of EU conditionality predicate the type, degree and nuance of EU influence that can be captured empirically. The prominent 'external incentives model', built on rationalist cost-benefit calculations relates 'effective conditionality' to basic requisites such as: consistent and credible conditions, and low domestic adoption costs (Schimmelfennig and Sedelmeier 2005). According to these criteria, the minority condition should not be very effective. It is neither consistent (in its application in any one accession country or across candidates) nor credible (the condition remains controversial in some member states, and the opening of the accession negotiations began when the first Copenhagen criterion was deemed 'fulfilled', thereby limiting the EU's subsequent scope for leverage). Moreover, the domestic costs (mostly political, but also financial) of adopting norms on minority protection and participation can hardly be considered to be 'low'. Most importantly, however, the link between low domestic adoption costs and effective conditionality undermines the very notion of conditionality. If the perceived or real domestic costs are low to begin with, the scope for testing the effect of conditionality is severely limited from the outset.

Amidst a number of empirical case studies of minority-sensitive legislative change, Kelley's study of the norm of minority protection in Central and Eastern Europe, as promoted by the EU, the Organization for Security and Co-operation in Europe (OSCE, Conference for Security and Co-operation in Europe, or CSCE, until 1994), and the Council of Europe, is the most detailed and conceptually informed analysis to date (Kelley 2004). It predates the final formulation of the 'external incentive model' but shares its basic assumptions and conclusions. Kelley emphasizes that EU membership conditionality was the key rationale behind changes towards minority-friendly legislation in Central and Eastern Europe. While she concludes that only membership conditionality has the capacity to overcome domestic opposition, her argument points to the importance of socialization in guiding policy change in the presence of membership conditionality. According to Kelley, socialization without membership conditionality fails to overcome domestic opposition. Similarly, Schimmelfennig and Sedelmeier or Jacoby point to mechanisms, such as EU-induced social learning and domestically motivated lesson-drawing or emulation, but ultimately find it hard to trace them empirically during the accession context, where they are difficult to separate from rationalist calculations (Jacoby 2004; Schimmelfennig and Sedel-meier 2005).

Research that frontloads the empirical analysis of conditionality tends to conclude by presenting the EU's effect as a 'reinforcement mechanism' or a 'lock-in' function (Schimmelfennig *et al.* 2003; Sasse 2005; Grabbe 2006). Some scholars have taken the next logical step leading to a re-conceptualization of our understanding of conditionality itself. This alternative approach to the study of conditionality, suggested by Hughes *et al.* (2004) questions the commonly held assumptions that conditionality itself is a clear-cut variable in a causal mechanism that explains policy or institutional change. Pointing to the flexible, continuously evolving and highly politicized content of conditionality itself, as it is being shaped by various actors at the EU level whose preferences change over time (e.g. inside the Commission) and domestic political actors in Central and Eastern Europe who regularly instrumentalize references to EU conditionality to shape an agenda or silence opposition, they question the existence of a variable called 'conditionality'. Instead, Hughes *et al.* (2004: 3–4) conceptualize conditionality itself as a process shaped by the interaction of multi-level actors, perceptions and interests, differentiated rewards and sanctions, temporal factors and different degrees of institutional or policy compliance. This definition highlights the pitfalls of linear causality models and the need to take seriously the inherent politicization of conditionality, but it is also quite open-ended and therefore calls for further conceptual and empirical elaboration.

Analysing conditionality as a construct, as this chapter suggests, is closely related to the conceptualization of conditionality as a process. A construct can have 'real' effects, but these are likely to be both direct and indirect, intended and unintended, due to the politicization of the process of (re-)construction and mobilization over time.

The post-enlargement context provides a new testing ground for the study of the effectiveness of EU conditionality. While the study of '*acquis* conditionality' is now turning into the study of the new member states' level of preparedness and compliance with the rules of the game, the study of 'democratic conditionality' – tied to the first Copenhagen criterion – regains in significance as a litmus test of the democratic consolidation of the polities in question. Isolating the EU effect in the post-accession context is potentially even harder than during the pre-accession phase. The question is whether the EU has created a certain momentum which carries over into the post-accession period. This momentum for reform might be reinforced either by the EU itself or by other international actors specializing in a particular issue area (e.g. the Council of Europe and the OSCE with their expertise in minority issues). Domestic actors might seek to enhance or limit the EU-induced pre-accession momentum in the post-accession phase depending on their own interests, thereby providing us with an insight into the domestic commitment to the EU's prescribed democratic norms. Similarly, the (dis-)continuity of structural or behavioural trends from the pre-accession phase forms part of the assessment of the EU's impact. The logical conclusion of presenting the minority condition as a construct is the recognition that any notion of compliance is a construct, as well as a political judgement.

Constructing the minority condition and turning it into policy

The explicit formulation of the conditions for accession and, in particular, the inclusion of the 'respect for and the protection of minorities' in the democracy criterion defined by the Copenhagen Council of 1993 marked a significant disjuncture for the EU. The nexus between human rights and conditionality had been an integral part of the EU's external relations since the Luxembourg European Council of 1991. The EU's eastward enlargement extended this normative conditionality at a time when the political salience of minority issues and the potential for conflict amidst multifaceted transition processes were paramount. The violent disintegration of former Yugoslavia and a number of intractable post-Soviet conflicts, as well as a perception of further conflict potential in view of sizeable minorities in many countries of Central and Eastern Europe shaped the EU's approach.

A mixture of 'hard' and 'soft' security concerns informed the push for a greater internationalization of minority rights in the early 1990s. While the EU borrowed the link between democracy and human (and later minority) rights from the Council of Europe, the CSCE/OSCE provided the EU with the security-based rationale for minority protection, a combination that resonated strongly with the member states in the early 1990s (Sasse 2005). Once the EU had formulated its loose first Copenhagen criterion, linking minority protection to the 'stability of institutions guaranteeing the rule of law and human rights', it faced the challenge of translating this new construct into a policy and enforcing it in the absence of a legal or political consensus on the norm of minority protection at international and European level (Vermeersch 2003, 2004; Sasse 2005; Schwellnus 2006).

The European Commission's annual Regular Reports, following on from the Opinions of 1997 and the Accession Partnerships, have been the EU's key instrument to monitor and evaluate the candidates' progress towards accession. Although not a source of inspiration and legitimacy at the outset of the accession process, over time the Council of Europe's Framework Convention for the Protection of National Minorities of 1995 became the Commission's primary instrument for translating the minority criterion into practice. Accordingly, the Regular Reports frequently reminded the candidate states to sign and ratify the Framework Convention − despite the fact that several EU member states, such as Belgium, France, Greece, Luxembourg and the Netherlands, had not done so at the time.

The Commission's reports are a compendium of results compiled from a variety of sources, including the candidate countries, the Council of Europe, the OSCE, international financial institutions, NGOs, as well as assessments made by member states, especially in the political sphere. It is difficult to measure the

relative weight of these inputs and to assess the process by which they were filtered and evaluated, but it is clear that in the area of minority issues, the Council
of Europe and the OSCE were privileged sources of information. During the
drafting stage, the Commission also scheduled a regular annual briefing session
in Brussels with the Council of Europe (including the chairman of the Advisory
Committee on the Framework Convention) and the OSCE (including the director
of the office of the High Commissioner on National Minorities). The involvement of the NGO sector in the preparation of the Reports is less apparent. Due to
the more specific NGO agendas, the Commission had no official 'privileged relations' with any one of them, although groups like Transparency International or
Human Rights Watch were regularly consulted. In general, issues would rather
be left out, if 'hard' evidence was missing: 'If a country had proven the Commission wrong on a single issue, the whole exercise would have suffered tre-
mendously.'[1]

The monitoring process, including co-operation between the Country Desks
in Directorate General (DG) Enlargement and the relevant line DGs, was overseen by a Horizontal Co-ordination Unit within DG Enlargement (comprising
about 25 people). Each year, this unit produced a manual listing the issues to be
addressed by the Country Desks,[2] and streamlined the draft reports in terms of
substance and language, in order to ensure consistency and comparability within
and across reports. As one official pointed out, 'there has been a tendency for
country teams to go native, both in terms of overly positive or negative assessments. It was our job to maintain the balance.'[3] A colleague from the same unit
detected 'a tendency to tone down or neutralize the language, while not dropping
issues completely'.[4] Over time, previous reports became a point of reference, in
particular their 'set phrases, such as the references to international or European
standards'.[5] The in-house drafting usually began around the end of June, once all
the different submissions had been received and the meetings with other international organizations had been held. Over the summer, both the relevant line DGs
and the Country Desks were involved in revising the drafts, overseen by the
Horizontal Unit. The texts were generally ready for consultation with the Legal
Service in September.

The reports were treated as confidential documents until their official release
in October or November. 'The candidate countries were often trying to find the
weakest link in the chain to obtain bits of the report in advance – and sometimes
it worked.'[6] About six weeks before the publication of the reports, high-level
civil servants from the candidate countries (usually the chief negotiators) were
briefed about the key findings by the Director General, the head of the Horizontal Co-ordination Unit, and further Commission officials involved in the monitoring exercise. At this stage, the conclusions to the reports had not been
finalized, leaving the candidate countries a final chance to submit documentation
regarding recent developments. In between the annual reports – usually once per
presidency – the Country Desks provided the Council with shorter updates along
the lines of the reports. The candidate countries and the EU delegations regularly
provided follow-up information for these updates. For the first-wave accession

countries, the Commission issued Comprehensive Monitoring Reports in the autumn of 2003, which dropped the political section and focused solely on the *acquis*. Minority-related issues were mentioned in the context of non-discrimination under chapter 13 (Social Policy), reflecting a wider institutional development: over time the line DGs had started to build more direct contacts with the candidate countries, thereby gradually moving the emphasis away from DG Enlargement. DG Justice and Home Affairs, DG Employment and DG Regional Policy were gradually becoming the Commission's focal point for minority-related issues and decisions about funding and follow-up.

The difficulty of measuring a construct

A comparative study of the Regular Reports reveals their three key characteristics with regard to the minority criterion: a hierarchy of minority issues, ad hocery and inconsistencies resulting from the lack of clear benchmarks and a dilemma of implementation (Hughes and Sasse 2003). Although most of the candidate countries of Central and Eastern Europe have significant minority populations, only two minority groups were consistently stressed in the Regular Reports: the Russophone minority in Estonia and Latvia, and the Roma minorities of Bulgaria, the Czech Republic, Hungary, Romania and Slovakia. This 'hierarchy' of minority issues reflects the EU's interest in good relations with its most powerful neighbour and energy supplier Russia and its own soft security concerns linked to migration. Furthermore, a non-territorialized, internally diverse and marginalized minority like the Roma is a politically less sensitive group to focus on, compared with territorialized and politically mobilized minorities, such as the Hungarians in Slovakia and Romania or the Turks in Bulgaria. Undoubtedly, the Roma face severe problems of systematic discrimination, political and social exclusion, segregation, and poverty, but this is not a feature specific to the candidate countries (Vermeersch 2003, 2004).

The Commission's Regular Reports have been a patchwork of formulaic codes encapsulating 'progress' on the road to membership. The commitment of candidate countries to improve minority protection is taken at face value and described positively as progress. Some candidate countries earn generic praise, for example through the statement that minorities are 'well integrated into Hungarian society' or that Hungary has a 'well-developed institutional framework protecting the interests of its minorities and promoting their cultural and educational autonomy' (European Commission 2001a, 2002c). The Regular Reports are designed in a way that renders them a cumulative success story for each candidate country. Positive developments are recorded, even when the previous Reports had not specified any problems in these areas.

The Regular Reports illustrate the EU's difficulties in measuring progress in the absence of clear benchmarks. The Reports track the adoption and amendment of laws on citizenship, naturalization, language and elections, the establishment of institutions that manage minority issues within the executive or legislative structures, and the launch of government programmes to address minority needs. Trends are evaluated by numerical benchmarks, such as the number of minority members obtaining citizenship, the number of requests for naturalization, the pass rate for language or citizenship tests, the number of schools or classes taught in the state or minority languages, the number of teachers trained to teach in the state or minority languages and the extent of media broadcasting in minority languages. The reports make frequent general references to 'international standards' or 'European standards' and cross-reference the recommendations, activities and documents of the Council of Europe and the OSCE. This practice is most evident in the case of Latvia and Estonia, where the Europe Agreements included a reference to the need to comply with the undertakings of the OSCE. The 1999 report on Latvia, for example, asserts that 'Latvia now fulfils all recommendations expressed by the OSCE in the area of naturalization and citizenship' (European Commission 1999a). Yet, fresh concerns over the linguistic rights of the Russophone minority are expressed in the 2001 report on Latvia, which broadly refers to the 'joint efforts' of the EU, the OSCE and the Council of Europe to establish guidelines for the new language law (European Commission 2001b). The reports indicate that the EU has also relied on the OSCE (and presumably also the Council of Europe) for some basic information and data gathering activities. For example, the 1998 report on Estonia quotes OSCE data on the number of minority members who gained citizenship (European Commission 1998).

Ad hocery and the borrowing of different external 'standards' have confounded the ambiguity and inconsistency inherent in the minority condition. The 2002 reports on Estonia and Latvia, for example, report on the one hand that the OSCE mission in these states closed in late 2001, but note on the other hand the EU's continued concerns. The report on Latvia, for example, 'urged' the country to ratify the Framework Convention and noted EU and OSCE concerns regarding the naturalization and effective political participation of minorities in the context of restrictive language laws. Nevertheless, the report concluded that 'the country has made considerable progress in further consolidating and deepening (. . .) respect for and protection of minorities' (European Commission 2002a, 2002b). As a Commission official put it: 'Although the closure of the OSCE missions was not a formal condition, the Commission had a clear interest in it'.[7]

The EU's own assessment of the Roma issue hovers uncomfortably between the realization that the socio-economic and political situation of the Roma has not improved and detailed lists of new activities and programmes targeting the needs of the Roma (see in particular: European Commission 1999b: 16–17, 2000b: 25–27). The fact that the Regular Reports harshly criticize the treatment of the Roma in the candidate countries, which are generally recognized as continuing 'to fulfil the political Copenhagen criteria', underlines that minority issues were not the EU's priority during the accession process. As a Commission official in DG Enlargement put it:

> There has been a constant inherent tension between the opening phrase about the fulfilment of the political criteria and the subsequent criticism

of the Roma treatment. We lack benchmarks to determine when the issue would be considered sufficiently 'resolved'. As long as the situation wasn't getting any worse, we tried to be as consistent as possible by focusing on the direction of policy-making.[8]

In the course of the accession process, the Commission's emphasis shifted gradually from the adoption of the *acquis* towards issues of 'capacity' and implementation. However, the Regular Reports demonstrate that the Commission is less equipped to monitor and follow up on problems of implementation. In the area of minority policies, these problems are dealt with in general terms, listing the lack of funding, weak administrative capacity, understaffing and the low levels of public awareness in the candidate countries as the main shortcomings. The 'gap between policy formulation and implementation' is addressed most explicitly with reference to the Roma, for example in the reports on Slovakia in 2000 and 2001 (European Commission 2000a: 22, 2001c: 31). The potential implications of weak policy implementation are referred to most explicitly in the 2002 report on Bulgaria, which obliquely notes that there are 'signs of increased tension between the Roma and ethnic Bulgarians' (European Commission 2002d: 39). On the other hand, the EU and the candidate countries at times appeared to be acting out a charade on Roma policy. For example, the 1999 report on Bulgaria states: 'Significant progress was achieved concerning further integration of Roma through the adoption of a Framework Programme for 'Full Integration of the Roma Population into the Bulgarian Society' and establishment of relevant institutions at central and regional level' (European Commission 1999c: 75). By what measure this formal adoption of a programme marks 'significant progress' is not clear, and two years later, little of this programme had been implemented (Rangelov 2001).

Assessing the impact of a construct

Through the involvement of international actors, the vaguely defined norm of minority protection has framed the debates and perceptions of domestic actors in the candidate countries. It has affected the timing and nature of specific pieces of legislation (e.g. the gradual modification of restrictive citizenship laws in Estonia and Latvia, the Slovak Language Law, the Hungarian Status Law), but the domestic political constellations with their inherent incentives and constraints have ultimately been critical for institutional and policy outcomes. The EU's actual impact has been described rather realistically in Commission circles: 'we help them do what they are already doing anyway'.[9] EU conditionality has anchored minority issues in the political rhetoric of the candidate states, but the EU had little to offer in terms of substantive guidance, as the lack of benchmarks, inconsistencies and the limited scope for follow-up on implementation in the Commission's Regular Reports demonstrate. There is now as much variation across the new member states as there is in the old member states with regard to the balance between ethnic and civic conceptions of statehood, the explicit recognition of national minorities (or lack thereof), and the state's responsibilities vis-à-vis its minorities (such as funding).

A meaningful assessment of the EU's impact on minority issues has to take stock of the EU's own measured criteria – despite their inconsistencies – and consider the wider domestic political context in which the minority condition has resonated. As subsequent chapters in this volume will provide detailed case studies, it will suffice here to point to two interesting settings: the variation in the extent to which international actors paid attention to minority issues during the accession process and the extent to which minority representation has been institutionalized in the domestic political scene. The intensity and visibility of international involvement in the area of minority protection singles out Latvia and Estonia as the strongest test case of the EU's transformative impact on legislative and behavioural change. The presence of ethnopolitical parties in Bulgaria, Romania, and Slovakia – three countries in which the EU concentrated on the Roma rather than on the politically mobilized minorities – provides for an instructive setting to assess the more indirect effects of the EU minority condition.

The EU's intense and continuous involvement in Estonia and Latvia was based on three benchmarks, highlighted in the Commission's Opinion and its Regular Reports: the amendments of citizenship and language legislation, the rate of naturalization, and the ratification of the Council of Europe's Framework Convention. The restrictive post-Soviet citizenship and language laws and naturalization procedures were amended step by step (Norgaard 1996; Kolsto 2002; Kelley 2004). The significant legal and constitutional changes during the accession period, however, have not fostered a conclusive trend of legislative activity and implementation in the post-accession period. Latvia's 1999 Language Law, which toned down its 1989 and 1992 precursors, still aims to regulate the use of the Latvian language down to private institutions and companies and self-employed persons. The law's definition of when these activities relate to public interests is vague, and reference is made to assessment procedures to check the required level of state language proficiency (Republic of Latvia 1999). The 2007 amendments to Estonia's Language Law have given equivalent language inspectorates extended powers. The Council of Europe's High Commissioner for Human Rights singled out this latest provision among his concerns (Commissioner for Human Rights 2007), following up on similar criticism by the Advisory Committee on the Framework Convention (Advisory Committee 2006).

In Latvia, the naturalization rate has dropped significantly after a temporary peak around the accession date in 2004–05, from 16,439 in 2006 to 6,826 in 2007 (Naturalization Board of the Republic of Latvia 2008). As of April 2007, there were 392,816 non-citizens (17 per cent of the population) and 41,439 aliens registered in Latvia (Naturalization Board of the Republic of Latvia 2008), whereas in Estonia, as of May 2006, there were 120,000 non-citizens (9 per cent of the population) (Estonian Ministry of Foreign Affairs 2008). The continuing problems with integration and occasional protests, including provocations by organizations from Russia, demonstrate that the legal changes promoted by EU accession were not sufficient for bringing about significant political will and behavioural change – on the part of the majority of the Russophones, as much as on the part of the political elites representing the majority. Deeper structural issues have remained unaddressed or have, in fact, been further ingrained through the politics of conditionality. Intensive international criticism has narrowed rather than widened the domestic scope for rethinking minority policies. The positive assessment by international institutions of the situation prior to EU accession has further eroded the space for political claim-making on the part of the minorities. The ethnic divide has become more pronounced over time, though this has not led to sustained societal mobilization on the part of the Russophones. The absence of an overarching ethnic identity among the Russophones and of a tangible avenue for political mobilization have hindered the formation of coherent minority parties or organizations. Latvia's political scene illustrates that even sizeable political representation at the national level does not necessarily guarantee influence over policy-making, especially if the other factions in parliament stand united on minority-relevant legislation. After Latvia's 2002 elections, 25 out of 100 deputies represented the loose bloc 'For Human Rights in a United Latvia', which combined a minority platform with a leftist outlook. The number of minority-friendly deputies decreased slightly to 23 in the 2006 elections. Despite their potential numerical strength, Latvia's minority-oriented deputies are easily outvoted by the overwhelming de facto majority Latvian 'ethnic' bloc, whenever minority-relevant issues are being decided in parliament.[10] Parliamentary representation of minority interests may even feed directly into more extremist rhetoric among the main right and centre-right parties in the run-up to elections.

The Framework Convention has served as the EU's shorthand for a measurable commitment to minority protection. The fact that Latvia did not heed the rhetorical pressure on this issue before accession demonstrates the lack of commitment to enforcement on both sides – Latvia delayed the process of ratification, and the EU did not make this a stumbling block on the way to membership. The declarations Latvia has added to the Framework Convention illustrate that the post-accession ratification of the document is a lukewarm endorsement of the principle of minority protection (Sasse 2008). During the accession process, the EU's leverage over minority issues was reinforced by the expertise and involvement of the OSCE and the Council of Europe. While the EU's own leverage on the various components of democratic conditionality by definition ends with accession, the leverage of the other two international institutions is significantly shaped by the politics of conditionality during accession. The OSCE's scope of action is limited, not least due to its tainted image resulting from the politically motivated decision on the mission closure in Estonia and Latvia (Hughes 2005). The Council of Europe's reputation is intact, and it is widely recognized as the only institution with a scope for action on minority issues beyond the date of EU accession. However, it can at best hope to gradually shape the ingrained structural, attitudinal and behavioural trends through its Framework Convention's monitoring cycles.

So far, there has been less analysis of the effects of the EU's minority condition in countries of Central and Eastern Europe with organized domestic minority representation. Bulgaria, Romania and Slovakia present variations on an instructive setting, where ethnopolitical parties have become a stable feature of the political systems (Brusis 2003; Vachudová 2005; Sasse 2006). In these countries, the incentive of EU membership, tied to a bundle of political criteria, helped to galvanize domestic political forces in favour of democratic regime change (the ouster of authoritarian leaders in Slovakia and Romania in 1996 and 1999 respectively, and a change in government in Bulgaria in 1997). Minority parties, which already existed as organized opposition forces, played a crucial and active role in this process. In Romania and Slovakia, the minorities' de facto political participation preceded a more detailed *de jure* elaboration of minority rights. Over time, the minority parties built a joint electoral platform with the moderate parties, cutting across ethnic divisions and forging new political majorities. The EU contributed to the creation of domestic political space for minority participation, but it did not intervene in the internal disputes over the subsequent formulation of institutional responses to minority demands, for example in the case of the amended Slovak Language Law of 1999, which remained unpopular among the Hungarian minority.

Recent elections in Bulgaria, Romania, and Slovakia have demonstrated that a minority's visibility in the political sphere, in particular in government, provides an easy platform for populist, nationalist or outright xenophobic counter-mobilization, without being necessarily the single or most important cause of the electoral success of nationalist parties. Political participation of an ethnic minority party and ethnic power-sharing, encouraged though not caused by the EU's minority condition, can thus prove stabilizing during one stage of the transition process and destabilizing during another. The political dynamics over time underpin the understanding of conditionality as a malleable construct that performs different functions over time.

The November 2000 elections in Romania saw a surge of extreme nationalist rhetoric. The second round of the presidential elections saw incumbent Ion Iliescu pitted against Corneliu Vadim Tudor, the leader of the nationalist Greater Romania Party. In the 2004 parliamentary elections, the Greater Romania Party received 13 per cent of the national vote. The rise of the xenophobic party *Ataka* (8.2 per cent) in Bulgaria's 2005 parliamentary elections and its leader Volen Siderov's strong showing in the presidential elections in 2006 (24 per cent in the second round) illustrate a similar trend towards successful nationalist parties. In the pre-term 2006 Slovak elections, the Hungarian Coalition Party obtained 11.7 per cent of the vote, a higher percentage than ever, but it is no longer represented in government. Instead, centre-left populist prime minister Robert Fico, leader of the Social Democratic Party, formed a government with Vladimír Mečiar's Movement for a Democratic Slovakia and the Slovak National Party, which obtained nearly 12 per cent of the vote. The price Fico had to pay for his coalition is the tacit acceptance of the nationalist rhetoric of his coalition partners. The moderate Hungarian party leader Bela Bugar has been replaced with the more outspoken Pal Csaky, an indication of how quickly polarization breeds.

Conclusions

This chapter has argued that the EU's condition of minority protection is best understood as a political construct. As a framing device, this construct can have 'real' effects on domestic actors, and these effects are best understood as contributing factors rather than primary causes. They are insufficiently captured by the focus on legislative change employed in most studies of EU conditionality. EU effects can be unintended and indirect. Methodologically, if we want to go beyond a formal or technical understanding of conditionality and compliance, we need to begin with the construction and malleability of the condition itself, taking seriously the political process by which it was devised originally and re-appropriated by different actors over time. Ultimately, medium to long term behavioural change is the best test of effective international conditionality. The discussion of the EU's minority condition has rightly been classified as a 'reinforcement mechanism' or 'lock-in effect'. However, what has not yet been appreciated is the second dimension of this lock-in effect: deeper structural issues facilitating polarization and segregation can also be 'locked in'. In the short run, the socialization effects of conditionality are almost impossible to trace. In the medium term, a wider range of socialization effects becomes apparent. Without at least a degree of socialization, the implementation of rationally adopted laws and policies from the accession period is bound to remain patchy. Rationalist calculations may inform legal changes but they do not necessarily go hand in hand with socialization effects supporting these changes. As this chapter has demonstrated, the socialization effects (revealed through behaviour) can point in the opposite direction from the rationalist motivation of legal change.

While the variation between cases and outcomes makes generalizations difficult, they suggest two dynamics that have so far been missing in the debate on EU conditionality: first, an intense and highly visible international involvement in a politicized issue (or one aspect of them) can produce an overlay of contradictory outcomes: a legal change can hide deeper political or societal problems which might, in fact, have become ingrained in the context of the EU's involvement. Second, the EU's minority condition can have an impact, even if and when the EU does not actively engage in it. The EU's encouragement of ethnic power-sharing as part of regime change and domestic political references to the EU's minority condition can fuel political mobilization, especially (but not only) in the presence of ethnopolitical parties. The political salience of minority issues can progress through various cycles of mobilization, including periods of power-sharing and polarization.

Notes

1 Author's interview with a Commission official, formerly Horizontal Co-ordination Unit, DG Enlargement, 13 January 2004.
2 The check-list on minority issues in the Unit's handbook for 2002 included the following: ratification and implementation of the Framework Convention; the situation of the Roma, ethnic Russians and other minorities; citizenship legislation, rate of nat-

uralization, stateless children, non-citizens' passports; active policies to integrate minorities; language legislation/language training programmes; professional restrictions; minority rights ombudsman (if relevant).

3 Author's interview with a Commission official, formerly DG Enlargement, 13 January 2004.

4 Author's interview with a Commission official, Horizontal Co-ordination Unit, DG Enlargement, 13 January 2004.

5 Author's interview with a Commission official, DG Enlargement, Brussels, 12 January 2004.

6 Author's interview with a Commission official, formerly Horizontal Co-Ordination Unit, DG Enlargement, 13 January 2004.

7 Author's interview with a Commission official, DG Enlargement, Brussels, 12 January 2004.

8 Author's interview with a Commission official, DG Enlargement, 13 January 2004.

9 Author's interview with a Commission official in the Horizontal Coordination Unit, 13 January 2004.

10 Author's interviews with members of the Latvian parliament, Riga, September 2005.

References

Advisory Committee (2006) *Second Opinion on Estonia, adopted on 24 February 2005*, Strasbourg: Advisory Committee on the Framework Convention for the Protection of National Minorities.

Brusis, M. (2003) 'The European Union and Interethnic Power-Sharing Arrangements in Accession Countries', *Journal on Ethnopolitics and Minority Issues in Europe*, 1: 1–21.

Commissioner for Human Rights (2007) *Memorandum to the Estonian Government. Assessment of the progress made in implementing the 2004 recommendations of the Commissioner for Human Rights of the Council of Europe*, Strasbourg: Council of Europe. Online, available at: https://wcd.coe.int/ViewDoc.jsp?id =1163131#P96_3581 (accessed 23 February 2008).

De Witte, B. (2000) 'Politics versus Law in the EU's Approach to Ethnic Minorities', EUI Working Paper RSC No. 2000/4.

Estonian Ministry of Foreign Affairs (2008) *Population by Nationality*. Online, available at: www.vm.ee/estonia/kat_399/pea_172/4305.html%20-%20Estonia %20 in %202006 (accessed 23 February 2008).

European Commission (1998) *1998 Regular Report on Estonia's Progress Towards Accession*, Brussels: European Commission.

—— (1999a) *Regular Report on Latvia's Progress Towards Accession*, Brussels: European Commission.

—— (1999b) *Regular Report on the Czech Republic's Progress Towards Accession*, Brussels: European Commission.

—— (1999c) *Regular Report on Bulgaria's Progress Towards Accession*, Brussels: European Commission.

—— (2000a) *Regular Report on Slovakia's Progress Towards Accession*, Brussels: European Commission.

—— (2000b) *Regular Report on the Czech Republic's Progress Towards Accession*, Brussels: European Commission.

—— (2001a) *Regular Report on Hungary's Progress Towards Accession*, Brussels: European Commission.

—— (2001b) *Regular Report on Latvia's Progress Towards Accession*, Brussels: European Commission.

—— (2001c) *Regular Report on Slovakia's Progress Towards Accession*, Brussels: European Commission.

—— (2002a) *Regular Report on Estonia's Progress Towards Accession*, Brussels: European Commission.

—— (2002b) *Regular Report on Latvia's Progress Towards Accession*, Brussels: European Commission.

—— (2002c) *Regular Report on Hungary's Progress Towards Accession*, Brussels: European Commission.

—— (2002d) *Regular Report on Bulgaria's Progress Towards Accession*, Brussels: European Commission.

Grabbe, H. (2006) *The EU's Transformative Power. Europeanization through Conditionality in Central and Eastern Europe*, Palgrave Macmillan: Houndmills.

Hughes, J. (2005) 'Exit in Deeply Divided Societies: Regimes of Discrimination in Estonia and Latvia and the Potential for Russophone Migration', *Journal of Common Market Studies*, 43 (3): 739–762.

Hughes, J. and Sasse, G. (2003) 'Monitoring the Monitors: EU Enlargement Conditionality and Minority Protection in the CEECs', *Journal on Ethnopolitics and Minority Issues in Europe*, 1: 1–36.

Hughes, J., Sasse, G. and Gordon, C. (2004) *Europeanization and Regionalization in the EU's Enlargement to Central and Eastern Europe. The Myth of Conditionality*, Palgrave Macmillan: Houndmills.

Jacoby, W. (2004) *The Enlargement of the European Union and NATO. Ordering from the Menu in Central Europe*, Cambridge: Cambridge University Press.

Kelley, J. (2004) *Ethnic Politics in Europe. The Power of Norms and Incentives*, Princeton: Princeton University Press.

Kolsto, P. (2002) *National Integration and Violent Conflict in Post-Soviet Societies: The Cases of Estonia and Moldova*, Oxford: Rowman and Littlefield.

Naturalization Board of the Republic of Latvia (2008) *Facts and statistics on residents*. Online, available at: www.np.gov.lv/index.php?en=fakti_en&saite=residents.htm (accessed 23 February 2008).

Norgaard, O. (ed.) (1996) *The Baltic States after Independence*, Cheltenham: Edward Elgar.

Rangelov, I. (2001) 'Bulgaria's Struggle to Make Sense of EU Human Rights Criteria', EUMAP online: European Standards in Minority Protection, 1 October 2001.

Republic of Latvia (1999) Official Language Law. Online, available at: http:// unpan1.un.org/intradoc/groups/public/documents/UNTC/UNPAN018409.pdf (accessed 25 February 2008).

Sasse, G. (2005) 'EU Conditionality and Minority Rights: Translating the Copenhagen Criterion into Policy', EUI Working Paper No. 2005/16, European University Institute, Robert Schuman Centre for Advanced Studies, Florence. Online, available at: http:// ideas.repec.org/p/erp/euirsc/p0154.html (accessed 23 February 2008).

—— (2006) 'The Political Rights of National Minorities: Lessons from Central and Eastern Europe', in: W. Sadurski (ed.) *Political Rights under Stress in 21st Century Europe*, Oxford: Oxford University Press: 239–282.

——. (2008) 'The Politics of EU Conditionality: The Norm of Minority Protection during and beyond EU Accession', *Journal of European Public Policy*, 15(6): 842–60.

Schimmelfennig, F., Engert, S., and Knobel, H. (2003) 'Cost, Commitment and Compliance: The Impact of EU Democratic Conditionality on Latvia, Slovakia and Turkey', *Journal of Common Market Studies*, 41 (4): 495–518.

—— and Sedelmeier, U. (eds) (2005) *The Europeanization of Central and Eastern Europe*, Ithaca: Cornell University Press.

Schwellnus, G. (2006) 'Double Standards? Minority Protection as a Condition for Membership', in: H. Sjursen (ed.) *Questioning Enlargement: The EU in search of identity*, London: Routledge: 186–200.

Vachudová, M. A. (2005) *Europe Undivided. Democracy, Leverage and Integration after Communism*, Oxford: Oxford University Press.

Vermeersch, P. (2003) 'EU enlargement and minority rights policies in Central Europe: explaining policy shifts in the Czech Republic, Hungary and Poland', *Journal on Ethnopolitics and Minority Issues in Europe*, (1): 1–32.

—— (2004) 'Minority policy in Central Europe: Exploring the impact of the EU's enlargement strategy', *The Global Review of Ethnopolitics*, 3 (2): 3–19.

3   Anti-discrimination legislation

Guido Schwellnus

Introduction

One way of protecting minorities besides the granting of specific minority rights is the adoption of anti-discrimination measures to ensure equal opportunities for members of minority groups and to combat discrimination and social exclusion. The adoption of anti-discrimination legislation in Central and Eastern Europe is closely related to European Union (EU) rules and conditions. Several reasons explain the predominance of EU influence in this area. First, although most post-communist constitutions contain general provisions on equality and non-discrimination (Pan and Pfeil 2002), specific anti-discrimination laws, in particular those that include positive measures to actively promote equal opportunities, have no tradition in Central and Eastern Europe. Unlike minority protection systems, which in several cases follow national traditions and peculiarities, the development of non-discrimination rules was mainly influenced by international or European norms.

Second, non-discrimination is one of the EU's focal points with regard to minority protection, which was demanded as part of the political conditions formulated in the Copenhagen criteria. Pressure was particularly put on countries with large Roma populations, as these tend to face large-scale discrimination and social exclusion. Finally, in contrast to other areas of minority protection where no respective EU rules exist, non-discrimination is a well-established norm of Community law, which has recently been extended towards the minority-relevant area of racial discrimination. Hence, the EU was neither confronted with the problem of setting 'double standards', i.e. demanding the implementation of rules from candidate states that did not apply to existing member states (De Witte 2000), nor did it face the need to refer to norms developed by other international institutions, as was the case with minority rights. Instead, the adoption of anti-discrimination legislation can predominantly be seen as the transposition of relevant EU directives.

EU non-discrimination rules

At the EU level, the issue of minorities is exclusively addressed through the concept of non-discrimination (Bell 2002; Toggenburg 2000). This norm has been a long-standing principle within Community law in the form of gender equality and the abolition of discrimination on the basis of nationality between member states, which were both already enshrined in the 1957 Treaty of Rome. In the following years, the European Court of Justice has consistently enforced the treaty provisions concerning nationality and gender discrimination, rendering non-discrimination one of the fundamental principles of Community law, and measures countering discrimination on the ground of gender in particular were specified in legislation such as the 1975 Equal Pay Directive and the 1976 Equal Treatment Directive.

Since the 1997 Amsterdam Treaty, the non-discrimination framework has been expanded to include ethnic and racial discrimination. Article 13 of the treaty states that the Community 'may take appropriate action to combat discrimination based on sex, racial or ethnic origin, religion or belief, disability, age or sexual orientation'. On this basis, two directives were passed in 2000: a 'Framework Directive on equal treatment in employment and occupation',[1] and, more significantly, a 'Directive on equal treatment between persons irrespective of racial or ethnic origin' (the so-called 'Race Equality Directive').[2] Finally, 'membership of a national minority' was included in the non-discrimination article (Art. 21) of the Charter of Fundamental Rights.[3] However, the last document has so far not become legally binding (Bell 2004).

The Race Equality Directive constitutes the cornerstone of Community law in the area of minority protection. It features detailed and in certain areas innovative provisions, such as a definition of direct and indirect discrimination, the legal concepts of harassment, victimization, and instruction to discriminate, provisions regarding the reversal of the burden of proof, and the establishment of specialized equality bodies. In contrast to the Framework Directive on equal treatment in employment and occupation, the scope of application of the Race Equality Directive goes beyond the sphere of the workplace and includes the fields of education, social protection and housing. Not mandatory, but explicitly allowed and encouraged, are positive measures to support or compensate disadvantaged groups. Moreover, the Commission has shown a strong preference towards the adoption of unified comprehensive anti-discrimination legislation, although the Directive allows for being implemented through several legal acts (Dimitrova and Rhinard 2005: 15).

EU conditionality in the field of non-discrimination

In theoretical terms, conditionality is expected to be effective if the benefits (i.e. the prospect of financial and institutional rewards by the EU) are sufficiently conditional, determinate, credible and high in order to exceed the domestic costs of compliance with EU conditions (Schimmelfennig and Schwellnus 2007). If we concentrate on the external factors that determine the effectiveness of conditionality, it is plausible to assume that the size of the reward (EU membership) and the credibility of the conditions, i.e. the ability to provide the reward if the conditions are fulfilled and to withhold it if they are not, are equal for all candidate states during the accession phase. There is, however, variation with regard to the determinacy of the conditions and the strength of conditionality over time as well as across countries. Hence, we can expect faster and more comprehensive rule adoption when conditionality is strong and rules are determinate, except in cases where domestic adoption costs are prohibitively high.

Two different forms of EU conditionality can be distinguished: *acquis* conditionality, which demands of all applicants the full implementation of the *acquis communautaire*, and democratic or political conditionality, which refers to the political conditions as formulated in the Copenhagen criteria (Schimmelfennig and Sedelmeier 2004). The latter include 'respect for and protection of minorities', which has been added to the membership conditions without being backed by EU rules or consistently applied in the old member states (De Witte 2000).

Among the conditions related to minority protection, the requirement to adopt anti-discrimination legislation takes a special place, because it belongs to both forms of conditionality. On the one hand, it falls under the scope of *acquis* conditionality, since it includes the transposition and implementation of EU Directives. On the other hand, however, combating discrimination on the basis of race or ethnicity is also part of the political condition to respect and protect minorities. This duality is obvious in the structure of the Commission's progress reports, which address both non-discrimination and special minority rights issues in the chapter on political criteria under the heading of 'minority rights and the protection of minorities', but exclusively refer to non-discrimination issues in the *acquis* part under the chapter on 'social policy and employment'.

In the case of *acquis* conditionality, variation in the determinacy of the conditions and the strength of conditionality is mainly over time, whereas the requirement to transpose the EU rules is uniform across countries. The implementation of anti-discrimination legislation became a clear requirement only after the adoption of the anti-discrimination directives in 2000, the transposition of which was from then on a constant reference point in the progress reports. Still, although the general condition to transpose the entire *acquis communautaire* was always in place, the vast amount of rules to be implemented is likely to have impeded the effect of this condition as long as the accession date was far away and the EU did not explicitly prioritize the particular rule earlier in the process. This situation changed only in the accession 'endgame' (Schimmelfennig, Engert and Knobel 2006: 239), when the states that could so far postpone the adoption of anti-discrimination legislation because of lacking specific EU demands had to catch up in order to fulfil the criterion of implementing the non-discrimination *acquis*.

The strength of political conditionality, however, varied considerably across countries. The question of whether the EU put a strong emphasis on non-discrimination depended heavily on the size of the Roma population in the respective applicant country, because the discrimination of the Roma was of particular concern to the EU. Hence, explicit, strong and repeated pressure was exerted on states with large Roma communities, whereas states with only small Roma populations did not face nearly as much political pressure. In five of the ten accession countries (Bulgaria, the Czech Republic, Hungary, Romania, and Slovakia), measures to combat Roma discrimination were specifically spelled out as a short-term priority in the 1999 Accession Partnerships and repeatedly demanded in the annual progress reports monitoring the compliance of candidate states with EU conditions. In the other five accession countries (Estonia, Latvia, Lithuania, Poland, and Slovenia), Roma issues were not given a prominent role. We can therefore distinguish countries that faced only the general *acquis* conditionality from those that additionally were confronted with strong political conditionality.

On the basis of the assumptions discussed so far we can now formulate theoretical expectations regarding the adoption of anti-discrimination legislation in Central and Eastern Europe. Three aspects of rule adoption are of interest: timing, scope, and form. Timing refers to the time when important pieces of anti-discrimination legislation are adopted. Scope refers to the degree to which transposition of the EU directives is fulfilled (e.g. whether all grounds and spheres of application are covered, or whether the necessary institutions are established). Form refers to the question whether transposition is achieved via a comprehensive anti-discrimination law or in a more piecemeal fashion through the inclusion of non-discrimination clauses in several different pieces of legislation (such as the labour code).

Regarding the timing of legislation, no legislative initiatives in the field of anti-discrimination are to be expected before the year 2000, when the relevant EU anti-discrimination directives were passed. After 2000, anti-discrimination legislation explicitly becomes part of *acquis* conditionality, but with the date of accession still far away, rule adoption is only to be expected in cases where it is linked with specific political conditionality. This situation changes in the enlargement 'endgame', i.e. the time directly before accession in 2004 (or 2007 for Bulgaria and Romania), when candidate states that have so far neglected or delayed transposition faced strong pressure to comply in order to gain membership. In contrast to other areas of minority protection, external incentives for compliance do not fade after accession, because member states that fail to transpose EU directives face infringement procedures. In the end, therefore, full transposition is to be expected from all new member states.

As to the scope and form of transposition, we should expect countries that face strong political conditionality in addition to general *acquis* conditionality not only to respond quicker with the adoption of anti-discrimination legislation, but they should also be more likely to fully transpose the *acquis communautaire* at an early stage, and to do so by adopting comprehensive anti-discrimination laws instead of opting for a piecemeal approach that initially transposes EU rules only partly by amending existing pieces of legislation.

The adoption of anti-discrimination legislation in Central and Eastern Europe

The following section tests whether the expectation that the adoption of anti-discrimination legislation in Central and Eastern Europe is predominantly a result of the implementation of EU rules prompted by conditionality holds. I will discuss first the five countries that were confronted with strong political conditionality regarding the discrimination against the Roma (Bulgaria, Czech Republic, Hungary, Romania, and Slovakia), and then the five countries that did not raise specific EU concerns, but only were submitted to the condition to fully adopt the *acquis communautaire* before accession (Estonia, Latvia, Lithuania, Poland, and Slovenia).

Countries with strong political conditionality

In Bulgaria, the reaction to the demand of transposing the EU directives was considerably delayed in comparison to other countries that faced strong political conditionality. While the EU reports reiterated the lack of progress in transposing the *acquis*, an NGO report still concluded in 2003 that '[n]o comprehensive anti-discrimination law or special anti-discrimination remedies, including bodies or procedures, exist' (Ilieva 2003: 1). In January 2004, however, 'comprehensive anti-discrimination legislation entered into force, through which a large degree of alignment with the anti-discrimination *acquis* has been reached' (European Commission 2004: 20). Although the timing appears close to the date of the first accession round, rule adoption cannot be attributed to a negotiation 'endgame' situation, since Bulgaria was only admitted in 2007. In the case of Bulgaria, a comprehensive anti-discrimination law transposing the EU directive was therefore adopted several years before accession.

In the Czech Republic, only the 'Employment Act' (amended in 1999) and the labour code (amended in 2001) included specific anti-discrimination clauses, but even here the formulations did not fulfil all requirements of the EU non-discrimination *acquis* (Bukovská and Taylor 2001: 14), so that further amendments were passed in 2003 and 2004 to align the laws with EU directives, e.g. by inserting definitions of discrimination (Boučková 2007: 3). In 2002, the social democrat government approved an expert report recommending the adoption of a single comprehensive anti-discrimination law instead of inserting respective clauses into existing bills (Bukovská and Boučková 2003: 2). Work on the anti-discrimination law was concluded in 2004, but its adoption was delayed, and when it finally passed the lower chamber of parliament in 2006, it was subsequently rejected in the Senate, which held a liberal-conservative majority. By November 2007, therefore, the Czech Republic had only partially transposed EU anti-discrimination law and still had to address the provisions of the Race Equality Directive that were not related to the workplace. Facing the imminent threat of infringement procedures to be initiated by the Commission, the new liberal-conservative government re-introduced a less far-reaching version of the anti-discrimination law in 2007 but, by November 2007, the law had still to be adopted.

In Hungary, Commission reports from 2001 onwards noted repeatedly the necessity to adopt legislation in order to transpose the *acquis*: 'Hungary does not have a unified law on anti-discrimination' (European Commission 2001b: 19).

'The current anti-discrimination legislation is fragmented [. . .]. Moreover, there is no comprehensive system to effectively enforce the implementation of anti-discrimination legislation' (European Commission 2002a: 27). The final assessment before accession also stressed that '[a]ttention is to be given to alignment with the anti-discrimination *acquis*, and considerable efforts should aim at improving the situation of the Roma minority' (European Commission 2003a: 36). The reaction to these explicit demands was initially delayed for domestic reasons. Plans for a comprehensive anti-discrimination law, which had been elaborated by an expert committee set up as early as 1997, were rejected in 2000 by the Minister of Justice. The minority ombudsman nevertheless forwarded a proposal, and after the Constitutional Court ruled that such a unified law would not be unconstitutional, a special committee was established to review existing legislation (Open Society Institute 2001: 223–224). However, it was only under a new government that a 'Law on Equal Treatment and the Promotion of Equal Opportunities' was adopted in 2003 (Bell *et al.* 2003: 66). This legislation covers all aspects of the Race Equality Directive and partly even exceeds the necessities of Community law. Thus, Hungary managed just in time to completely transpose the *acquis* in this area (European Commission 2005a: 15; Cormack and Bell 2005: 15).

In Romania, the adoption of the EU's Race Equality Directive led to a very quick legislative reaction. Already in 2000 the Romanian government passed a special 'Ordinance on the Prevention and Punishment of All Forms of Discrimination', which was approved by parliament in 2002. This regulation gave Romania 'the most comprehensive anti-discrimination framework among EU candidate countries' (Open Society Institute 2001: 393) at the time. Although in the follow-up to this rapid rule transfer some inconsistencies arose, because the anti-discrimination clauses of other laws – e.g. in the labour code – still featured differing formulations and had to be amended, Romania has been one of the first countries to fully transpose the EU non-discrimination *acquis*.

In Slovakia, the government reacted swiftly to the Race Equality Directive. In 2001 a comprehensive anti-discrimination law was drafted in collaboration with human rights non-governmental organizations (NGOs) (Open Society Institute 2001: 442). This proposal, which was specifically endorsed by the party of the Hungarian minority, was adopted by the government in February 2002 and forwarded to the parliament. There, however, the bill failed, because one of the coalition partners (the Christian Democrats) voiced massive concerns and finally forced the withdrawal of the bill. Hence, the first attempt to transpose the non-discrimination *acquis* failed at the hands of veto players in the governing coalition (Dimitrova and Rhinard 2005: 13). At least partial transposition was achieved in 2002 by adopting a new labour code which incorporated the workplace-related areas of the anti-discrimination directives.

Still, the Commission held that '[t]he adoption of comprehensive anti-discrimination legislation would be a major step forward' (European Commission 2002c: 32), and despite a further amendment of the labour code, the final monitoring report in 2003 came to the conclusion that '[l]egislation remains to be fully aligned with the *acquis* and the equality body required by the *acquis* needs to be established' (European Commission 2003c: 33–34). In the end, the anti-discrimination law was passed in May 2004 – i.e. shortly after accession – with the help of the opposition, despite continuing resistance of the Christian Democrats. This did not, however, end the contestation of the issue, because the Minister of the Interior (a member of the Christian Democrat party) brought the case before the Constitutional Court in order to check the compatibility of positive measures with the equality principle enshrined in the Slovak constitution. The court decided in October 2005 that the respective regulations were not in conformity with Slovak constitutional law and had to be dropped (Dimitrova and Rhinard 2005: 14). The bill was subsequently passed without affirmative action provisions, but is still compliant with the non-discrimination directives, which allow for, but do not prescribe, positive measures.

Countries with weak political conditionality

In Estonia, progress to transpose the EU directives was slow, although the Ministry of Justice already in 2002 elaborated a draft equal opportunities law. The draft was forwarded to the parliament in October of the same year, but was withdrawn again after the elections in March 2003 (Bell *et al.* 2003: 59). The new government immediately decided on preparing a new draft, but at the time of accession still no non-discrimination legislation had been passed. Only the 'Law on Work Contracts' was amended just in time for accession in April 2004 (European Commission 2005a: 14). In summary, Estonia has so far only partly complied with the condition of fully transposing the non-discrimination *acquis* (European Commission 2003e), because the areas of the Race Equality Directive not related to the workplace are not yet covered by any legislation (European Commission 2005a: 16). Only after an official letter by the Commission, the Ministry of Justice in 2006 finalized a draft 'Law on Equal Treatment' to fully transpose the Directives but, by November 2007, it had not yet been adopted (Poleshchuk 2007: 6).

In Latvia, transposition of the EU anti-discrimination directives in workplace-related areas was achieved by adopting a new labour code in 2001, which was amended in May 2004, i.e. at the time of accession. However, Latvian non-discrimination legislation remains fragmented and does not cover the areas of the Race Equality Directive that are not related to the workplace (Bell *et al.* 2003: 72; European Commission 2005a: 15). A comprehensive anti-discrimination law was passed in the first parliamentary reading in April 2004 immediately before accession, but the government decided to withdraw it, obviously because it planned to amend several pieces of existing legislation instead (European Commission 2005a: 16). Hence, Latvia is among the countries that have so far only partially transposed the *acquis*.

In Lithuania, no progress on transposing the anti-discrimination acquis was noted until the final report of the European Commission, which noted that draft legislation was in the parliamentary process (European Commission 2003b). In

November 2003, with the accession date drawing closer, the 'Law on Equal Treatment' was passed, and it came into force in January 2005. 'This law regulates equality on the basis of age, sexual orientation, disability, race and ethnic origin, religion and belief. This Law covers the prohibition of discrimination on all grounds listed in Directives 2000/78/EC and 2000/43/EC' (Ziobiene 2007: 3). Hence, Lithuania managed only in the accession 'endgame' to fully comply with EU rules, but in the end did so comprehensively and through a unified law.

In Poland, as in most of the countries not facing strong political conditionality, the necessary implementation of the Race Equality Directive as part of the transposition of the *acquis communautaire* is mentioned – albeit in a rather cursory manner – in the Commission reports from 2000 onwards: 'Legislation transposing the EC directive based on Article 13 of the Treaty relative to discrimination on the grounds of race or ethnic origin will have to be introduced and implemented' (European Commission 2000: 57). The fact that legislative measures to implement the Directive did not follow for some time was noted in the progress reports, but not with a very strong emphasis (European Commission 2001a: 22 and 68, 2002b: 28). Only shortly before accession, in November 2003, an amendment of the labour code at least transposed the part of the directive relating to the workplace. Still, full alignment of the Polish legal system to EU law in this area remains to be achieved.

In Slovenia, the necessity to adopt legislation transposing the EU non-discrimination *acquis* was mentioned since the 2000 progress report, and the first success was reported in 2002, when the workplace-related aspects of the directives were addressed.

> With regard to the transposition of EC anti-discrimination legislation, the Employment Relations Act adopted in April 2002 includes provisions on direct and indirect discrimination on a number of grounds. Further progress is needed to ensure the full transposition and implementation of the EC anti-discrimination legislation.
>
> (European Commission 2002d: 24)

In its final monitoring report a year later, the Commission concluded that 'legislative alignment is advanced but remains to be completed as regards the Equality Body, which needs to be established' (European Commission 2003d: 32). However, it was only in April 2004, i.e. at the time of accession to the EU, that a comprehensive 'Implementation of the Principle of Equal Treatment Act' was adopted, which covers all grounds of discrimination covered by the EU directives and even additional grounds, so that Slovenia since then 'generally complies with the Directives protecting against discrimination' (Tratar 2005: 2).

Implementation

If the story ended with the formal transposition of the directives by way of adopting anti-discrimination legislation, the EU's efforts to promote non-discrimination rules were a success story. Despite the variation in the speed and scope of rule adoption, all candidate countries finally moved towards complete and comprehensive transposition of the directives. However, formal rule adoption is only the first step and must be followed by effective implementation to bring about the desired result. As the Commission formulated it in its framework strategy on non-discrimination and equal opportunities:

> These efforts have produced results, including the development of some of the most comprehensive and far-reaching anti-discrimination legislation to be found anywhere in the world. However, further action is required in order to ensure the full and effective implementation and enforcement of this legal framework.
>
> (European Commission 2005b: 2)

Theoretically, the prospects for effective implementation should be higher in cases of *acquis* conditionality, such as the transposition of the EU anti-discrimination directives, than in areas of purely political conditionality (as in the case of group-specific minority rights), where the EU often possesses neither the expertise nor the sanction mechanisms to monitor and enforce the post-accession implementation of formally adopted rules. But even with regard to compliance with EU rules, research has highlighted the existence of different 'worlds of compliance', ranging from observance through dependence on domestic politics to complete neglect (Falkner *et al.* 2005: 317–341). Hence, whether formally adopted rules are effectively implemented or remain 'empty letters' is not a foregone conclusion.

Since legal protection against discrimination (with the exception of affirmative action measures) is predominantly a negative right that needs to be claimed individually (Niessen 2003: 254), one important obstacle to implementation, once the necessary legislation is in place, is the lack of willingness or ability of victims to bring cases of discrimination before a court. In many countries in Central and Eastern Europe, only a few cases regarding discrimination have been reported directly after the introduction of anti-discrimination legislation. One reason is the lack of information on the part of both claimants and state authorities, so that either victims of discriminatory practices are unaware of their rights or authorities fail to prosecute them as cases of discrimination.

An even more fundamental impediment to implementation is deep-rooted prejudice against ethnic minorities, which further enhances both the likelihood of authorities failing to prosecute acts of discrimination due to 'institutionalized racism' and the likelihood of victims being discouraged to claim their rights. Given the problems of a purely passive, individual rights-based system of legal protection against discrimination, specialized equality bodies, whose establishment is required by the Race Equality Directive, are of central importance for the implementation of anti-discrimination law. Their mandate not only includes awareness-raising and the dissemination of information, but also active support for claimants and in many cases even the competence to issue direct sanctions in cases of detected discrimination. The frequency and severity of such sanctions can be taken as an indicator for the status of implementation of non-discrimination rules beyond the mere letter of the law.[4]

Among the new EU member states, in 2006 comparatively severe sanctions were only reported in Hungary (fines of €1,600–2,800) and Romania – notably two countries that faced strong EU conditionality in this area and reacted with comprehensive anti-discrimination laws. All other countries still show considerable deficiencies with regard to sanctioning acts of discrimination through the new equality agencies. In Poland, no information on the number of complaints or sanctions in 2006 was available, whereas in the Czech Republic, no operational specialized equality body exists due to the still-not-completed formal transposition of the Race Equality Directive. In Latvia, sanctions were neither severe nor frequent, while Lithuania and Slovakia reported no sanctions at all in 2006. In Estonia and Slovenia, only very few complaints regarding ethnic discrimination were made (one in Estonia in the period 2004–06, and six in Slovenia in 2005–06), which is not to be interpreted as the absence of discrimination in these countries (European Union Agency for Fundamental Rights 2007: 8).

> The very low number of recorded complaints in some Member States, despite NGO reports and independent research surveys pointing towards the existence of ethnic discrimination in these countries, could indicate a lack of awareness of the existence and functioning of these specialised bodies.
> (European Union Agency for Fundamental Rights 2007: 38)

This fact points again to the important role of awareness-raising and the dissemination of information to both state authorities and the wider public as preconditions for the effective implementation of anti-discrimination legislation. Although such a requirement is also explicitly incorporated into both relevant directives, it has been noted that '[o]f all the Directives' articles, it is those on the dissemination of information and social and civil dialogue that have seen the least formal implementation by the Member States' (Bell *et al.* 2006: 94). It may, however, be argued that the specialized agencies mandated with dissemination and awareness-raising in many cases only have been set up with the transposition of EU law, so that implementation gaps in this area may be temporary. In any case, as both the specialized bodies and dissemination are part of the non-discrimination *acquis*, the EU retains some leverage to press for implementation. In addition, the Commission has identified awareness-raising as a fruitful field for EU funding (European Commission 2005b: 3).

Conclusions

What conclusions can be drawn from this brief overview of anti-discrimination legislation in the ten new EU member states from Central and Eastern Europe? All candidates have addressed questions of discrimination with specific legislation as a result of pressure to adopt the EU's non-discrimination *acquis*.

Furthermore, we can observe an increase in legislative activity towards the end of accession negotiations. This corroborates the theoretical expectation that in the absence of specific conditionality, the urgency of the general condition to transpose the entire *acquis* increases sharply in the accession 'endgame'.

Countries that faced explicit and repeated EU demands to apply the non-discrimination *acquis* in order to combat discrimination against the Roma in general reacted more quickly and comprehensively and were also more likely to achieve transposition by passing unified anti-discrimination legislation at a comparatively early stage. However, domestic opposition in several cases delayed the adoption of already drafted laws considerably, in one case (the Czech Republic) even beyond the accession date. Among the candidate countries that were not confronted with strong political conditionality, we more often observe a period of negligence regarding anti-discrimination legislation, and the response to increased pressure in the later stages of accession negotiations is piecemeal and often results in only partial or fragmented adoption.

The most important legislative gap in several countries is the failure to transpose those aspects of the Race Equality Directive that are not related to the workforce. This is predominantly the effect of a piecemeal approach of introducing non-discrimination clauses in existing legislation, most notably the labour code. However, with continuing pressure after accession through the threat of infringement procedures in case of non-compliance with EU rules, there seems to be a general trend towards comprehensive and unified anti-discrimination laws, even among those countries that initially opted for a piecemeal approach (Bell *et al.* 2006: 8).

Whereas the formal adoption of anti-discrimination legislation as a result of EU pressure can be considered a success, the results regarding the implementation of legal rules are so far mixed. If the frequency and severity of sanctions issued by the specialized equality agencies established with the transposition of the Race Equality Directive is taken as an indicator for the current status of implementation, a similar picture to the speed and scope of formal transposition prior to accession emerges: two countries facing strong conditionality (Hungary and Romania) are the front-runners with frequent and severe sanctions against detected acts of discrimination – although again the Czech Republic is a laggard due to its not yet completed formal transposition and therefore not yet operational specialized body, and Slovakia's equality agency does not issue any sanctions – and countries facing weak conditionality (Estonia, Latvia, Lithuania, Slovenia) generally show a low number of complaints and a lack of sanctioning, which does not so much show that discrimination is absent in these countries but rather that awareness is missing.

However, it may be that current shortcomings can be attributed to the recent transposition of anti-discrimination rules (and hence little knowledge about them) and especially the short time that has elapsed since the establishment of specialized bodies created to support claimants and to disseminate information. As in the case of formal transposition, variation across countries could be largely a temporary issue. Still, it remains to be seen, whether these newly created institutions will have the desired impact in the longer run. More fundamental societal obstacles, such as deep-rooted prejudices against discriminated groups, are in any case a long-term issue that needs to be addressed.

Notes

1 Council Directive 2000/78/EC of 27 November 2000 establishing a general framework for equal treatment in employment and occupation: Dir. 2000/78, OJ 2000 L303, 16–22.
2 Council Directive 2000/43/EC of 29 June 2000 implementing the principle of equal treatment between persons irrespective of racial or ethnic origin: Dir. 2000/43, OJ 2000 L180, 22–26.
3 Charter of Fundamental Rights of the European Union [2000] OJ C364/13.
4 For a recent comparative analysis of all 27 EU member states covering the time period of 2005–06, see: European Union Agency for Fundamental Rights 2007: 20–39.

References

Bell, M. (2002) *Anti-Discrimination Law and the European Union*, Oxford: Oxford University Press.

—— (2004) 'Equality and the European Union Constitution', *Industrial Law Journal*, 33 (3): 242–260.

Bell, M., Chopin, I., Hendriks, I. and Niessen, J. (2003) *Equality, Diversity and Enlargement. Report on measures to combat discrimination in acceding and candidate countries*, European Commission Directorate-General for Employment, Social Affairs and Equal Opportunities Unit D.4, Luxembourg: Office for Official Publications of the European Communities.

Bell, M., Chopin, I. and Palmer, F. (2006) *Developing Anti-Discrimination Law in Europe – The 25 EU Member States compared*, Brussels: European Network of Legal Experts in the Non-Discrimination Field.

Boučková, P. (2007) *Report on Measures to Combat Discrimination – Directives 2000/43/EC and 2000/78/EC: Country Report Czech Republic*, Brussels: European Network of Legal Experts in the Non-Discrimination Field.

Bukovská, B. and Boučková, P. (2003) *Report on Measures to Combat Discrimination in the 13 Candidate Countries (VT/2002/47). Country Report Czech Republic*, Brussels: European Network of Legal Experts in the Non-Discrimination Field.

Bukovská, B. and Taylor, L. (2001) *Legal analysis of national and European anti-discrimination legislation. A comparison of the EU Racial Equality Directive & Protocol No. 12 with anti-discrimination legislation in Czech Republic*, Brussels: European Network of Legal Experts in the Non-Discrimination Field.

Cormack, J. and Bell, M. (2005) *Developing Anti-Discrimination Law in Europe. The 25 EU Member States compared*, Brussels: European Network of Legal Experts in the Non-Discrimination Field.

De Witte, B. (2000) 'Politics Versus Law in the EU's Approach to Ethnic Minorities', *EUI Working Paper* No. RSC 2000/4, Florence: European University Institute.

Dimitrova, A. and Rhinard, M. (2005) 'The power of norms in the transposition of EU directives', *European Integration Online Papers*, 9 (16).

European Commission (2000) *2000 Regular Report from the Commission on Poland's Progress Towards Accession*; Brussels: European Commission.

—— (2001a) *2001 Regular Report on Poland's Progress Towards Accession*, Brussels: European Commission.

—— (2001b) *2001 Regular Report on Hungary's Progress Towards Accession*, Brussels: European Commission.

—— (2002a) *2002 Regular Report on Hungary's Progress Towards Accession*, Brussels: European Commission.

—— (2002b) *2002 Regular Report on Poland's Progress Towards Accession*, Brussels: European Commission.

—— (2002c) 2002 *Regular Report on Slovakia's Progress Towards Accession*, Brussels: European Commission.

—— (2002d) *2002 Regular Report on Slovenia's Progress Towards Accession*, Brussels: European Commission.

—— (2003a) *Comprehensive monitoring report on Hungary's preparations for membership*, Brussels: European Commission.

—— (2003b) *Comprehensive monitoring report on Lithuania's preparations for membership*, Brussels: European Commission.

—— (2003c) *Comprehensive monitoring report on Slovakia's preparations for membership*, Brussels: European Commission.

—— (2003d) *Comprehensive monitoring report on Slovenia's preparations for membership*, Brussels: European Commission.

—— (2003e) *Comprehensive monitoring report on Estonia's preparations for membership*, Brussels: European Commission.

—— (2004) *2004 Regular Report on Bulgaria's progress towards accession*, Brussels: European Commission.

—— (2005a) *Equality and non-discrimination Annual report 2005*, European Commission Directorate-General for Employment, Social Affairs and Equal Opportunities Unit D.3, Luxembourg: Office for Official Publications of the European Communities.

—— (2005b) *Non-discrimination and equal opportunities for all – A framework strategy. Communication from the Commission to the Council, the European Parliament, the European Economic and Social Committee and the Committee of the Regions*, Brussels: European Commission.

European Union Agency for Fundamental Rights (2007) *Report on Racism and Xenophobia in the Member States of the EU*, Brussels: European Union Agency for Fundamental Rights.

Falkner, G., Treib, O., Hartlapp, M. and Leiber, S. (2005) *Complying with Europe. EU Harmonisation and Soft Law in the Member States*, Cambridge: Cambridge University Press.

Ilieva, M. (2003) *Report on Measures to Combat Discrimination in the 13 Candidate Countries (VT/2002/47). Country Report Bulgaria*, Brussels: European Network of Legal Experts in the Non-Discrimination Field.

Niessen, J. (2003) 'Making the Law Work. The Enforcement and Implementation of Anti-Discrimination Legislation', *European Journal of Migration and Law*, 5: 249–257.

Open Society Institute (2001) *Minority Protection in the EU Accession Process. Monitoring the EU Accession Process: Minority Rights*, Budapest: Open Society Institute.

Pan, C. and Pfeil, B.S. (2002) *Minderheitenrechte in Europa. Handbuch der europäischen Volksgruppen Band 2* [Minority Rights in Europe. Handbook of European Ethnic Groups Volume 2], Wien: Braumüller.

Poleshchuk, V. (2007) *Report on Measures to Combat Discrimination – Directives 2000/43/EC and 2000/78/EC: Country Report Estonia*, Brussels: European Network of Legal Experts in the Non-Discrimination Field.

Schimmelfennig, F., Engert, S. and Knobel, H. (2006) *International Socialization in Europe: European Organizations, Political Conditionality, and Democratic Change*, Basingstoke: Palgrave Macmillan.

Schimmelfennig, F. and Schwellnus, G. (2007) 'Politiktransfer durch politische Konditionalität. Der Einfluss der EU auf die Nichtdiskriminierungs- und Minderheitenschutzgesetzgebung in Mittel- und Osteuropa' [Policy Transfer via Political Conditionality: The EU's Impact on Non-Discrimination and Minority Protection Legislation in Central and Eastern Europe], in: K. Holzinger *et al.* (eds.) *Transfer, Diffusion und Konvergenz von Politiken* [Transfer, Diffusion and Convergence of Policies], Wiesbaden: VS-Verlag, 271–296.

Schimmelfennig, F. and Sedelmeier, U. (2004) 'Governance by conditionality: EU rule transfer to the candidate countries of Central and Eastern Europe', *Journal of European Public Policy*, 11 (4): 661–679.

Toggenburg, G. (2000) 'A Rough Orientation Through a Delicate Relationship: The European Union's Endeavours for (its) Minorities', *European Integration online Papers*, 4 (16).

Tratar, M.K. (2005) *Report on Measures to Combat Discrimination – Directives 2000/43/EC and 2000/78/EC: Country Report Slovenia*, Brussels: European Network of Legal Experts in the Non-Discrimination Field.

Ziobiene, E. (2007) *Report on Measures to Combat Discrimination – Directives 2000/43/EC and 2000/78/EC: Country Report Lithuania*, Brussels: European Network of Legal Experts in the Non-Discrimination Field.

4 The Framework Convention for the Protection of National Minorities

Rainer Hofmann

Introduction

The Council of Europe Framework Convention for the Protection of National Minorities (FCNM) was opened for signature on 1 February 1995 and entered into force on 1 February 1998. All ten European Union (EU) accession countries from Central and Eastern Europe are member states to the FCNM, although Latvia only ratified the FCNM after accession to the EU. While recognizing that there are disagreements about what the FCNM requires, the focus of this chapter is on the formal and substantive compliance of these countries from an FCNM perspective.

The monitoring system

The evaluation of the implementation of the FCNM is entrusted to the Council of Europe Committee of Ministers (consisting of the Ministers of Foreign Affairs of the Council of Europe member states), assisted by the Advisory Committee (AC). States parties are required to submit a report within one year of the entry into force of the FCNM for the respective state party. Further reports are due on a five-yearly basis or at the Committee of Ministers' request.

For the first monitoring cycle, the following monitoring procedure applied. After receipt of a state report by the Council of Europe, it was transmitted to all 18 members of the AC. The members of the country-specific working group set up within the AC also received the often quite voluminous annexes to the state reports and reports by NGOs and organizations representing national minorities. The working group then drafted a questionnaire, requesting additional information from the respective state. Country visits constituted the most important part of the process leading to the formulation of a draft opinion. Such country visits included not only meetings with government officials, but also with representatives of other state organs and representatives of national minorities and civil society. As a rule, such visits also included travels into regions where national minorities reside. The respective working group then drafted an opinion which was discussed at the AC plenary. All opinions were adopted by the AC with overwhelming majorities, quite often unanimously.

The actual discussion of the opinions of the AC as well as of government comments took place in the Rapporteur Group on Human Rights (GR-H), a sub-body of the Committee of Ministers. Most government comments were constructive and consisted of information on developments after adoption of the opinion, most frequently prompted by critical remarks made during a country visit.

The Committee of Ministers concluded the monitoring procedure by adopting its country-specific resolutions, consisting of conclusions and recommendations. The resolutions of the Committee of Ministers largely followed the opinions of the AC. The Committee of Ministers also called on governments to keep the AC informed about measures taken. An important element of this follow-up procedure concerns follow-up seminars. Such seminars were open to the public and attended by competent government officials, representatives of national minorities, members of civil society, and representatives of the AC.

The second cycle of monitoring follows more or less the same pattern as the first. The major difference consists in the different outline for state reports: member states are asked to indicate all practical arrangements made for following up the first monitoring cycle and to answer specific questions by the AC.

Compliance with the formal aspects of the monitoring system

The compliance record of the ten EU accession countries with the formal aspects of the FCNM monitoring system differs considerably (see Tables 4.1, 4.2 and 4.3).

Among the ten countries of interest, Latvia constitutes a special case. Due to very strong internal opposition, it took Latvia more than ten years to ratify the FCNM. Therefore, it is too early to assess Latvia's post-ratification compliance. Among the nine remaining countries, only Bulgaria has a truly poor compliance record as concerns the formal aspects of the FCNM monitoring system. Both state reports have been delayed by more than two years, government comments

Table 4.1 Accession to the Council of Europe and the FCNM

	Accession to the Council of Europe	FCNM signed	FCNM ratified	FCNM entering into force
Bulgaria	7 May 1992	9 October 1997	7 May 1999	1 September 1999
Czech Republic	30 June 1993	28 April 1995	18 December 1997	1 April 1998
Estonia	14 May 1993	2 February 1995	6 January 1997	1 February 1998
Hungary	6 November 1990	1 February 1995	25 September 1995	1 February 1998
Latvia	10 February 1995	11 May 1995	6 June 2005	1 October 2005
Lithuania	14 May 1993	1 February 1995	5 March 2000	1 July 2000
Poland	26 November 1991	1 February 1995	20 December 2000	1 April 2001
Romania	2 October 1993	1 February 1995	11 May 1995	1 February 1998
Slovakia	30 June 1993	1 February 1995	14 September 1995	1 February 1998
Slovenia	14 May 1993	1 February 1995	25 March 1998	1 February 1998

Table 4.2 First monitoring cycle

	State report due	State report received	Advisory Committee opinion	Government comments	Committee of Ministers resolution	Follow-up seminar
Bulgaria	1 September 2000	9 April 2003	27 May 2004	14 May 2005	5 April 2005	–
Czech Republic	1 April 1999	1 April 1999	6 April 2001	27 August 2001	6 February 2002	1 December 2003
Estonia	1 February 1999	22 December 1999	14 September 2001	20 February 2002	13 June 2002	26 September 2002
Hungary	1 February 1999	21 May 1999	22 September 2000	14 May 2001	21 November 2001	2 December 2002
Latvia	1 October 2006	11 October 2006	–	–		–
Lithuania	1 July 2001	31 October 2001	21 February 2003	23 September 2003	10 December 2003	18 October 2004
Poland	1 April 2002	10 July 2002	27 November 2003	19 May 2004	30 September 2004	26 September 2005
Romania	1 February 1999	24 June 1999	6 April 2001	28 August 2001	13 March 2002	28 October 2002
Slovakia	1 February 1999	4 May 1999	22 September 2000	5 June 2001	21 November 2001	8 July 2003
Slovenia	1 July 1999	29 November 2000	12 September 2002	14 March 2003	28 September 2005	–

Note
Status as of 1 October 2007.

Table 4.3 Second monitoring cycle

	State report due	State report received	Advisory Committee opinion	Government comments	Committee of Ministers resolution	Follow-up seminar
Bulgaria	1 September 2005	–	–	–	–	–
Czech Republic	1 April 2004	2 July 2004	24 February 2005	18 July 2005	15 March 2006	–
Estonia	1 February 2004	16 July 2004	24 February 2005	22 July 2005	15 February 2006	9 October 2006
Hungary	1 February 2004	7 May 2004	9 December 2004	25 April 2005	14 December 2005	30 November 2006
Lithuania	1 July 2006	3 November 2006	–	–	–	–
Poland	1 April 2007	–	–	–	–	–
Romania	1 February 2004	6 June 2005	24 November 2005	5 December 2006	23 May 2007	–
Slovakia	1 February 2004	3 January 2005	26 May 2005	4 November 2005	21 June 2006	–
Slovenia	1 July 2004	6 July 2004	26 May 2005	1 December 2005	14 June 2006	–

Note
Status as of 1 October 2007.

were late, and no follow-up seminar has been organized. Lithuania has a good record for the first monitoring cycle and has started well into the second. Poland has also done well during the first monitoring cycle. For the remaining six countries, the second monitoring cycle has been more or less concluded. Whereas Slovenia had a rather modest compliance record as regards the first monitoring cycle, its second monitoring cycle was characterized by considerable improvement, with only a follow-up seminar missing. Romania, in contrast, had a good record for the first monitoring cycle, but was late in submitting its second state report and its government comments; moreover, no follow-up seminar has yet been organized. The Czech Republic, Estonia, and Slovakia have a good compliance record for both the first and second monitoring cycle. As regards compliance with the formal aspects of the monitoring system, only Hungary can claim an excellent record: timely submission of state reports and government comments, as well as organization of two follow-up seminars.

Compliance with the substantive aspects of the monitoring system

As Latvia is still at the very beginning of the first monitoring cycle, an assessment of its compliance with the substantive aspects of the FCNM system is not yet possible. With regard to Bulgaria, Lithuania and Poland, an assessment can only be based on the first monitoring cycle. In the case of all countries, the AC noted in its opinions positive developments as well as shortcomings.

Bulgaria

In its first opinion on Bulgaria, the AC encouraged the authorities to reconsider the exclusion of groups such as the Macedonians and Pomaks with regard to the personal scope of the FCNM's application. The AC also called on the authorities to address the poor school attendance among Roma children and the unwarranted placement of Roma children in schools for the mentally disabled. The AC further held that special attention should be paid to the participation of persons belonging to national minorities in Bulgarian public life, and that additional measures were necessary in order to promote these persons' access to, and presence in, the media. Moreover, the AC asked the authorities to fully observe the rights to freedom of peaceful assembly and of association. Furthermore, the AC concluded that the implementation of the FCNM remained 'problematic' (a term which in the AC practice reflects most serious doubts as to the compatibility of domestic legislation and practice with the obligations resulting from the FCNM) as regards the use of minority languages, both in dealings with administrative authorities and in criminal procedures, and also where topographical indications were concerned. Finally, as regards education, the AC found, inter alia, that teaching of minority languages within the compulsory curriculum remained limited and their use as languages of instruction was 'virtually non-existent' (AC 2006b: 4).

The government comments were characterized by an outright rejection of the AC's findings. As regards a possible extension of the personal scope of application of the FCNM, the government insisted on the view that Macedonians and Pomaks do not show any identifiable objective 'distinctive features' (Government of Bulgaria 2006: 4) and, therefore, would not be eligible for protection under the FCNM. As concerns the Roma, the government maintained that the findings of the AC did not correctly reflect the actual situation. Likewise, the government rejected the notion that there were undue limitations of the freedoms to peaceful assembly and association and that numerically smaller national minorities were in need of increased access to the media. With respect to the use of minority languages in contacts with administrative and judicial authorities, as well as topographical indications, the government declared that the relevant provisions of the FCNM did not establish any obligation on states parties. The same argument was made with regard to the teaching in, and instruction of, minority languages.

Notwithstanding the rather strong wording of the government comments, the Committee of Ministers' resolution, as in almost all cases, was almost identical to the findings of the AC. Overall, Bulgaria's compliance with the substantive aspects of the FCNM system appears to be as poor as its compliance with the formal requirements of membership.

Czech Republic

In its first opinion on the Czech Republic, the AC was 'particularly concerned about the discrimination faced by the Roma in various fields, and the manner in which this minority is treated by the police' (AC 2002a: 15). More generally, it considered that 'appropriate measures should be adopted in order to improve the situation of numerically small minorities in areas such as the education system, access to the media and the use of minority languages in relations with authorities' (AC 2002a: 3).

The government comments were remarkable insofar as they accepted, at least implicitly, almost all of the critical assessments contained in the AC opinion. The Czech government stressed that with the entry into force, on 2 August 2001, of the new Act on the Rights of Members of National Minorities there was now a comprehensive legislative framework regulating a number of issues addressed in the AC opinion. The government also reported on various programmes to improve the situation of the Roma and to increase access of all national minorities to the media (Government of the Czech Republic 2002). Since the Czech government had mostly accepted the shortcomings identified in the AC opinion, the Committee of Ministers' resolution reinforced the findings of the AC.

In its opinion on the second state report the AC noted, as 'positive developments', that the Czech Republic had pursued and diversified its action to protect persons belonging to national minorities. The AC noted that the authorities had adopted measures to supplement and clarify the legislation on the use of minority languages in relations with administrative authorities, for topographical indications, as well as the teaching of, and in, minority languages. Similarly, Czech legislation would now provide for the participation of representatives of national minorities in decision-making affecting them at the central and regional level. Progress had also been made as regards the protection against discrimination and the enactment of specific measures to promote inter-ethnic tolerance and to improve inter-ethnic dialogue. The AC also noted that the situation of the Roma had continued to be a priority of the government (AC 2005a).

As 'issues of concern' the AC found shortcomings in the practical implementation of provisions on the use of minority languages in relations with administrative authorities, for topographical indications, as well as the teaching of, and in, minority languages. The AC also held that the situation of the Roma was still a matter for deep concern. The AC called on the authorities to address, as a matter of priority, the following issues: the employment and housing situation, the continuing isolation of Roma children within the education system, as well as allegations regarding cases of sterilization of Roma women without their informed prior consent (AC 2005a).

The government comments were clearly less appreciative of the findings of the AC than the comments on the first opinion. The Czech government maintained that some AC remarks did not reflect 'the true state of affairs' (Government of the Czech Republic 2005: 3). Moreover, the Czech government stated that 'the bulk of the AC Opinion are numerous negative and critical remarks on the situation of Roma communities' (Government of the Czech Republic 2005: 3).

Notwithstanding this rather harsh critique, the Czech government's specific comments on 'issues of concern' were more constructive, in particular with regard to the use of minority languages in relations with administrative authorities and for topographical indications, and the participation of national minority representatives in the conduct of the public affairs concerning them. Most of the government comments dealt with the situation of the Roma and the measures taken to address it. As most government comments did not really challenge the factual correctness of the AC's findings, the Committee of Ministers' resolution was, once more, an almost verbatim reproduction of the concluding remarks of the AC opinion.

In the first monitoring cycle, the Czech Republic showed a remarkably good compliance with its substantive obligations and adopted a wide range of legislative and other measures. Considerable shortcomings persist, but overall the compliance record is quite positive.

Estonia

In its first opinion on Estonia, the AC expressed concern about legislation pertaining to the use of minority languages in private signs visible to the public. The AC also found that the then applicable National Minorities Cultural Autonomy Act was problematic with regard to its personal scope of application, as it excluded non-citizens. The AC also held that naturalization should be made more accessible and that initiatives aimed at increasing knowledge of the Estonian language were coupled with improved guarantees for persons belonging to national minorities to receive instruction in or of their language (AC 2002b).

The government comments noted that several legislative amendments which had been recently enacted had been inspired by the FCNM. The government stated that the Language Act regulating the use of minority languages in private signs visible to the public has been made less restrictive. The government also reported on measures simplifying the naturalization procedure (Government of Estonia 2002). In view of these comments, the Committee of Ministers' resolution was an almost verbatim reproduction of the AC opinion.

The AC opinion on the second state report indicated, as 'positive developments', that measures had been adopted resulting in a more accessible and streamlined process of naturalization. Estonia had also made it possible for minority schools to apply for an exemption from the requirement to introduce Estonian as the main language of instruction as from 2007. Finally, Estonia had reduced obstacles to the posting of private signs in minority languages (AC 2005b).

As 'issues of concern' the AC noted that the number of persons without citizenship remained 'disconcertingly high' (AC 2005b: 1). It also found that the envisaged transfer to Estonian as the main language of instruction in minority schools had not yet been adequately prepared by the authorities. It noted that the Language Act still contained problematic elements, including as regards private signs. It also criticized the language proficiency requirements in public employment. The AC further noted that the proportion of persons belonging to national minorities employed in public service remained relatively low, and that the National Minority Cultural Act had remained unchanged despite the fact that it was generally considered to be ineffective (AC 2005b).

The remarkably positive government comments spoke of a recently established programme to further facilitate naturalization, including by offering free language training. It also reported on the initiation of a new teacher training programme supported from EU funds. The government also reported that various initiatives had been implemented with a view to increase proficiency of Estonian among members of the public services (Government of Estonia 2005). In view of these comments, the Committee of Ministers' resolution was fully in line with the AC findings.

Overall, Estonia has shown a remarkable resolve to engage in a constructive dialogue with the FCNM monitoring bodies. With respect to most issues of concern, improvements could be recorded and Estonia has made increasing use of EU funds to address shortcomings in its compliance with the FCNM.

Hungary

In its first opinion on Hungary, the AC considered that the situation of the Roma gave rise to 'deep concern' (AC 2001a: 2). In respect of other national minorities, the AC found that issues to be addressed concerned mainly access to media, education and participation in public life. Most of the government comments were devoted to existing or planned programmes in order to improve the socio-economic situation of the Roma and their access to education (Government of Hungary 2005). In view of these constructive comments, the Committee of Ministers' resolution reflected to a very large extent the findings of the AC.

The AC opinion on the second state report noted as 'positive developments' that Hungary had 'improved markedly its anti-discrimination legal and institutional framework' (AC 2005c: 30). It also noted improvements as regards access to the media and the teaching of minority languages within the public education system. As 'issues of concern' the AC stressed that the 1993 Law on the Rights of National and Ethnic Minorities was in need of reform, in particular as regards the election process and funding of minority self-governments and the financial implications of national minorities running their own schools. With respect to the Roma, the AC expressed its 'deep concern' about the 'persistence of various exclusion and segregation practices at the expense of a high number of Roma pupils' (AC 2005c: 31). The AC also criticized that little progress had been made as far as bilingual education was concerned and noted that specific new mechanisms were needed for the representation of minorities in parliament.

The government comments stated that a bill had been introduced to amend the Law on the Rights of National and Ethnic Minorities in such a way as to remedy the shortcomings indicated by the AC. It also advised about new Roma integration programmes (Government of Hungary 2005).

As these comments recognized the issues of concern as indicated by the AC, the Committee of Ministers' resolution was, to a very large extent, a verbatim reproduction of the AC opinion. The only significant difference was that the Committee of Ministers welcomed the legislation adopted in 2005 with a view to improving the operation and financing of minority self-governments, the election of their representatives, and their participation in local municipal government.

Hungary has shown a remarkably good compliance record. With respect to many issues of concern, improvements have been achieved. However, Hungary has not yet succeeded in considerably improving the integration of the Roma, a failure which Hungary shares with most countries faced with this task.

Lithuania

In its first opinion on Lithuania, the AC noted certain shortcomings in such fields as education, use of minority languages, participation in public affairs and intercultural dialogue. It urged the authorities to pay particular attention to the discriminatory effect of provisions relating to dual citizenship. The AC also held that further efforts were 'needed to remedy the legal uncertainty' (AC 2003a: 2) as regards the use of minority languages in dealings with administrative authorities and as regards topographical indications.

The government comments showed a remarkable resolve to take the findings of the AC into consideration in then-ongoing legislative work. The government also noted that the then new Law on Education guaranteed the right of persons belonging to national minorities to learn their mother tongue and receive secondary education in their language (Government of Lithuania 2003). Since the legislative reforms referred to in the government comments had not yet been concluded, the Committee of Ministers' resolution constituted a near verbatim reproduction of the main findings of the AC opinion.

The Lithuanian authorities seem to wish to continue the constructive dialogue with the FCNM monitoring bodies which has been established during the first monitoring cycle. However, a number of the points of major concern have not yet been effectively addressed.

Poland

In its first opinion on Poland, the AC noted that the legal and institutional framework protecting persons belonging to national minorities showed 'important shortcomings' (AC 2004a: 3). This was particularly the case for the use of minority languages in relations with administrative authorities and for topographical indications. The AC also asked the authorities to 'pursue the efforts made to solve the issues linked to monuments and cemeteries affecting many national minorities' (AC 2004a: 3). The AC further found that there was scope for 'improvement in the media sector, especially concerning additional radio programmes' (AC 2004a: 3). The AC also expressed 'concern about the threats of closure of a number of Lithuanian schools' (AC 2004a: 3). Finally, the AC noted that there remained 'problems in the implementation of the Framework Convention as concerns Roma' (AC 2004a: 3), in particular as regards education, and found that, 'while participation in public affairs at local and regional level is satisfactory, there is a clear need to reinforce participation of persons belonging to national minorities at national level' (AC 2004a: 30).

The government comments explicitly accepted a number of the most critical findings of the AC. This applied in particular to the use of minority languages in contact with administrative authorities and for topographical indications. The Polish government also acknowledged the serious problems connected with monuments and cemeteries of particular importance to national minorities. The government further acknowledged the shortcomings identified with respect to radio and televisions programmes and informed on recent steps taken to improve the situation. It also reported on measures recently taken with a view to ensure the availability of sufficient financial means to effectively support the Lithuanian schools. The government also accepted the AC findings concerning the situation of the Roma, and informed about recent steps abolishing so-called 'Roma classes' and introducing a programme aimed at improved integration of Roma pupils in the general education system (Government of Poland 2004).

Since the Polish government had, to a very large extent, accepted the findings of the AC, the Committee of Ministers' resolution mirrored these findings. It can be concluded that during the first cycle of monitoring Poland was fully prepared to comply with its substantive obligations.

Romania

In its first opinion on Romania, the AC noted that the 'situation of the Roma gives rise to deep concern' (AC 2002c: 2). The AC was also 'concerned by the persistence of cases of police brutality and the way in which those are being prosecuted' (AC 2002c: 2). With regard to other minorities, the AC found that issues to be addressed related mainly to the media, public employment and education.

The government comments mainly consisted of information on measures recently enacted or under discussion. In view of the fact that the comments largely acknowledged the findings of the AC, the Committee of Ministers' resolution reiterated these findings.

The AC opinion on the second state report noted as 'positive developments', that Romania had taken '[n]ew legislative, institutional and practical measures [. . .] in fields such as non-discrimination, the use of minority languages in the public sphere as well as education' (AC 2006a: 1). As 'issues of concern', the AC noted that 'access to the existing mechanisms for participation and state support does not extend to all potentially interested organizations and communities' (AC 2006a: 1). It also noted 'financial difficulties affecting many fields of relevance to the protection of national minorities, such as education' (AC 2006a: 36). Furthermore, the AC considered that further measures were needed 'to ensure more effective implementation of the anti-discrimination legislation [. . .] especially concerning full and effective equality of the Roma' (AC 2006a: 1). The AC concluded that the social and economic situation of the Roma remained 'problematic and increased efforts, including of a financial nature' (AC 2006a: 1), were needed. Finally, the AC stressed that a balanced approach should 'prevail in the current process of property restitution, with due consideration for its impact on the situation of persons belonging to more vulnerable groups, such as the Roma' (AC 2006a: 1).

The government comments consisted mainly of information on recent developments. In particular, the government reported on the results of a meeting between government authorities and representatives of national minorities organized in order to discuss the AC opinion. With respect to the Roma, the government informed on a number of new programmes initiated or under discussion. In view of the fact that the government to a very large extent recognized the 'issues of concern' indicated in the AC opinion, the Committee of Ministers' resolution was, once again, an almost verbatim reproduction of the AC opinion.

Romania has shown a strong resolve to engage in a constructive dialogue with the FCNM monitoring bodies. Despite the measures taken by the Romanian authorities, many problems persist, in particular as regards the socio-economic situation of the Roma. Yet, the compliance record of Romania with respect to the substantive obligations can be considered as good.

Slovakia

In its first opinion on Slovakia, the AC found that the content of some provisions of the State Language Law needed clarification with regard to the legal status of minority languages. Moreover, it called for more detailed regulations on education in minority languages. Finally, the AC expressed its particular concern 'about the discrimination encountered by Roma in various fields as well as the treatment of this minority by law-enforcement officials' (AC 2001b: 2).

The government comments mostly informed about recent initiatives, including with regard to the Roma. However, the Slovak government emphasized in many instances its disagreement with the findings of the AC. It stated, *inter alia,* that Slovak legislation provided for a sufficient framework to effectively combat discrimination. It also considered that there was no need to change the existing legislation concerning the public use of minority languages or the education in minority languages (Government of Slovakia 2001). Despite these critical statements, the Committee of Ministers' resolution constituted an almost verbatim reproduction of the AC opinion.

The AC opinion on the second state report noted as 'positive developments' the substantial increase in the allocation of financial support to national minorities. The AC also held that 'serious efforts have been made to address ethnically motivated crimes more vigorously' (AC 2006c: 31). Finally, the AC welcomed the 'setting up of the Selye János University in Komárno, which [. . .] will [. . .] expand the possibilities available for persons belonging to the Hungarian minority to receive higher education in their language' (AC 2006c: 31).

As 'issues of concern' the AC noted the constitutional dispute which had so far prevented the entry into force 'of positive measures to address disadvantages linked to racial or ethnic origin' (AC 2006c: 32). It also found that there were still shortcomings as concerns the 'financing of minority cultures and instruction in minority languages' (AC 2006c: 32) and that there was scope for improvement in the participation of persons belonging to national minorities in the decision-making process. The AC also found that the 'overall situation of the Roma continues to be a matter of deep concern' (AC 2006c: 1).

The government comments offered a number of critical remarks on the findings of the AC. However, as they did not really challenge the overall adequacy of the AC assessment, the Committee of Ministers' resolution was, again, an almost verbatim reproduction of the respective findings of the AC opinion.

Slovakia has taken a more cooperative stance in the second round of monitoring. While real problems remain as to the full integration of Roma, the overall compliance record on the substantive obligations can be considered as good.

Slovenia

In its first opinion, the AC found that there was 'scope for improvement in the media sector' (AC 2005d: 2) concerning the Hungarian minority and in the field of education with respect to the Italian minority. Moreover, the AC held that, as regards the use of Hungarian and Italian in relations with administrative authorities, there remained 'shortcomings in the practical implementation of existing legal provisions' (AC 2005d: 2). Finally, the AC noted that problems remained as concerns the Roma. The AC mentioned the 'removal of a significant number of persons from the register of permanent residents in Slovenia in 1991' (AC 2005d: 9) and that the protection of the FCNM is only afforded by the Slovenian state to the Hungarian and Italian minorities, but did not include these issues in its concluding remarks.

Most of the government comments consisted of information on recent developments, including a judgement of the Constitutional Court which had resulted in new legislation improving the political participation of Roma in local government, a number of Roma integration programmes, the establishment of new radio and TV broadcasting facilities for the Hungarian minority, and initiatives to increase the number of qualified staff for Italian language education (Government of Slovenia 2005). In view of these comments, which acknowledged the accuracy of the findings of the AC, the Committee of Ministers' resolution fully reproduced the AC findings.

The AC opinion on the second state report noted as 'positive developments' the adoption of anti-discrimination legislation and the Roma integration programmes. As 'issues of concern' the AC noted the situation of the Roma and that there were still shortcomings in the resources allocated to national minorities. Almost all of the government comments related to measures taken with respect to the findings of the AC. In view of these constructive comments, the Committee of Ministers' resolution was, once again, a verbatim reproduction of the AC opinion.

Overall, Slovenia has shown a strong resolve to strengthen the constructive dialogue with the FCNM monitoring bodies and has a very good compliance record as regards its substantive obligations.

Conclusions

This chapter aimed to assess, from an FCNM perspective, the compliance record of the ten EU accession states from Central and Eastern Europe. Since Latvia did not ratify the FCNM until 6 June 2005, it fell outside the scope of this study. Among all remaining nine states, only Bulgaria shows a poor compliance record. All other countries have a good or very good compliance record. There can be no doubt that the situation of the Roma, in particular as regards education, employment, housing, health care, and political participation, remains a real problem. On the other hand, a large number of measures and programmes were adopted in recent years. It seems justified to assess the degree of compliance not only by looking at the results, but also by taking into account the quality and quantity of measures taken. Similar considerations apply with respect to the assessment of the compliance of Estonia as regards the situation of the Russian-speaking minority and justify a positive assessment of compliance as regards the substantive obligations.

References

AC (2001a) *Opinion on Hungary, adopted on 22 September 2000*, Strasbourg: Council of Europe, Advisory Committee on the Framework Convention for the Protection of National Minorities.

—— (2001b) *Opinion on Slovakia, adopted on 22 September 2000*, Strasbourg: Council of Europe, Advisory Committee on the Framework Convention for the Protection of National Minorities.

—— (2002a) *Opinion on the Czech Republic, adopted on 6 April 2001*, Strasbourg: Council of Europe, Advisory Committee on the Framework Convention for the Protection of National Minorities.

—— (2002b) *Opinion on Estonia, adopted on 14 September 2001*, Strasbourg: Council of Europe, Advisory Committee on the Framework Convention for the Protection of National Minorities.

—— (2002c) *Opinion on Romania, adopted on 6 April 2001*, Strasbourg: Council of Europe, Advisory Committee on the Framework Convention for the Protection of National Minorities.

—— (2003a) *Opinion on Lithuania, adopted on 21 February 2003*, Strasbourg: Council of Europe, Advisory Committee on the Framework Convention for the Protection of National Minorities.

—— (2004a) *Opinion on Poland, adopted on 27 November 2003*, Strasbourg: Council of Europe, Advisory Committee on the Framework Convention for the Protection of National Minorities.

—— (2005a) *Second Opinion on the Czech Republic, adopted on 24 February 2005*, Strasbourg: Council of Europe, Advisory Committee on the Framework Convention for the Protection of National Minorities.

—— (2005b) *Second Opinion on Estonia, adopted on 24 February 2005*, Strasbourg: Council of Europe, Advisory Committee on the Framework Convention for the Protection of National Minorities.

—— (2005c) *Second Opinion on Hungary, adopted on 9 December 2004*, Strasbourg: Council of Europe, Advisory Committee on the Framework Convention for the Protection of National Minorities.

—— (2005d) *Opinion on Slovenia, adopted on 12 September 2002*, Strasbourg: Council of Europe, Advisory Committee on the Framework Convention for the Protection of National Minorities.

—— (2005e) *Second Opinion on Slovenia, adopted on 26 May 2005*, Strasbourg: Council of Europe, Advisory Committee on the Framework Convention for the Protection of National Minorities.

—— (2006a) *Second Opinion on Romania, adopted on 24 November 2005*, Strasbourg: Council of Europe, Advisory Committee on the Framework Convention for the Protection of National Minorities.

—— (2006b) *Opinion on Bulgaria, adopted on 27 May 2004*, Strasbourg: Council of Europe, Advisory Committee on the Framework Convention for the Protection of National Minorities.

—— (2006c) *Second Opinion on Slovakia, adopted on 24 November 2005*, Strasbourg: Council of Europe, Advisory Committee on the Framework Convention for the Protection of National Minorities.

Government of Bulgaria (2006) *Comments of the Government of Bulgaria on the Opinion of the Advisory Committee on the Implementation of the Framework Convention for the*

Protection of National Minorities in Bulgaria (received 14 March 2005), Strasbourg: Council of Europe.

Government of the Czech Republic (2002) *Comments of the Government of* the Czech Republic *on the Opinion of the Advisory Committee on the Implementation of the Framework Convention for the Protection of National Minorities in the Czech Republic (received 27 August 2001)*, Strasbourg: Council of Europe.

—— (2005) *Comments of the Government of the Czech Republic on the Second Opinion of the Advisory Committee on the Implementation of the Framework Convention for the Protection of National Minorities in the Czech Republic (received 18 July 2005)*, Strasbourg: Council of Europe.

Government of Estonia (2002) *Comments of the Government of Estonia on the Opinion of the Advisory Committee on the Implementation of the Framework Convention for the Protection of National Minorities in Estonia (received 20 February 2002)*, Strasbourg: Council of Europe.

—— (2005) *Comments of the Government of Estonia on the Opinion of the Advisory Committee on the Implementation of the Framework Convention for the Protection of National Minorities in Estonia (received 22 July 2005)*, Strasbourg: Council of Europe.

Government of Hungary (2001) *Comments of the Government of Hungary on the Opinion of the Advisory Committee on the Implementation of the Framework Convention for the Protection of National Minorities in Hungary (received 14 May 2001)*, Strasbourg: Council of Europe.

—— (2005) *Comments of the Government of Hungary on the Second Opinion of the Advisory Committee on the Implementation of the Framework Convention for the Protection of National Minorities in Hungary (received 25 April 2005)*, Strasbourg: Council of Europe.

Government of Lithuania (2003) *Comments of the Government of Lithuania on the Opinion of the Advisory Committee on the Implementation of the Framework Convention for the Protection of National Minorities in Lithuania (received 23 September 2003)*, Strasbourg: Council of Europe.

Government of Poland (2004) *Comments of the Government of Poland on the Opinion of the Advisory Committee on the Implementation of the Framework Convention for the Protection of National Minorities in Poland (received 19 May 2004)*, Strasbourg: Council of Europe.

Government of Slovakia (2001) *Comments of the Government of Slovakia on the Opinion of the Advisory Committee on the Implementation of the Framework Convention for the Protection of National Minorities in Slovakia (received 5 June 2001)*, Strasbourg: Council of Europe.

Government of Slovenia (2005) *Comments of the Government of Slovakia on the Opinion of the Advisory Committee on the Implementation of the Framework Convention for the Protection of National Minorities in Slovakia (received 14 March 2003)*, Strasbourg: Council of Europe.

5   The Roma

Peter Vermeersch and Melanie H. Ram[1]

Introduction

More than other populations in Europe, the Roma are a minority of pan-European concern and attention. Although they are far from a single bounded ethnic group, many of them share a similar social status in a large number of European states, and they are increasingly conceptualized as a non-territorial European nation. Organizations who claim to speak in the name of the Roma are, in certain cases, indeed active across state borders. In the 1990s, the European Union (EU) became increasingly concerned about the situation of the Roma in the Central and East European candidate countries and on various occasions criticized their governments for their poor record on the protection of the Roma. Governments in the region have responded differently to these appeals and to those from other international organizations, Roma activists, and international non-governmental organizations (NGOs). In this chapter, we describe the situation of the Roma, the variety of policy responses in the new EU member states, Roma mobilization, the role of EU conditionality, the degree to which policy initiatives were implemented, and perspectives for the future.

The situation of the Roma in Europe

The Roma are a minority in practically every country in Europe and, as it has now become commonplace for activists to emphasize, are the largest minority in the EU following the 2004 and 2007 enlargements. They were formerly called 'Gypsies', but many now consider this term pejorative. The exact size of the Roma population is an issue of question and controversy, since many of the people who are seen as Roma reject the classifications offered to them in censuses. As a result, census figures undercount the number of people who in less official circumstances would be willing to identify themselves as Roma. Estimates indicate that there are between seven and nine million Roma living in Europe (Liégeois 2005), the large majority in Central and Eastern Europe and the Balkans. Bulgaria, Hungary, Romania, Slovakia, and Spain are each estimated to have a population of over half a million Roma, with Romania having the largest Roma population in absolute terms, numbering perhaps as many as 2.5 million (see Table 5.1).

1   This chapter is a collaborative work for which the authors share equal credit and responsibility.

Table 5.1 Estimated Roma populations in Europe

Countries with the largest Roma populations in Europe	Roma as a percentage of the total population	Roma population in absolute figures
Romania	11.6	2,500,000
Bulgaria	10.4	800,000
Slovakia	9.6	520,000
Macedonia	8.0	160,000
Hungary	5.9	600,000
Serbia and Montenegro*	5.6	450,000
Albania	3.2	100,000
Czech Republic	2.9	300,000
Greece	2.7	300,000
Spain	1.8	800,000

Sources: Roma population figures are maximum estimates offered by Liégeois (2005: 21). Total population estimates come from the *World Bank Data Profiles* available at http://www.worldbank.org/data/countrydata/countrydata.html (figures for 2006).

Note
*Montenegro became independent from Serbia in 2006.

In the ten new EU member states from Central and Eastern Europe that are the focus of this chapter, the percentage of Roma varies widely. While the Roma constitute less than 2 per cent of the population in Estonia, Latvia, Lithuania, Poland, and Slovenia, they are estimated to represent a much larger part of the total population in the Czech Republic (2–4 per cent), Hungary (4–8 per cent), and Bulgaria, Romania, and Slovakia (8–12 per cent in each) (Liégeois and Gheorghe 1995: 7). Not only is the Roma population in the enlarged EU significant, it is also growing, and these two aspects were certainly influential in bringing EU attention to this population.

The Roma, however, are not a single, coherent group. Their existence as a 'group' is the result of a complex process of labelling, categorization, and counter-categorization by political authorities, cultural elites, self-proclaimed representatives and the wider population (see Vermeersch 2006: 13–20). Although most historical research now agrees that they have common cultural and historical roots, Roma communities in different countries often have little if any direct connection with each other.[2] Even within particular countries, Roma communities are often quite distinct and see themselves linked only in that they are not *gadje* (non-Roma) or in that they are the target of the same government policy. Thus, while internal heterogeneity and contestation for leadership is typical of many ethnic minority groups (just as it is for so-called ethnic majority populations), the divisions and differences among those known or labelled as Roma are perhaps more acute. What has tied the Roma in Central and Eastern Europe together in recent years is that they have met with similar disadvantages and difficulties following the collapse of communism, have generally been subject to social exclusion and discrimination, and tend to be economically worse off than the majority populations.

Discrimination against the Roma is hardly a new phenomenon. While there was toleration and occasionally protection of Roma in Europe during some historical periods and under some rulers, with the Ottoman Empire for example being more tolerant than the Habsburg Empire (Barany 2002: 84–88), Roma began to face anti-'Gypsy' legislation and to be expelled from territories across Europe (often under penalty of death) beginning from the mid-fifteenth century (Kenrick 1998). They were enslaved in the Romanian principalities of Moldavia and Wallachia from the fourteenth until the mid-nineteenth century (Guy 2002: 6). German policies against the Roma culminated in the Nazis' attempt to annihilate them during the Holocaust. Hundreds of thousands of Roma, and perhaps as many as 1.5 million, were killed. The communist era in Central and Eastern Europe was primarily one of forced assimilation, but education and employment levels were generally raised through mandatory education and employment policies. When the communist system collapsed, and along with it many industries in which the Roma had been employed, many Roma lost their jobs. Lacking the necessary skills and education to compete in the intense new labour markets, the Roma were the group most adversely affected by the transition to market economies. The problems faced by the Roma today in most European countries are twofold. First, they face discrimination by the majority population and public authorities, particularly affecting opportunities for education, housing, health care, and employment, as has now been catalogued in numerous reports by both NGOs and EU institutions (see for example Open Society Institute 2002; European Commission 2004). Second, most are subject to economic hardship and often extremely poor living conditions, frequently as a result of the aforementioned discrimination (either past or present) and the transition to a market economy.

Domestic policies towards the Roma in the new EU member states

In the decade that followed the collapse of communism, all the countries in Central and Eastern Europe that we discuss in this chapter started to adopt special policies, legal regulations or institutional arrangements with the explicit aim of improving the living conditions of their Roma populations. When governments first began to step up their efforts in this area in the 1990s, they did so with a double purpose in mind. They wanted to create more integrated societies, but they also sought to improve their standing in the international community in anticipation of their accession to the EU. By the time of EU enlargement, however, these policies had achieved only mixed results, as we will discuss below. Today, policies for the integration of Roma are still in the process of being further developed.

The initiatives of each country differed, as is not surprising, given their diverse political legacies and traditions. There were, however, some similar trends across the region. First, the policies that countries introduced emerged in a complicated way, due to the evolving and relatively fluid institutional environment and the very broad field of problems at which they were aimed, including unemployment, poverty, segregated education, discrimination, ill health, and residential isolation. It was clear to policy-makers that they needed to devise measures in different policy fields simultaneously in order to address the difficulties Roma faced in many areas of life. This explains in part the complexity of the policy-making processes that preceded the introduction of new measures.

Second, all of the countries were increasingly prepared to adopt newly emerging European legal standards on minority protection and anti-discrimination. For example, all of the acceding countries except Latvia[3] signed and ratified the Council of Europe's Framework Convention for the Protection of National Minorities (FCNM) before becoming EU members; the convention has still not been signed or ratified by all of the older EU members (see Chapter 4 on the Framework Convention).

Third, EU accession countries were required to transpose legislation that has become known as the Race Equality Directive (Directive 2000/43/EC implementing the principle of equal treatment between persons irrespective of racial or ethnic origin) into domestic law. Although the transposition of the directive is an obligation for all EU members, there is variation in the level of implementation (see Chapter 3 on anti-discrimination legislation).

While the examples above indicate a number of common trends in the way in which minority protection mechanisms have gained increasing acceptance in Central and Eastern Europe, there is also significant variation among countries when it comes to the finer details of institutional and policy designs for minority protection, especially regarding the place given to the protection of the Roma in these developing minority protection regimes. This variation is partly a reflection of different citizenship traditions in the region, but it also reflects the different ways in which governing politicians have interpreted the problems facing the Roma.

A basic distinction can be made between countries that have followed what can be called a 'minority rights' model and those that have tended to apply a model of 'undifferentiated citizenship'. The minority rights model endorses the strategy of granting members of national minorities special, group-differentiated rights with regard to culture, language, traditions, and participation in the social and economic domain. The 'undifferentiated citizenship' model, on the other hand, is based on the idea that nobody must be exempted generally applicable laws. The underlying logic is that the problems that ethnic minorities face need to be disassociated from culture; the problems are rather seen to arise from socioeconomic and class factors (see Barry 2001). In the cultural domain, this model suggests that 'the neutral attitude of the state will permit different cultures to coexist' (Entzinger 2000: 109).

Hungary is the prime example of a new EU member state that endorsed the minority rights model. It did so already in the beginning of the 1990s. Through the 1993 Law on the Rights of National and Ethnic Minorities, Hungary granted its thirteen officially recognized 'historical' minorities (the Roma as an 'ethnic minority' as well as twelve 'national minorities' with outside kin-states) a far-reaching form of cultural autonomy, which was realized through a system of elected local and national self-governments. Since the mid-1990s, members of local minority self-governments in Hungary have been elected by minority populations, while the members of national minority self-governments (representing the minority at the national level) have been elected by an electoral body that consists of the members of local minority self-governments. According to the above-mentioned law, local minority self-governments are fully responsible for the development and management of local minority educational and cultural institutions. With regard to public policies, however, minority self-governments in Hungary remain essentially consultative bodies, and there is little minority representation in the country's parliament.

Other countries in the region, including those that were less inclined to give full cultural autonomy to ethnic minority communities, moved in the direction of the minority rights model by granting certain rights to recognized minorities, but not introducing elected minority councils. In Romania, for example, the Roma, as other minorities, are entitled to one seat in parliament when they fail to pass the 5 per cent electoral threshold.

The problem with the minority rights model, at least when it is focused narrowly on cultural autonomy or special representation rights, has been that it did not provide a powerful answer to many direct needs of the Roma. This was clearly felt in Hungary. During the period from 1989 to 1995, when Hungarian policy-makers were primarily concerned with ensuring a well-protected position for the Roma as a culturally self-governing community, little attention was given to socio-economic matters or issues of discrimination. After 1995, however, the Hungarian government, increasingly pressured by the EU and domestic and international NGOs, began to see the need to develop additional policy programmes that would more directly deal with discrimination, unemployment, lack of education, bad housing, spatial isolation, and poverty among the Roma. In a report published in 1997, the government admitted that the self-government system was not suited to alter economic predicaments (Government of the Republic of Hungary 1997). In response to this conclusion, the government adopted the Medium-Term Package of Measures for improving the situation of Roma, a package that was substantially revised in the following years (see Chapter 9).

The self-government system has also been criticized for its tendency to ingrain difference rather than promote equality. As one observer formulated the matter:

> There is an inconsistency between the fundamental dynamic of Roma politics to achieve the equality of Roma people with regard to the rights and opportunities enjoyed by other citizens and the primary role of the self-government system to promote the 'difference' of minority identities through facilitating cultural autonomy.

> (Kovats 2001: 21)

While other countries in Central and Eastern Europe did not go as far as Hungary in their endorsement of the minority rights model (such as Poland, Romania, Slovakia, and Slovenia) or opted as much as possible for an undifferentiated citizenship model (such as Bulgaria and the Czech Republic), in the latter half of the 1990s all countries with substantial Roma populations designed special policy programmes for them. Five of the ten countries under discussion here (Bulgaria, the Czech Republic, Hungary, Romania, and Slovakia) have since 2005 also been part of the Decade of Roma Inclusion. Together with the governments of Croatia, Macedonia, Montenegro, and Serbia, these countries have pledged to step up their efforts in key policy areas in order to reach, by 2015, the full inclusion and acceptance of the Roma in society. The initiative is unique, since it involves not only governments and international organizations, but also NGOs. It remains to be seen whether the initiative moves beyond a declaratory one, as there are no mechanisms to ensure that governments keep their promises. Progress has begun to be monitored by civil society through a new initiative called DecadeWatch, supported by the Open Society Institute and the World Bank, co-sponsors of the Decade of Roma Inclusion.

Roma mobilization

Where are the Roma themselves in this picture? The Roma movement in the countries under discussion represents a remarkable mixture of successes and failures. Since the beginning of the 1990s, a considerable number of Roma activists and organizations have been actively engaged in one form or another of ethnic politics. They have been able to attract the attention of international organizations and have sometimes found access to domestic governmental institutions. They have also relatively successfully constructed and disseminated the term 'Roma', which now, as the director of one advocacy group described it, 'has come to dominate the official political discourse, at least in Europe, and has acquired the legitimacy of political correctness' (Petrova 2003: 111). At the same time, however, they have manifestly failed to mobilize the Roma into a political mass movement and activists remain divided on crucial issues such as interests and identity (see Vermeersch 2006). At present, Roma mobilization is still in its early stages and shows little signs of progress.

Roma activists in the region have experimented with different routes of mobilization. They have been involved in electoral politics, as well as NGOs, and have sometimes worked in cooperation with non-Roma NGOs that support Roma causes. Some have sought access to state institutions, as administrative bodies for the implementation of special Roma policies have increasingly employed Roma activists or organized consultations with them.

Each of these strategies has proven to be associated with specific problems. For example, it has been difficult for Roma to gain access to politics through participation in elections, due to lack of electoral support, even among Roma communities. Some Roma activists have established their own ethnic parties, especially in countries where other political parties had been successful in mobilizing ethnic constituencies, such as in Bulgaria, Romania, and Slovakia. So far, however, Roma parties based solely on ethnic affiliation have done very poorly in elections, with a few exceptions at the municipal level. Structural reasons for this include a youth bulge among Roma communities (and thus a smaller voting age population) and often widely dispersed communities. In addition, coordination, cooperation, and support among Roma activists have tended to be weak. The few Roma party representatives who were elected in the past (e.g. in Czechoslovakia in the beginning of the 1990s) were not in a strong position to introduce tangible changes and have therefore not been able to secure much trust among potential voters. Moreover, it has proven difficult for Roma parties to devise a programme that represents the widely diverse demands and concerns among Roma communities. Finally, Roma voters sometimes feared that casting votes for ethnic parties would further marginalize them.

Participation in mainstream parties has turned out to be a relatively more successful strategy. Since the beginning of the 2000s, there has been an increase in the number of elected Roma politicians from lists of large non-ethnic parties in some of the countries under discussion. In Bulgaria, the Czech Republic, Hungary, and Romania, a few Roma politicians have been able to gain parliamentary seats through mainstream parties. In 2004, Hungary hit international news headlines for being the first country with two Roma politicians in the European Parliament. While some of these Roma elected at national or European level have gained a position from which they might influence policy, others have been criticized for not actively standing up for their community.

Outside electoral politics, some Roma activists have been able to gain a high profile as Roma spokespersons through their activity in independent organizations or through their appointment to special administrative bodies. In Slovakia, for example, a well-known Roma activist in an international NGO (Klára Orgovánová) was selected to become Government Commissioner for Roma Affairs. While in some countries, such as Bulgaria, the number of Roma state employees remains very low, in most countries there has been a gradual increase in the number of Roma hired as employees by appointed Roma officials, which some see as a positive trend (Gheorghe 2006). At the same time, however, some Roma activists have questioned the role of appointed government officials from the viewpoint of their lack of accountability and democratic representation.

The role of the EU and the impact of conditionality

What role did the EU play in influencing government policies and programmes regarding the Roma? Was EU conditionality effective in the case of the Roma? The answer is yes and no. On the one hand, the Roma may be considered a dramatic success case of conditionality. The majority of activists lobbying for Roma rights would wholeheartedly agree that the Roma would not have emerged on the agenda of the Central and East European countries had their situation not been brought up as an important issue by the EU (see for example Grigore 2004; Koreck 2004; Szakáts 2004). On the other hand, if one evaluates the success of

EU conditionality in terms of bringing about a substantial improvement in the lives of most of the minority population, few if any would attest to such a success.

The Roma are an interesting and in some ways unique case for testing EU conditionality, in that they appeared rather suddenly on the EU agenda (see Ram 2004), have been the subject of often vague but nonetheless continuous demands from the EU, and have not had any homeland or kin-state to lobby on their behalf. When the possibility of EU enlargement to Central and Eastern Europe emerged on the political agenda in the early 1990s, the EU's attention to minorities focused on potential (and actual) violence against minority populations, especially on conflicts that might spill over borders or create calls for secession. Thus, although they were subject to violent racist attacks, the Roma were virtually ignored by the EU at first, in part due to a lack of knowledge and awareness. As the EU began to formally enumerate the necessary conditions for membership and international NGOs began to raise the issues of violence and discrimination against the Roma, the Roma began to be mentioned more and more in EU documents. The EU's attention to the situation of the Roma also grew as enlargement drew closer. EU demands to acceding countries regarding the Roma were primarily outlined in the Commission's 1997 Opinion on each country's application for membership and the subsequent annual Regular Reports from 1998 to 2003. In addition, Accession Partnership documents in 1999 and 2001 emphasized priority areas for attention. For Romania and Bulgaria, there was an additional Accession Partnership in 2003, an additional Regular Report in 2004, and subsequent monitoring reports in 2005 and 2006. For all countries, these documents were supplemented by periodic statements and commissioned studies of the European Commission, the European Council, and the European Parliament, which became more numerous over time.

The situation of the Roma was consistently mentioned in the 1997 Opinions and the subsequent annual Regular Reports on candidate countries as among the issues that had to be addressed in order to attain membership. The Accession Partnership documents in 1999, 2001, and 2003 identified integration of the Roma as a priority for Bulgaria, the Czech Republic, Hungary, Romania, and Slovakia. Over time, the EU described the problems faced by the Roma in each country with increased specificity, and put greater emphasis on the need to address these problems. At the beginning of the monitoring process, a lack of information (on the part of the EU and the candidate country governments) was an impediment to prescribing specific actions. While some issues specific to individual countries (such as the citizenship law in the Czech Republic)[4] were mentioned, a number of the assessments in 1997 were very similar. The Opinions on the Czech Republic, Romania and Slovakia each included a short paragraph that mentioned, in almost identical language, the daily discrimination faced by the Roma, the lack of adequate protection by the police, and the 'difficult' social situation of the Roma (due in part to 'sociological factors'). The Czech and Slovak reports also noted violence by skinheads against the Roma (European Commission 1997a: 18, 1997b: 22, 1997c: 16).

The EU's conditions at the beginning were as general as its assessments. Those countries wishing to do what was necessary in order to meet the EU criteria (and usually nothing more) were given little indication of how to address the identified problems or at what point the necessary 'attention' or 'improvement' would be considered to have been met. For example, the Opinion on Romania provided the government with only the following prescription regarding the Roma: '[i]t is important that the Government step up the integration measures recently announced to take full account of the difficulties encountered by this section of the population' (European Commission 1997a: 18). The Opinion on the Czech Republic indicated only that 'the already substantial efforts of the Czech authorities in the cultural sphere [. . .] must be stepped up in the future' (European Commission 1997c: 16). The Opinion on Slovakia provided this particularly vague advice: 'The position of the Roma (gypsies) also requires attention from the authorities' (European Commission 1997b: 23). Later reports more specifically catalogued some of the problems faced by Roma in particular countries, although some reports remained rather vague with regard to the solutions to these problems. Ultimately, despite 'requiring' improvement in the situation of the Roma, it seems quite clear that the countries with significant Roma populations joined the EU without genuinely meeting this requirement.

Implementation issues

In the accession process, implementation has always lagged behind policy adoption and minority rights are no exception. As the Commission's 2001 Regular Report on Slovakia stated, 'further progress can be noticed in developing approaches to tackle the problems of minorities, but there remains a gap between policy formulation and implementation on the ground' (European Commission 2001: 14). This statement could be made about most, if not all, of the new EU member states. The accession process inherently encouraged form over practice. In their rush to adopt an enormous amount of EU-required legislation, and sometimes in the face of domestic opposition, acceding countries adopted new legislation (and sometimes emergency ordinances that bypassed parliament), fully realizing that implementation would have to follow at some later date, would not be easy, and could possibly be ignored altogether (Ram 2002).

Moreover, in the case of the Roma, adopting new policies and institutions has been far easier than fixing institutionalized problems, many of which are not easy to resolve and require measures that are unpopular among the wider electorate. Where political will to improve the lives of the Roma has been present at the national level, implementation has often been confronted with impediments at the local level. Moreover, funding for projects to help the Roma often goes to non-Roma NGOs, in part because of the complex nature of EU funding requirements. Thus, especially in the case of many EU-funded projects, those deciding how to address the concerns of the Roma, though usually well-intentioned, are often not the Roma themselves. An empirical study evaluating EU-funded projects targeting Roma in poor communities in the Czech Republic, Hungary, and Slovakia found that the effectiveness of projects 'was very limited', and 'the increased centralisation of larger initiatives marginalised the input of Roma people themselves' (Guy and Kovats 2006: 3). The conclusion of this report is a sobering one: EU projects could have achieved more, had they been better implemented.

Post-membership perspectives

There are reasons to believe that the benefits of EU conditionality for the Roma are now over. The leverage of the EU over countries hoping to join, which was used to pressure countries to improve the situation of the Roma, has mostly disappeared. NGOs that previously lobbied the EU to include certain issues regarding the Roma in monitoring reports on candidate countries have lost this useful tool with regards to the new member states. EU leverage is still being employed towards current candidate countries (Croatia, Macedonia, and Turkey), some of which also have large Roma populations, but new member states cannot be as readily criticized on minority rights as they could in the past. This is due in part to the EU's limited competence on internal minority rights issues. It also reflects the fact that if 'old' member states were to highlight continuing problems in other member states, they would invite criticism regarding the situation of their own Roma populations. Thus, the 'double standards' decried by minority rights activists in recent years remain an obstacle to further progress. In addition, prejudice among the majority populations towards the Roma remains widespread, limiting public support for further reforms (Ram 2007).

On the other hand, the EU provides some avenues for improvement. Probably the biggest driver of change now is the Race Equality Directive, adopted by the EU in 2000 (see Chapter 3 on anti-discrimination legislation). Unlike other EU policies and conditions regarding the Roma, the Directive is (relatively) clearly outlined and applies to all member states, rather than only to acceding countries. It was not designed or adopted with the intention of protecting the Roma and many believe it would not be adopted if it were introduced today.[5] Nonetheless, the Directive has triggered new legislation and institutions that can be used to address discrimination against the Roma. Although the Commission has found substantial shortcomings in new and old member states with regard to the transposition and implementation of the Directive, and has initiated infringement procedures against many of them, the Directive has already been used successfully in the courts in some countries. In Bulgaria, for example, adoption of the Protection against Discrimination Act in 2003 has been followed by several 'landmark' judgements regarding the Roma (European Roma Rights Centre 2006). The Directive has provided a new tool for Roma rights activists and brought additional attention to the Roma through reports monitoring its implementation, such as those by the Commission's DG for Employment and Social Affairs' European Network of Independent Legal Experts in the non-discrimination field (Ram 2007).

Another post-enlargement opportunity for improving the situation of the Roma relates to funding. Leading up to enlargement, the EU provided over €100 million to Roma-targeted projects under the Poland and Hungary: Assistance for Restructuring their Economies (PHARE) programme (European Commission 2007). After accession, new member states have access to significant resources, especially from the EU's structural funds, that may be used for Roma projects, for example in areas such as employment, education, and social exclusion. While there is no requirement to use any of these funds for Roma projects, some countries have already agreed to do so. Others have at least included the Roma in their national plans for the use of EU funds and will continue to be pressured by NGOs to keep their promises. It remains to be seen exactly how much money will be spent on Roma projects, and if the projects will be more effective and more numerous than those supported under the PHARE programme.

Finally, the participation of Roma themselves in EU institutions offers some possibilities for sustaining attention on Roma issues. The two new Roma members of the European Parliament (MEPs) who achieved their posts with Hungary's accession have vowed to keep the Roma on the EU's agenda. They have already had some success in this regard with the adoption of two European Parliament resolutions on the Roma. The Parliament's 2005 Resolution on the Situation of Roma in the European Union emphasized 'the importance of urgently eliminating continuing and violent trends of racism and racial discrimination against Roma', recounted the numerous disadvantages faced by the Roma, and called on various EU bodies, EU member states, and candidate countries to take specific actions to address these concerns (European Parliament 2005). The Roma MEPs could help to promote change and to raise awareness about the Roma, but two Roma women within a body of limited power in a slowly moving institution can only hope to achieve incremental success without other facilitating factors, no matter how tirelessly they may work.

Conclusions

Throughout Central and Eastern Europe, the Roma continue to face economic difficulties and discrimination. Over the past decade and a half, the governments of the region have developed various policies and programmes to address the situation of the Roma. They have also adopted European legal standards on minority protection and anti-discrimination. Moreover, there has been an emergence of many Roma activists and NGOs, although this has not been matched by significant political participation. EU conditionality has been influential in bringing attention to the Roma and in getting programmes and institutional reforms adopted by governments of accession countries, but implementation has lagged behind reform, and countries were admitted to the EU while substantial problems remained. Despite the disappearance of EU leverage post-enlargement, the EU provides some possibilities for improving the situation of the Roma. These include continued monitoring of the implementation of the Race Equality Directive, EU regional aid funding, and increased Roma activism at the EU level. It remains to be seen whether the next decade will bring any substantial improvements in the lives of the Roma living in Central and Eastern Europe.

Notes

2 Even the term 'Roma' has not been universally adopted by the populations often denoted as such by outsiders. The Sinti in Germany, for example, consider themselves a distinct group.
3 Latvia had signed the convention prior to accession, but did not ratify it until January 2005.
4 The citizenship law, which took effect when the Czech Republic and Slovakia became independent countries on 1 January 1993, was criticized because its requirements prevented many Roma from attaining citizenship.
5 The quick adoption of the Race Equality Directive in 2000 was to a large extent the result of an extraordinary amount of political will, which was present at that particular moment in time among all the member states, because they wanted to respond forcefully to the inclusion of the Freedom Party in the Austrian government. Since 2000, the political context has become much more complicated (not in the least because of EU enlargement and new security debates) and commission officials have pointed out to activists and NGOs that finding unanimous support for new legislation proposals in the field of anti-discrimination will not be that easy anymore.

References

Barany, Z. (2002) *The East European Gypsies: Regime Change, Marginality, and Ethnopolitics*, Cambridge: Cambridge University Press.
Barry, B. (2001) *Culture and Equality*, Cambridge: Polity Press.
Entzinger, H. (2000) 'The Dynamics of Integration Policies: A Multidimensional Model,' in R. Koopmans and P. Statham (eds.) *Challenging Immigration and Ethnic Relations Politics: Comparative European Perspectives*, Oxford: Oxford University Press, 97–118.
European Roma Rights Centre (2006) 'Justice for Romani Victims of Racial Discrimination in Bulgaria,' World Conference Against Racism listserv. Online, available at: www.hrea.org/lists/wcar/markup/msg00269.html (10 June 2006).
European Commission (1997a) *Agenda 2000 – Commission Opinion on Romania's Application for Membership of the European Union*, Brussels: European Commission. Online, available at: http://ec.europa.eu/enlargement/archives/ pdf/dwn/opinions/romania/ro-op_en.pdf (accessed 18 August 2007).
—— (1997b) *Agenda 2000 – Commission Opinion on Slovakia's Application for Membership of the European Union*, Brussels: European Commission. Online, available at: http://ec.europa.eu/enlargement/archives/pdf/dwn/opinions/slovakia/   sk-op_en.pdf (accessed 18 August 2007).
—— (1997c) *Agenda 2000 – Commission Opinion on the Czech Republic's Application for Membership of the European Union*, Brussels: European Commission. Online, available at: http://ec.europa.eu/enlargement/archives/pdf/dwn/opinions/czech/cz-op_en.pdf (accessed 18 August 2007).
—— (2001) *2001 Regular Report on Slovakia's Progress Towards Accession*, Brussels: European Commission. Online, available at: http://ec.europa.eu/enlargement/ archives/pdf/key_documents/2001/sk_en.pdf (accessed 18 August 2007).
—— (2004) *The Situation of Roma in an Enlarged European Union*, Brussels: European Commission. Online, available at: www.ec.europa.eu/ employment_social/fundamental_rights/pdf/pubst/roma04_en.pdf (accessed 15 August 2007).
—— (2007) *The EU and Roma*, Brussels: European Commission. Online, available at: http://ec.europa.eu/employment_social/fundamental_rights/roma/rfund/   ren_en.htm (accessed 26 September 2007).

European Parliament (2005) *European Parliament resolution on the situation of the Roma in the European Union*, Brussels: European Parliament. Online, available at: www. europarl.europa.eu/sides/getDoc.do?pubRef=-//EP//TEXT+TA+P6-TA-2005–0151+0+DOC+XML+V0//EN (accessed 1 November 2006).

Gheorghe, N. (2006) 'The Decade of Roma Rights', *Roma Rights*, 2–3. Online, available at: www.errc.org/cikk.php?cikk=2648 (accessed 30 September 2007).

Government of the Republic of Hungary (1997) *Report No. J/3670 of the Government of the Republic of Hungary to the National Assembly on the Situation of the National and Ethnic Minorites Living in the Republic of Hungary*, Budapest: Government of the Republic of Hungary.

Grigore, D. (2004) 4 June, President of Aven Amentza, Bucharest, Romania, interview by Melanie Ram.

Guy, W. (2002) 'Romani identity and post-Communist policy,' in W. Guy (ed.) *Between Past and Future: the Roma of Central and Eastern Europe*, Hatfield: University of Hertfordshire Press, 3–32.

Guy, W. and M. Kovats (2006) *EU-funded Roma programmes: Lessons from Hungary, Slovakia and the Czech Republic*, London: Minority Rights Group International.

Kenrick, D. (1998) *Historical Dictionary of the Gypsies (Romanies)*, Maryland: Scarecrow Press.

Koreck, M. (2004) 17 June, Project on Ethnic Relations, Tirgu Mureş, Romania, interview by Melanie Ram.

Kovats, M. (2001) 'The Political Significance of the First National Gypsy Self-Government (Országos Kisebbségi Önkormányzat),' *Journal of Ethnopolitics and Minority Issues in Europe*, 1.

Liégeois, J.-P. and N. Gheorghe (1995) *Roma/Gypsies: A European Minority*, London: Minority Rights Group International.

Liégeois, J.-P. (2005) 'Les Roms au cœur de l'Europe', *Le Courrier des Pays de l'Est*, 6 (1052): 19–29.

Open Society Institute (2002) *Monitoring the EU Accession Process: Minority Protection*, Budapest: Open Society Institute.

Petrova, D. (2003) 'The Roma: between a myth and the future', *Social Research*, 70 (1): 111–161.

Ram, M.H. (2002) 'Built by Association: Transplanting Democracy through European Integration', paper presented at University of Toronto conference on 'The European Union's Eastern Enlargement: Surveying the Social and Economic Divides', Toronto, 7–10 February.

—— (2004) 'Lobbying the European Union from Afar: NGO Advocacy on Minority Rights in Candidate States', paper presented at Institut d'Etudes Politiques conference on 'Organized Civil Society and European Governance: Training, Recruitment and Practices of Interest Group Representatives in the European Union', Strasbourg, 21–23 June.

—— (2007) 'Anti-Discrimination Policy and the Roma: Assessing the Impact of EU Enlargement', *Croatian Yearbook of European Law and Policy*, 3.

Szakáts, R. (2004) 15 June, Ethnocultural Diversity Resource Center (EDRC), Cluj, Romania, interview by Melanie Ram.

Vermeersch, P. (2006) *The Romani Movement: Minority Politics and Ethnic Mobilization in Contemporary Central Europe*, New York and Oxford: Berghahn Books.

Part II
Country case studies

6   Bulgaria

Minority rights 'light'

Bernd Rechel

Introduction

Minority rights in Bulgaria present a paradox. While the protection of minorities has played a prominent role in the accession of the country to the European Union (EU), minority rights in Bulgaria have remained remarkably restricted. There are hardly any positive minority rights and some minorities, notably Macedonians and Pomaks (Bulgarian-speaking Muslims), are not afforded any minority rights at all (Rechel 2008a).

A major reason for this is that the legislative framework for minority protection was largely established in the first half of the 1990s and has little changed since then. Under communism, the long-term regime of Todor Zhivkov increasingly relied on overt nationalism and pursued a number of coercive assimilation campaigns against the country's minorities. These were originally directed against Roma and Pomaks, but culminated in the 'Revival Process' of 1984–85, in which the country's Turks were forced to change their names, while Turkish language and culture were outlawed. The 'Revival Process' eventually led to the

Map 6.1 Bulgaria (source: http://maps.mygeo.info/maps_eu_bg.html – accessed 1 February, 2008)

Table 6.1 Key indicators for Bulgaria

Total population (millions)[a]	7.7 (2006)
Urban population (% of total)[a]	70.3 (2006)
GDP per capita, PPP (US$)[a]	10,127 (2006)
Unemployment rate (%)[b]	10.1 (2005)
Ethnic composition (2001 census)[c]	Bulgarian: 83.9%
	Turkish: 9.4%
	Roma: 4.7%
	Others: 2.0%

Sources: a World Bank 2007; b UNICEF 2007; c National Statistical Institute 2004.

Notes
PPP: purchasing power parity; unemployment rate is based on registered unemployment as a percentage of 15–59 year olds; GDP per capita is given in current international US$.

exodus of over 300,000 Turks in the summer of 1989 and discredited Bulgaria's communist regime. Zhivkov was ousted in November 1989 and the reversal of the 'Revival Process' in December 1989 by the new communist regime was one of the first steps towards democratizing the country. However, the communist legacy was to exert a lasting influence on minority rights in Bulgaria, as it shaped public attitudes, minority rights demands, and accommodations by the state in the post-communist period.

With regard to the country's ethnic composition, the Turks and the Roma are Bulgaria's largest minorities, comprising 9.4 and 4.7 per cent of the population respectively, according to the 2001 census (Table 6.1). However, as in other countries in Central and Eastern Europe, due to processes of stigmatization, the Roma are undercounted in censuses and may account for as much as 9 per cent of Bulgaria's population (National Council on Ethnic and Demographic Issues 2003b). The number of self-identified Pomaks has been omitted in the official census results, but was later reported to have been 49,764 persons (Republic of Bulgaria 2006: 5), i.e. 0.63 per cent of the population. There are several smaller ethnic minorities, including the Macedonians, who have faced considerable state pressure when striving to assert an ethnic self-identification different from the Bulgarian one. The 2001 census was the first since 1965 that recorded the number of self-identified Macedonians, at 0.06 per cent of the population (National Statistical Institute 2004).

Key policy changes

Key policy changes in the area of minority rights in Bulgaria after 1989 were the reversal of communist assimilation campaigns, the adoption of the post-communist constitution of 1991, the re-introduction of minority language education in 1991–99, the ratification of the Framework Convention for the Protection of National Minorities in 1999, the adoption of a programme for the integration of the Roma minority (the 'Framework Programme') in 1999, and the adoption of a comprehensive anti-discrimination law in 2003.

Although the reversal of communist assimilation campaigns was the single most important policy change in the area of minority rights in Bulgaria since 1989, it was only done half-heartedly and over a prolonged period of time. The decision of the communist regime to revert the 'Revival Process' in December 1989 was met with nationalist protests, in particular in areas with a large share of Turkish populations. At a meeting of all sides, concessions were made to the nationalists. In January 1990, the National Assembly adopted a 'Declaration on the National Question' that banned organizations or activities directed against 'territorial integrity, the unity of the nation or aiming at the separation of parts of its territory on the basis of religious, ethnic or other principles' (State Gazette 1990). At round table talks with the emerging anti-communist opposition, a more specific prohibition of parties along ethnic or religious lines was agreed that was transposed into the 1991 constitution.

Bulgaria's post-communist constitution was one of the most illiberal in Central and Eastern Europe (Elster 1997: 135) and did not recognize the existence of minorities in the country. The new constitution was particularly directed against the political participation of minorities. Most importantly, Article 14(4) provided that there 'shall be no political parties on ethnic, racial or religious lines' (State Gazette 1991a). Although this article was criticized by UN treaty bodies, the EU, and the Council of Europe, it remained intact throughout the post-communist period. Article 14(4) had important implications for minority policies in Bulgaria. In a crucial case concerning the Movement for Rights and Freedoms, the party with a largely Turkish electorate, the Constitutional Court found in 1992 that the party conformed with the constitution (Constitutional Court 1992). In turn, the Movement for Rights and Freedoms abstained from far-reaching minority rights demands (Rechel 2007).

The only article of the constitution that referred to 'citizens whose mother tongue is not Bulgarian' (State Gazette 1991a: Art. 36.2) granted them the right to 'study and use their own language alongside the compulsory study of the Bulgarian language'. The right of minorities to be taught their language in public schools, however, was fiercely contested in the beginning of the 1990s. Amid nationalist protests, 'mother tongue' education was re-introduced in 1991 as an optional, extracurricular subject for grades 3–8 (State Gazette 1991b). In 1994, minority language education became a freely elective subject for grades 1–8 (State Gazette 1994) and in 1999 it entered the regular curriculum as an obligatory elective subject for grades 1–12 (State Gazette 1999b). The teaching of other topics in minority languages in state schools is so far not even subject to debate.

In 1997, Bulgaria's new government of the Union of Democratic Forces signed the Framework Convention for the Protection of National Minorities, which was two years later than the other nine EU candidate countries of Central and Eastern Europe. At the domestic level, ratification remained contested, as accession to the convention implicitly acknowledged that minorities existed in Bulgaria. The Constitutional Court, however, decided that the convention conformed to the constitution (Constitutional Court 1998). Ratification followed in 1999, although with the accompanying declaration that the ratification and implementation of the Framework Convention for the Protection of National Minorities do not imply any right to engage in any activity violating the territorial integrity and sovereignty of the unitary Bulgarian State, its internal and international security.

(State Gazette 1999a)

In 1997, the government of the Union of Democratic Forces also established a governmental body for minority issues, the National Council on Ethnic and Demographic Issues. As similar bodies in other countries in Central and Eastern Europe, however, this council was only an advisory body without authority or resources to develop, implement and monitor minority-related policies. The need to strengthen the capacity of the National Council on Ethnic and Demographic Issues was noted by the European Commission in all its Regular Reports between 2000 and 2004 and by the 2001 resolution of the European Parliament on Bulgaria's application for membership and the state of negotiations, and it was also included in the short-term priorities of the Accession Partnerships of 1999 and 2001. In 2004, the new government of the Simeon II National Movement turned the council into the National Council for Cooperation on Inter-ethnic and Demographic Issues and the administration of the council into the Directorate on Ethnic and Demographic Issues. However, as their predecessors, these new agencies remained advisory bodies with limited capacity and no executive power.

Adoption of the Framework Programme for Equal Integration of Roma into Bulgarian Society ('Framework Programme') was another key policy change. The Framework Programme had been developed in 1998 by a broad alliance of Roma organizations and has been described as the 'most significant accomplishment' of Roma in Bulgaria's public life (Russinov 2001). The Bulgarian government, after pressure from the Council of Europe, reluctantly adopted the programme in April 1999. The Framework Programme set out strategic objectives for a period of ten years in the areas of minority protection, economic development, health care, development of Roma neighbourhoods, and education (National Council on Ethnic and Demographic Issues 2003a).

The Law on Protection against Discrimination, finally, was adopted in September 2003, after the Regular Reports in 2000, 2001, and 2002 reminded Bulgaria that it needed to transpose the EU anti-discrimination *acquis* (European Commission 2000, 2001, 2002).

When considering the key policy changes adopted by Bulgaria after 1989, it can be concluded that the country has moved from a state policy that aimed to eliminate ethnic differences towards a minority rights regime that offers non-territorial cultural minority rights. However, this impression is superficial. As will be discussed in some more detail in the next section of this chapter, non-territorial cultural rights have only been granted to the country's Turkish minority. The Roma enjoy only very limited cultural minority rights and the state response towards them could be categorized as some form of 'immigrant multiculturalism'. Pomaks and Macedonians, finally, fall outside any minority rights regime and, as under communism, the state response towards them continues to fall into the category of 'eliminating diversity'.

Implementation

The failure of implementing measures for the protection of minorities was a key feature of many of the policy changes adopted in Bulgaria after 1989. As already mentioned, the reversal of communist assimilation campaigns was only done hesitantly, as it was met with nationalist protests. The government seemed to follow the course of 'administering democracy [to the country's minorities] only in homeopathic doses' (Troebst 1992: 200). Of particular relevance for the post-communist development were attempts to outlaw the Movement for Rights and Freedoms, with its largely Turkish electorate. After having participated in the June 1990 elections, the Sofia city court refused to register the party in August 1991, a ruling that was confirmed by the Supreme Court in September 1991. Following pressure from Western European countries, however, the Central Electoral Committee decided in September 1991 that the Movement for Rights and Freedoms would be allowed to take part in the upcoming elections, preventing an escalation of ethnic tension.

As mentioned above, it took until 1999 for minority language education to be included in the regular curriculum. This prolonged period of time was largely due to the unpopularity of granting minority rights to the country's minorities, and to the domestic political constellation, in which the former communists, the Bulgarian Socialist Party, exerted considerable influence until 1997, when it lost elections to the opposition Union of Democratic Forces. In practice, the new minority language provision only started to be implemented in the 2002/03 school year. There are, however, several obstacles to implementation, one of the most important of which is that children from minorities have to choose between foreign languages and their mother tongue. There are also huge differences across the country's minorities: although most Turkish children receive minority language education, hardly any Roma children do so, and minority language education for self-identified Macedonian children remains unthinkable.

Ratification of the Framework Convention for the Protection of National Minorities was a key policy change, as it made the notion of 'national minorities' explicit. Yet, ratification did not seem to lead directly to any domestic policy change. In its Opinion on Bulgaria, adopted on 27 May 2004, the Council of Europe Advisory Committee criticized both the scope and depth of minority rights afforded by the Bulgarian state. It recommended to allow the use of minority languages in dealings with authorities and for topographical indications and to expand the protection of the convention to Macedonians and Pomaks (Advisory Committee on the Framework Convention 2006). These suggestions were dismissed in the comments of the Bulgarian government which argued that Macedonians and Pomaks do not constitute ethnic minorities (Republic of Bulgaria 2006).

For the first years after its adoption, the Framework Programme for Equal Integration of Roma into Bulgarian Society remained nothing more than a piece of paper. Following pressure from the European Commission, the Bulgarian government finally adopted an Action Plan for its implementation in October 2003, shortly before the new Regular Report of the Commission was published. Since then, several more policy documents on Roma integration were adopted, including the launch of the Decade of Roma Inclusion 2005–2015 in Sofia in February 2005. However, the government does not seem to follow a clear strategic direction and many of the original goals of the Framework Programme have remained elusive. This particularly applies to the critical area of education, where a comprehensive government policy and instruments for implementation remain lacking (Open Society Institute 2007). The National Action Plan for the Realization of the Decade of Roma Inclusion appears at first sight to thoroughly address the key areas of the Roma Decade. However, 'a closer look reveals that it is conceived more as a pro forma, bureaucratic document which acts as a catch-all for existing policies that affect either Roma specifically or all disadvantaged groups, including Roma' (Tashev and Bechev 2007: 57). As for the Framework Programme, there is a reliance on external donors and no special, earmarked funding from the state budget has been allocated for the Roma Decade. What 'gets reported as implementation consists of various activities undertaken by state institutions from their general budget' (Tashev and Bechev 2007: 59).

The Law on Protection against Discrimination entered into force on 1 January 2004, considerably improving the legislative framework for addressing discrimination. A growing number of rulings by first and second instance courts have since then been made. After some delays associated with its politically charged membership, the Anti-Discrimination Commission began functioning in November 2005. In 2006, 48 proceedings instigated by the commission were concerned with ethnic or racial discrimination and the Anti-Discrimination Commission established discrimination in seven of these cases (Commission for Protection against Discrimination 2007).

The impact of the new anti-discrimination framework on society at large, however, remains to be seen. Simultaneous to the emergence of the new anti-discrimination framework, hate speech and anti-minority rhetoric have been on the rise. In the 2005 parliamentary elections, the extreme nationalist party Attack (*Ataka*) received 9 per cent of the vote and its leader Volen Siderov received 24 per cent of the vote in the second round of the presidential elections in October 2006. Throughout the summer of 2006, *Ataka* organized protests in front of mosques throughout the country and this was for several months tolerated by the local authorities (Bulgarian Helsinki Committee 2007). With the electoral success of the new nationalist party, the societal climate for minorities worsened and this does not bode well for the time after EU accession.

Indeed, in the elections to the European Parliament in May 2007, *Ataka* received 14.2 per cent of the vote, resulting in three seats in the European Parliament. Already in January 2007, new ultra-nationalist Members of European Parliament (MEPs) from Bulgaria and Romania delivered the 20 MEPs necessary to form the new right-wing bloc 'Identity, Tradition and Sovereignty'. Although this political group ceased to exist in November 2007, following the retreat of the Greater Romania Party, the electoral success of ultra-nationalist parties in the new EU member states is now shaping policy-making within the EU.

Overall, a number of reasons for lacking implementation of policy changes in Bulgaria can be identified. Public attitudes seem to be of particular importance. These are related to several aspects of minority rights. First, nationalist sentiments impeded the reversal of the communist assimilation campaigns and the re-introduction of minority language education. Second, a consensus in Bulgarian society on the Bulgarian ethnicity of Pomaks and Macedonians makes the granting of minority rights to these groups politically very difficult. Third, anti-Roma racism remains widespread and what are regarded as 'special measures' for Roma are highly unpopular among the non-Roma population (including other ethnic minorities). Finally, minority rights in general find little support in the ethnic Bulgarian population. In light of these public perceptions, it comes as no surprise that the political will of Bulgarian governments to extend the protection of minorities was generally absent and that there was often a lack of direction, weak institutional capacities, limited budgetary allocations, and lacking minority involvement (Rechel 2008b).

Explanatory factors

Bulgaria's minority rights regime is the result of a combination of internal and external factors. Among the internal factors, the historical legacy from communism, domestic party constellations, popular attitudes to minorities and minority rights, and factors specific to the minorities themselves (such as their size, ethnic self-identifications, socio-economic standing, and political clout) stand out. Among the external factors, the Council of Europe and the EU have played a key role.

In the early 1990s, the reversal of the communist assimilation campaigns was undertaken with the aim of overcoming Bulgaria's international isolation. It was thus driven by a broad move towards Europe, without yet any clear association with conditionality or EU membership. Similarly, the 1991 constitution was enacted without any direct involvement of Western organizations and this explains to some degree why very illiberal provisions were included. An exception to the subordinate role of Western actors in the early 1990s was the decision of the Central Electoral Committee in September 1991, which allowed the Movement of Rights and Freedoms to take part in the upcoming elections. This decision seems to have been the direct result of Western pressure. Overall, however, in the first half of the 1990s, the West did not play a major role in shaping minority rights policies in Bulgaria. Clearly more important were domestic factors. In the early 1990s, the Bulgarian public and political elite continued to be opposed to the notion that minorities existed in Bulgaria at all. The demands of the Movement for Rights and Freedoms were primarily concerned with a reversal of the communist assimilation policies and the reintroduction of minority language education. In the context of virulent nationalist demonstrations and the potential exclusion from the political process, the demand for wider-reaching minority rights was politically not feasible. The two main political parties in the first years of transition, the Bulgarian Socialist Party and the Union of Democratic Forces were both wary of the nationalist electorate. After the 1991 elections, however, the Movement for Rights and Freedoms emerged as a crucial third force and minority language education was reintroduced. Between 1994 and 1997, the former communists returned to power and progress in minority rights stalled.

In 1997, both the domestic party constellation changed and the EU started to articulate its expectations with regard to minority protection in Bulgaria. The reform-oriented government of the Union of Democratic Forces was more responsive to Western expectations and this interplay resulted in a number of domestic policy changes, including the introduction of minority language education in the regular curriculum, the ratification of the Framework Convention, the adoption of the Framework Programme, and the establishment of a National Council on Ethnic and Demographic Issues. The 2001 elections resulted in a government coalition between the Simeon II National Movement and the Movement for Rights and Freedoms, under which the Law on Protection against Discrimination was enacted in 2003.

Remarkably, however, the institutional framework for minority rights in Bulgaria has remained largely unaffected by these policy changes, with the exception of the area of anti-discrimination. One reason for this was that, in contrast to those countries in Central and Eastern Europe with sizeable Russian or Hungarian minorities, minority kin-states have not played a significant role with regard to minority rights policies in Bulgaria. Turkey was largely satisfied with the reversal of the assimilation campaign, while relations between Bulgaria and Macedonia were more affected by the so-called 'language dispute' in 1994–97, during which Bulgaria refused to recognize the existence of a separate Macedonian language and nation. As a result of the constraint of minority kin-states with regard to minorities in Bulgaria, the High Commissioner on National Minorities of the Organization for Security and Co-operation in Europe (OSCE) never became involved, in marked contrast to all of Bulgaria's neighbouring countries.

Furthermore, some of Bulgaria's minorities have faced serious obstacles when aiming for influence in the political arena and this has contributed to a restrictive minority rights regime. The Roma, despite their numerical size, have failed to gain any political leverage at the national level. Their political participation is undermined by stigmatization, a variety of ethnic self-identifications, and socio-economic exclusion. As far as the Macedonian minority is concerned, despite several rulings of the European Court of Human Rights, the Bulgarian government continues to refuse the registration of Macedonian parties (Rechel 2007).

Finally, the role of public attitudes can hardly be overestimated. In addition to deeply entrenched anti-Roma racism, minority rights in general remain highly unpopular. In a survey in 2005, for example, 29 per cent of ethnic Bulgarian interviewees disagreed with minorities having representatives in parliament, while 76 per cent stated that they would not vote for their preferred party if it nominated a qualified Roma candidate, 64 per cent would not vote for a party with Turkish candidates and 50 per cent would not vote for a party with Jewish candidates (Voynova 2005).

Assessing the impact of the EU

Despite the change on the domestic political scene in 1997, it can be assumed that most of Bulgaria's policy changes after 1997 would not have happened without direct pressure from the EU. The European Commission expected Bulgaria to adopt the Framework Convention, to take steps towards the integration of the Roma minority, and to transpose the anti-discrimination *acquis*. In all three cases, Bulgarian governments complied with the expectations.

While the Council of Europe was instrumental in the process leading to the adoption of the Framework Programme, the European Commission played a crucial role in pressuring Bulgaria to adopt a plan for implementation, although it is remarkable how long it has taken to do so. Ratification of the Framework Convention ranked highly both in the European Commission reports and in the post-accession monitoring by the Parliamentary Assembly of the Council of Europe. Where institutions of the Council of Europe were not vested with additional leverage from the European Commission, however, they were regularly ignored or dismissed. This happened, for example, with regard to a report of the European Commission against Racism and Intolerance in 2004. In a long appendix, the Bulgarian authorities rejected most findings of the report (European Commission against Racism and Intolerance 2004). The rulings of the European Court of Human Rights against Bulgaria, on the other hand, both with regard to the human rights of Roma and those of Macedonians, seem to have been ignored by both the European Commission and the Bulgarian government. Finally, as mentioned above, the recommendations of the Advisory Committee on the Framework Convention were simply brushed off by the Bulgarian authorities (see: Republic of Bulgaria 2006).

This suggests that the EU was far more influential than Council of Europe institutions, in particular when these acted in isolation. Even after having found Bulgaria in compliance with the political Copenhagen criteria in 1998, the European Commission continued to exert influence in the sphere of minority rights and did so until its final monitoring report prior to accession, which was published in September 2006. Yet, post-accession monitoring by the EU in the sphere of minority rights can be said to be nearly non-existent. While the September 2006 report stated that the European Monitoring Centre on Racism and Xenophobia (EUMC, in 2007 transformed into the EU Agency for Fundamental Rights, or FRA) will continue its monitoring after accession (European Commission 2006: 7), it had until then not been involved in the drawing up of European Commission monitoring reports and is unlikely to have a significant impact on the new EU member states.

It is also worth noting where, despite its leverage, the EU failed to matter. As mentioned above, Bulgaria refused to amend its constitutional provisions directed against the political participation of minorities, despite the fact that these were criticized by UN treaty bodies, the Council of Europe, and the European Commission. This may be due to the fact that the European Commission has not consistently included this issue in its monitoring reports.

A more general impediment to the leverage of the EU was that it was not concerned with minority rights as such. What it was concerned with, were issues of regional stability and migration, and the question of minority protection was framed in this context. The inclusion of the Roma played a prominent role in the monitoring reports on Bulgaria, but it was mainly perceived as a socio-economic issue and the question of positive minority rights was generally ignored, as was the situation of other minorities in the country.

Crucially, the European Commission equated nominal policy changes with a success of conditionality. According to Morten Jung-Olsen, the former Head of the Bulgaria Team in the European Commission, 'the philosophy has [. . .] been that credible commitments were acceptable as a way of moving the agenda forward' (Jung-Olsen 2005). It is true that the European Commission also pressured Bulgaria to establish a plan for implementation of the Framework Programme, but once such a plan had been drawn up, its mere existence was taken to be sufficient indication of meeting the Accession Partnership priorities. This emphasis on nominal changes encouraged the Bulgarian government to adopt superficial policy changes without any intention to implement them in practice. An example of this approach is the Framework Convention, which does not seem to have resulted in any domestic policy change.

Another omission of the EU was to ignore public attitudes towards minorities and minority rights. As this chapter suggests, these are crucial, not only for embarking on policy changes, but also for their actual implementation. Too often, Roma, rather than the existence of racism and discrimination, were portrayed in the Bulgarian media as an obstacle to EU accession.

Conclusions

The lessons that emerge from the Bulgarian case are mixed. Beginning in the second half of the 1990s until Bulgaria's accession in 2007, the EU played a pivotal role in shaping the agenda of Bulgarian governments in the sphere of minority rights. Responding to the expectations of the European Commission, Bulgaria adopted a programme for the integration of the Roma minority, established a governmental agency for ethnic and demographic issues, and ratified the Framework Convention. Finally, in 2003, Bulgaria brought its legislation into line with the EU's anti-discrimination directives. In the years after 1989, the EU was clearly the most important international actor influencing minority rights policies in Bulgaria.

Despite the nominal emphasis on minority protection in the EU accession process, positive minority rights in Bulgaria have remained fairly limited. The use of minority languages as a language of instruction in state schools remains unthinkable, as does its use in dealings with authorities or for topographical indications. Furthermore, Pomaks and Macedonians continue to be considered as ethnic Bulgarians and do not enjoy any minority rights.

A major reason for this apparent contradiction is that the course of Bulgaria's minority rights trajectory had been set when the country departed from communism in the period 1989–91. When the communist regime started to reverse the assimilation campaigns against the country's minorities in late 1989, this was met with nationalist protests and, as a compromise, very restrictive provisions were included in the post-communist constitution, including a prohibition of parties along 'ethnic, racial or religious lines'. Faced with its potential exclusion from the political arena, the Movement for Rights and Freedoms embarked on a non-confrontational course that was minimalist in terms of minority rights. It is now an established and generally accepted party on the Bulgarian political scene, but its minority rights agenda remains modest, and this has left its mark on the country's minority rights regime.

When the EU started to seriously enter the fray with its Opinion on Bulgaria's application for membership in 1997, a government more responsive to Western expectations had taken office in form of the Union of Democratic Forces. However, the EU lacked both the interest in and competence on minority rights per se and was mainly concerned with the socio-economic integration of the Roma minority, and, later, with the transposition of anti-discrimination directives. The Turkish minority was described by the European Commission as being integrated into society and other minorities were ignored, despite the growing attention they received by Council of Europe bodies.

A marked implementation gap can be observed with regard to most of Bulgaria's policy changes in the sphere of minority rights. This is partly due to the approach of the European Commission, which paid insufficient attention to actual implementation, implicitly encouraging superficial policy changes. The only nominal adoption of new policy instruments can also be attributed to public attitudes and prejudices, of which policy-makers must have been acutely aware. Although the nationalist attitudes towards the country's Turkish minority have been receding since the days of Zhivkov, xenophobia and anti-Roma racism remain widespread. Addressing and overcoming these deeply entrenched attitudes may be one of the most important challenges for effecting a better protection of minorities in Bulgaria.

References

Advisory Committee on the Framework Convention (2006) *Opinion on Bulgaria, adopted on 27 May 2004*, Strasbourg: Advisory Committee on the Framework Convention for the Protection of National Minorities, Council of Europe.

Bulgarian Helsinki Committee (2007) *Human Rights in Bulgaria in 2006*, Sofia: Bulgarian Helsinki Committee.

Commission for Protection against Discrimination (2007) *Godishen Otchet 2006 [Annual report 2006]*, Sofia: Republic of Bulgaria.

Constitutional Court (1992) 'Reshenie No. 4 ot 21 april 1992 g. po konstitutsionno delo No. 1 ot 1991 g. [Decision Nr. 4 of 21 April 1992 on constitutional case Nr. 1 of 1991]', *State Gazette No. 35 of 28 April 1992*. Sofia: Konstitutsionnen süd [Constitutional Court].

—— (1998) 'Reshenie No. 2 ot 18 fevruari 1998 g. po konstitutsionno delo No. 15 ot 1997 g. [Decision Nr. 2 of 18 February 1998 on constitutional case Nr. 15 of 1997]', *State Gazette No. 22 of 24 February 1998*. Sofia: Konstitutsionnen süd [Constitutional Court].

European Commission (2000) *2000 Regular Report on Bulgaria's Progress Towards Accession*, Brussels: European Commission.

—— (2001) *2001 Regular Report on Bulgaria's Progress Towards Accession*, Brussels: European Commission.

—— (2002) *2002 Regular Report on Bulgaria's Progress towards Accession*, Brussels: European Commission.

—— (2006) *Monitoring report on the state of preparedness for EU membership of Bulgaria and Romania*, Brussels: European Commission.

European Commission against Racism and Intolerance (2004) *Third report on Bulgaria, adopted on 27 June 2003, published on 27 January 2004*, Strasbourg: European Commission against Racism and Intolerance, Council of Europe.

Elster, J. (1997) 'Ways of constitution-making', in A. Hadenius (ed.) *Democracy's victory and crisis*, Cambridge: Cambridge University Press, 123–142.

Jung-Olsen, M. (2005) Interview of the author with Morten Jung-Olsen, former Head of Unit of the Bulgaria Team in the European Commission, Brussels, 14 June 2005.

National Council on Ethnic and Demographic Issues (2003a) 'Framework Programme for Equal Integration of Roma in Bulgarian Society, adopted on 8 April 1999', *Bulletin of the National Council on Ethnic and Demographic Issues (English edition)*: 19–24.

—— (2003b) *Informatsiia za politikata na Bŭlgarskoto pravitelstvo za podobriavane na polozhenieto na romskoto naselenie v Bŭlgariia [Information on the policy of the Bulgarian government for the improvement of the situation of the Roma population in Bulgaria]*, Sofia: National Council on Ethnic and Demographic Issues, prepared for the conference "Roma in an Expanding Europe", Budapest, 30 June–1 July 2003. Online, available at: www.ncedi.government.bg/8.Doklad-Budapest-1.07.03.htm (accessed 27 February 2004).

National Statistical Institute (2004) *Prebroiavane na naselenieto, zhilishtniia fond i zeme-delskite stopanstva prez 2001, Tom 1, Naselenie, Kniga 1, Demografski i sotsialni kharakteristiki na naselenieto [Census of Population, Housing Stock and Agriculture in 2001, Volume 1, Population, Book 1, Demographic and Social Characteristics of the Population]*, Sofia: Natsionalen Statisticheski Institut [National Statistical Institute].

Open Society Institute (2007) *Equal Access to Quality Education for Roma: Bulgaria*, New York: Open Society Institute.

Rechel, B. (2007) 'State Control of Minorities in Bulgaria', *Journal of Communist Studies and Transition Politics*, 23 (3): 352–370.

—— (2008a) *The long way back to Europe: minority protection in Bulgaria*, Stuttgart: ibidem-Verlag.

—— (2008b) 'Neuspechŭt pri izpŭlnenieto na merkite za zashtita na maltsinstvata [The failure of implementing measures for the protection of minorities]', *Sotsiologicheski Problemi*, special issue.

Republic of Bulgaria (2006) *Comments of the Government of Bulgaria on the Opinion of the Advisory Committee on the Implementation of the Framework Convention for the Protection of National Minorities in Bulgaria (received on 14 March 2005)*, Strasbourg: Council of Europe.

Russinov, R. (2001) 'The Bulgarian Framework Programme for Equal Integration of Roma: participation in the policy making process', *Roma Rights, journal of the European Roma Rights Centre*, 2–3.

State Gazette (1990) 'Deklaratsiia na Narodnoto sŭbranie na Narodna republika Bŭlgariia po natsionalniia vŭpros ot 15 ianuari 1990 g. [Declaration of the National Assembly of the People's Republic of Bulgaria on the National Question of 15 January 1990]', *Dŭrzhaven vestnik [State Gazette] No. 6 of 19 January 1990*.

—— (1991a) 'Konstitutsiia na Republika Bŭlgariia [Constitution of the Republic of Bulgaria], adopted on 12 July 1991', *Dŭrzhaven vestnik [State Gazette] No. 56 of 13 July 1991*.

—— (1991b) 'Ministerski Suvet, Postanovlenie No. 232 ot 29 noemvri 1991 g. za izuchavane na maĭchin ezik v obshtinskite uchilishta [Council of Ministers Decree No. 232 of 29 November 1991 on the Study of Mother Tongue in Municipal Schools]', *Dŭrzhaven vestnik [State Gazette] No. 102 of 10 December 1991*.

—— (1994) 'Postanovlenie No. 183 na MS ot 5.09.1994 g. za izuchavane na maĭchin ezik v obshtinskite uchilishta v Republika Bŭlgariia [Council of Ministers Decree No. 183 of 5 September 1994 on the Study of Mother Tongue in Municipal Schools in Bulgaria]', *Dŭrzhaven vestnik [State Gazette] No. 73 of 9 September 1994*.

—— (1999a) 'Zakon za ratifitsirane na Ramkovata konventsia za zashtita na natsionalnite maltsinstva [Law on Ratification of the Framework Convention for the Protection of National Minorities]', *Dŭrzhaven vestnik [State Gazette] No. 18 of 26 February 1999*.

—— (1999b) 'Zakon za stepenta na obrazovanie, obshtoobrazovatelniia minimum i uchebniia plan [Law on Educational Level, General Educational Minimum and Curricula]', *Dŭrzhaven vestnik [State Gazette] No. 67 of 27 July 1999*.

Tashev, T. and Bechev, T. (2007) 'Bulgaria', in: M. Nicoara (ed.) *Decade Watch. Roma Activists Assess the Progress of the Decade of Roma Inclusion. 2005–2006*, Hungary: Createch Ltd, 57–66.

Troebst, S. (1992) 'Nationalismus als Demokratiehemmnis in Bulgarien. Von der Verfassungsdiskussion zur Präsidentschaftswahl (Mai 1991–Januar 1992) [Nationalism as an impediment to democracy in Bulgaria. From the discussion on the constitution to the presidential elections (May 1991–January 1992)]', *Südosteuropa*, 41 (3–4): 188–227.

UNICEF (2007) TransMONEE Database 2007.

Voynova, S. (2005) *Roma Participation in the 2005 Parliamentary Elections*, Washington: National Democratic Institute for International Affairs.

World Bank (2007) *World Development Indicators*, Washington: World Bank.

7 Czech Republic

Exceptionality and conditionality at work

Eva Sobotka

Introduction

This chapter argues that the policies adopted towards minorities in the Czech Republic throughout the 1990s were to a large degree influenced by the notion of 'Czech exceptionality', which was at odds with international human and minority rights standards. Beginning in 1997, European Union (EU) conditionality resulted in significant policy changes, in particular with regard to the Roma minority, but challenges remain in the protection of members of ethnic minorities against discrimination. Following the predominant focus of the international community, this chapter pays particular attention to the policies adopted towards the Roma.

The independent state of Czechoslovakia was created in 1918. With the Munich Agreement in 1938, Czechoslovakia lost about one third of its territory, the *Sudetenland* (the western regions mainly inhabited by ethnic Germans) and the regions largely inhabited by the Hungarian and Polish minorities. In 1939 Slovakia became independent and the Czech territory a protectorate of Germany.

Map 7.1 The Czech Republic (source: http://maps.mygeo.info/maps_eu_cz.html – accessed 1 November, 2007).

Table 7.1 Key indicators for the Czech Republic

Total population (millions)[a]	10.2 (2006)
Urban population (% of total)[a]	73.5 (2006)
GDP per capita, PPP (US$)[a]	22,791 (2006)
Unemployment rate (%)[b]	7.9 (2005)
Ethnic composition (2001 census)[c]	Czechs: 90.4%
	Moravians: 3.7%
	Slovaks: 1.9%
	Undeclared: 1.7%
	Poles: 0.5%
	Other: 1.8%

Sources: a World Bank 2007; b UNICEF 2007; c Czech Statistical Office 2007.

Notes
PPP: purchasing power parity; unemployment rate is based on registered unemployment as a percentage of 15–59 year olds; GDP per capita is given in current international US$.

In 1945 the Czechoslovak Republic was reinstituted within its former territories, with the exception of sub-Carpathian Ukraine which was annexed to the Soviet Union. Czechoslovakia did not recognize minorities until the introduction of federalism in 1968, when the state officially recognized the Germans, the Hungarians, the Poles and the Ukrainians/Ruthenians as nationalities and defined their rights constitutionally. The 'velvet divorce' of 1 January 1993 led to the dissolution of the former Czechoslovakia into the Czech Republic and Slovakia, but issues related to the German, Jewish and Roma minorities had resurfaced already in 1989 and 1990.

According to the 2001 census, 90.4 per cent of the population self-identified by ethnicity (*národnost*) as Czechs, 3.7 per cent as Moravians, and 1.9 per cent as Slovaks (see Table 7.1). When compared to the 1991 census, this constituted a significant decline in the number of Moravians, from 13.2 per cent in 1991.[1] In the 2001 census, 11,746 self-identified as Roma (0.1 per cent of the population), a decline from 32,903 (0.3 per cent) in 1991. The decline in the size of the Roma and Moravian minorities between 1991 and 2001 can be explained by the fact that, while in the 1991 census the declaration of ethnicity was obligatory, in 2001 it was optional.

Key policy changes

The protection of minorities is specified by the constitution, specific laws, international treaties, and bilateral agreements with neighbouring countries, in particular Germany, Poland, and Slovakia. In Czechoslovakia, minority rights were enshrined in the 1968 Constitutional Law on the Status of National Minorities. This law was superseded by the Charter of Fundamental Rights and Freedoms, which was adopted by the Czechoslovak Federal Assembly in January 1991. After the break-up of the Czechoslovak federation in January 1993, the Charter became part of the constitutional order of the Czech Republic.

In 1994, the government of the Czech Republic adopted resolution No. 63 on the Concept of the Government's Approach to Issues Concerning National

Minorities in the Czech Republic. Although this political document was not legally binding, it set out basic principles concerning 'national minorities', including the status of minorities and the protection of their rights. The right to use minority languages could also be derived from the 1991 Charter of Fundamental Rights and Freedoms. Apart from general non-discrimination clauses, the Charter specified certain minority rights, including the right to develop one's culture, the right to mother tongue education, and the use of minority languages in public. The use of minority languages is further specified by the Act on the Rights of Members of National Minorities of 10 July 2001 (the 'Minority Law'). The Minority Law defined a 'national minority' as 'a community of citizens of the Czech Republic who live on the territory of the present Czech Republic and as a rule differ from other citizens by their common ethnic origin, language, culture and traditions' (Czech Republic 2001).

Minority policy is informed by the work of the Council for National Minorities (also known as the Council for Nationalities), which was established in accordance with the Minority Law. The Council is a consultative and coordinating body of the Czech government. It is chaired by a government member, and its meetings are currently attended by representatives of 12 'national minorities': Bulgarians, Croats, Germans, Greeks, Hungarians, Poles, Roma, Russians, Ruthenians, Serbs, Slovaks, and Ukrainians, with each minority nominating up to three representatives. At the regional and municipal level, there are Committees for National Minorities. These are self-governing bodies in regions or municipalities, where at least 10 per cent of the population belongs to a national minority (5 per cent at the regional level and in Prague, the capital). At present, there are seven regional and 39 municipal committees.

In terms of international law, the Czech Republic acceded to the Council of Europe Framework Convention for the Protection of National Minorities on 18 December 1997 and to the European Charter for Regional or Minority Languages on 15 November 2006.

It is possible to distinguish four stages of minority policy, roughly corresponding with changes in government. In the first stage, between 1990 and 1992, the Czechoslovak government sought to create a Western style liberal democracy. Securing membership in EU and NATO was a major foreign policy goal, and Czechoslovakia acceded to the international mechanisms of human and minority rights protection of the Organization for Security and Co-operation in Europe (OSCE, until 1994 named Conference for Security and Co-operation in Europe, CSCE) and the Council of Europe and developed political alliances with neighbouring countries.

In the second stage of minority policy, between June 1992 and November 1997, the government still aimed for EU and NATO membership, but it perceived the state through the prism of Czech exceptionality, which was a form of Czech nationalism mainly propagated by the cabinets of prime minister Václav Klaus. In this period, developments in a number of policy areas, including minority rights, were surprisingly insulated from international influences. Until 1997, international pressure in the area of minority protection only forced change in one clear case: the 1993 Citizenship Law that disproportionably impacted on Roma.

In the third stage, between 1997 and 2004, a 'wake-up call' from the EU resulted in substantial policy changes. This 'wake-up call' made clear that, in order to be included in the first wave of EU enlargement, certain criteria will have to be met. The basis of policy-making switched from Czech exceptionalism to EU requirements (Vachudová 2001: 359). In 2001 and 2002 respectively, public administration reforms had a significant impact on the implementation of minority policies. In the fourth stage, the period since 2004, the Czech Republic has continued to recognize the rights of minorities, but had still a long way to go with regard to the fight against racism and discrimination, in particular in relation to the Roma minority.

Phase I (1990–92): Czechoslovakia – dissidents' 'return to Europe'

The question of whether to include 'national minorities' and Roma in a single policy package was immediately on the agenda of the provisional Czechoslovak government formed in December 1989. A growing number of racially motivated attacks, as well as increased activism of the Roma elite within the structures of the Civic Movement (a liberal group founded in 1991 inside the dissident Civic Forum that won the 1990 elections in the Czech part of Czechoslovakia), contributed to the formulation of a new state policy towards the Roma. In early 1990, Roma were recognized as a nationality *(národnost)* or 'national minority' and the government declared that it aimed to speed up the 'societal rise' of the Roma population by disbanding the pre-1989 departments overseeing 'Gypsy affairs' and by involving newly established Roma non-governmental organizations (NGOs) in Roma policy-making (Sulitka: 1998: 224). Roma members of parliament (MPs) in the Czech and Slovak National Councils and the Federal Assembly took an active part in drafting a new policy towards the Roma, as did representatives of Roma organizations and the Roma political party, the Roma Civil Initiative (RCI). In October 1991, the government approved resolution No. 619 on 'Principles of the Policy towards the Roma minority of the Government of the Czech and Slovak Federal Republic', setting out comprehensive Roma integration principles. With adoption of the 'Principles of Policy of the Government of the Czech and Slovak Federal Republic towards National and Ethnic Minorities' in 1992, more concrete steps towards formulating a Roma policy were taken. Due to the upcoming elections and growing tension over the dissolution of the state, policy-making on national minorities, however, dropped from the policy agenda of the federal, as well as the national, level. In the elections in June 1992, the economic pragmatism of the Civic Democratic Party (CDP) won out over the human rights oriented former dissidents.

Phase II (1992–97): the civic principle, racism and discrimination

After the CDP had won the 1992 national elections, it formed a coalition government with the Civic Democratic Alliance and the Christian Democratic Union –

Czechoslovak Popular Party.[2] The overarching goal of the two CDP-led governments under prime minister Klaus (June 1992 – June 1996 and June 1996 – November 1997) was to create a market economy, consolidate democracy, and join EU and NATO. The Klaus governments, while successful in projecting a very positive image of the Czech Republic to the West, had fostered an 'ideology of Czech exceptionalism' (Pehe 1998: 6–7) at home that had no place for human rights and minority issues (Hala 1995: 21–22). Within this period, racially motivated violence against Roma intensified, with many attacks and murders (Trojan 1994: 34–35). Norms relating to ethnic minorities were conservatively interpreted and affirmative action or a multicultural policy towards minorities were deemed incompatible with the civic principle *(občanský princip)*, that was set out in the 1991 Charter of Fundamental Rights and Freedoms, but misinterpreted in the spirit of CDP's neo-liberal ideology.

Overall, the period between 1992 and 1997 was characterized by exclusion and assimilation, and previous Roma policy efforts were given low priority or considered to be inapplicable. Roma civil society organizations were cut off from any cooperation with the government. Between June 1992 and February 1993, the government policy towards Roma made a U-turn from the objective of increasing the rise of Roma within society to one of controlling migratory flows from Slovakia, increasing repressive measures against what was perceived as a high level of Roma criminality, and allowing municipalities to evict Roma under the guise of increasing public order and implementing the Citizenship Law. Political parties, such as the 'Club of Committed Non-party Members' *(Klub angažovaných nestraníků)*, called for the formation of civic self-defence groups, to protect citizens 'from the Gypsy disorder' (Landergott 1992). A number of politicians from across the political spectrum, but mainly from right wing parties, such as the Association for the Republic – Republican Party of Czechoslovakia (the Republicans), differentiated between 'citizens' or 'moral citizens' on the one hand, and 'Gypsy', 'socially unadaptable', 'migrating population', 'asocial inhabitants' and 'scum' on the other.

In 1990 and 1991, many Roma migrated from the Slovak to the Czech Federal Republic, mostly to the industrial cities of north-Bohemia, such as Most and Ústí nad Labem. During this time, several municipalities enacted ordinances to control the migration of 'asocial inhabitants' (US State Department 1994). These policy initiatives were inspired by an effort of Germany to deport a large number of asylum seekers and migrants through readmission treaties with neighbouring countries and Romania (Dengler and Kovařík 1993; *Rudé Právo* 1993; Kovařík 1993). The public discussion surrounding Roma policy in the Czech Republic revolved around lowering criminality and increasing control over this segment of the population (Czech Television 1 1993; Šídlo 1993).

When the Czechoslovak federation dissolved on 1 January 1993, the Czech Republic implemented the narrowly crafted Citizenship Law, which had been adopted on 29 December 1992. Thousands of Roma who had been long-term or life-long residents and who were former Czechoslovak citizens were left stateless and told to go to Slovakia. After adoption of the Citizenship Law, many

Roma migrated out of the Czech Republic. Municipalities started to call Roma 'socially unadaptable' and evicted them en masse. Some families, rejected by Slovak authorities, returned and spent some time living in public parks and unsuitable industrial spaces.

Racially motivated violence against Roma grew in intensity. The Documentation Centre for Human Rights recorded 1,210 racially motivated attacks in the period 1990–97, with only 10 per cent ending in court. Of the 19 incidents in which people were killed, only two were qualified by the authorities as racially motivated (Sobotka 2004: 215). Racial discrimination in access to services, such as by denying entrance to restaurants and swimming pools, became a widespread phenomenon (Tichý and Kastnerová 1996; *Lidové Noviny* 1996; Žák 1996). According to studies of the Ministry of Interior, a large part of the Czech population agreed with pronouncements of racism against Roma and foreigners (Vachudová 2001). In response to continuing attacks by skinheads and police inaction, Roma self-defence units began being formed in January 1993 (*Mladý Svět* 1995: 10–11). Racial discrimination and racially motivated incidents were also met with protest marches and demonstrations by Roma, and complaints were filed with the Constitutional Court.

Between 1992 and 1997, participation of minorities, including Roma, in policy-making was marginal, partly because no legislative framework was created for the emerging civil society. Political parties did not promote ethnic diversity, nor were their internal structures inclusive of minorities. At a government meeting in February 1993, prime minister Klaus expressed his shock over the activities of skinheads, but excluded the possibility of amending the Citizenship Law. However, he tasked the Minister of Labour and Social Affairs, Jindřich Vodička, to prepare a report on the situation of Roma in the Czech Republic. The report, published in 1993, rejected the notion of Roma criminality and acknowledged their dramatic socio-economic decline (*Lidové Noviny* 1993). While four subsequent government resolutions tasked ministries to prepare practical proposals, these resolutions were mostly declaratory and between 1994 and 1996 no proposals had been prepared.

Phase III (1997–2003): institutionalization

In 1997, private and public TV channels in the Czech Republic broadcast dubious news reports about thefts and crime in the Roma community. These broadcasts continued for several weeks, resulting in renewed anti-Roma hysteria (Uhl 1998: 222; Sobotka 2003: 95). At this time, the Citizenship Law had still not been adequately amended and large numbers of Roma were excluded from the social security system (Zoon 1997: 5). Calls for Roma to leave the Czech Republic were numerous (Uhl 1998: 225; Sobotka 2004: 230) and contributed to a climate that accelerated Roma emigration (Sobotka 2003: 95).

The migration of Roma from the Czech Republic to Canada and the United Kingdom in the summer of 1997 served as an important focusing event. The immediate reaction of the Czech government was to downplay the significance of the process (Sobotka 2003: 95). Prime minister Klaus emphasized that 'the government [had] done everything it [could] for the Roma in the last few years' (Sobotka 2004: 230). Following a meeting with the Roma Civic Initiative in August 1997, however, he proposed to increase the representation of Roma in the state administration and to establish a central government body to coordinate Roma issues (Sobotka 2004: 230). In October 1997, the number of asylum seekers from the Czech Republic in Canada in this year reached 1,300 (compared to 144 in the previous year), and Canada imposed a visa regime for Czech citizens. Only after 90 per cent of asylum applications resulted in refugee status, did the Czech government officially acknowledge the existence of a 'Roma issue', and initiated the process of establishing the Inter-Ministerial Commission for Roma Community Affairs, a body responsible for drafting a government policy towards the Roma.

Qualified debates about a suitable policy towards the Roma started to take place on the pages of the Czech daily newspapers *Právo*, *Mladá Fronta Dnes* and *Lidové Noviny* in autumn 1996. In these articles, leading intellectuals debated principles of affirmative action, equality, segregation and attitudes of the majority population towards the Roma. These debates facilitated a new approach towards the Roma, but also provoked controversial responses, such as the rejection of affirmative policies by the Minister without Portfolio, Pavel Bratinka, who had been tasked with preparing a Roma policy draft (Sobotka 2004: 219). Public debate, however, dismissed Bratinka's rejection (Uhl 1996a) and commentators challenged widespread perceptions of the Roma and argued for the development of a strong, tolerant and multicultural Czech society (Uhl 1996b). Most protagonists of the debate became involved in the formulation of Roma policies in governmental advisory bodies, first in the Inter-Ministerial Commission, since 1998 in the Council for Roma Community Affairs, and since 1999 in the Council for Human Rights.

The embarrassment of the Czech Republic over growing numbers of Roma asylum seekers in Canada and the United Kingdom in the late summer of 1997, in conjunction with the negative evaluation on the treatment of the Roma in the Opinion of the European Commission from October 1997, prompted the government to reformulate its Roma policy. In October 1997, the government published its first substantial report on the situation of the Roma, entitled 'Report on the Situation of the Roma Community in the Czech Republic and Government Measures Assisting its Integration into Society', familiarly called the 'Bratinka Report' (after the Minister without Portfolio). The report provided comprehensive information on the situation of the Roma and included proposals in a number of policy areas (Sobotka 2001).

The Inter-Ministerial Commission for Roma Community Affairs, a body initiating, drafting, and overseeing policy formation towards the Roma, was established in September 1997. In April 1999, the government approved the 'Concept of Governmental Policy Towards Members of the Roma Community Supporting Their Integration into Society' (the 'Concept Proposal'), consisting of a brief political programme aimed primarily at supporting the emancipation of the

Roma (Government of the Czech Republic 1999). This policy document covers the period 2001–20. Between 1998 and 2001, the Inter-Ministerial Commission for Roma Community Affairs brought together deputy ministers and members of the Roma community for regular discussions of policy issues. In December 2001, the Commission was replaced by the Council for Roma Community Affairs.

While several Roma members of the Council (14 in 2002) came from the country's regions, a fact that strengthened the link between the Council and Roma advisors at the regional or municipal level, the relationship between the central government and the municipalities on Roma and minority issues has never been easy. With the institutionalization of Roma policy-making, although in an advisory role, the resistance of municipalities to proposed changes grew in some places, and some of the measures introduced, such as the appointment of Roma advisors and assistants, only met with partial success (Open Society Institute 2002: 137–138). Decentralized units of self-administration have been under no obligation to follow proposed changes in Roma policy or have simply ignored efforts of the national government. In particular, efforts to segregate Roma re-emerged in municipality housing policies in Ostrava, Přerov, Olomouc, Brno and Ústí nad Labem, and intensified after 1999. Perhaps the best known segregation attempt of a local municipality is the wall in Matiční Street in Ústí nad Labem, separating Czech and Roma inhabitants. Following international protests, including in the 1999 Regular Report by the European Commission, the wall was torn down in November 1999, six weeks after it had been erected.[3]

Since adoption of the first Opinion of the Advisory Committee on the Framework Convention for the Protection of National Minorities in April 2001 and the Committee of Ministers' resolution in February 2002, the Czech Republic has diversified its action to protect persons belonging to minorities. An annual assessment of their situation is carried out by the government's Council for National Minorities, with the participation of representatives of minorities. Both minority representatives and Czech authorities have confirmed that the protection of minorities has developed positively in recent years. In the legislative field, in accordance with the Minority Law, the authorities have adopted measures to supplement and clarify the legislation on the protection of 'national minorities'. For instance, the use of minority languages in relations with administrative authorities and for topographical indications, as well as the teaching of, and in, minority languages is now regulated by specific legislation. Similarly, Czech legislation now contains provisions on the participation of representatives of 'national minorities' in decision-making affecting them at the central, regional, and municipal level.

Phase IV (2004–07): post-accession

The Minority Law has been helpful in facilitating participation of minorities in public affairs and the Czech Republic has adopted a number of laws and policies directed at the integration and cultural development of minorities. Nevertheless, the Minority Law has been criticized by NGOs and minority representatives, since it offers considerably less protection than earlier drafts of the law and may have little relevance for Roma, given the 10 per cent threshold for its application. Moreover, the UN Commission for Elimination of all Forms of Racial Discrimination criticized the lack of legal provisions for the protection of minorities from discrimination (CERD 2007), an area not addressed by the Minority Law.

The current legislation on protection against discrimination is fragmented, with anti-discrimination measures dispersed in more than ten different legal regulations. Furthermore, the legislation does not implement all requirements of the EU Race Equality Directive.[4] The European Commission pointed out that definitions of discrimination are lacking, that national legislation transposing the Race Equality Directive does not cover all types of employment, social protection or access to goods and services, that the sharing of the burden of proof is not applied in all fields covered by the directive, that protection against victimization does not apply outside the field of employment, that a body for the promotion of equal treatment with the competences required under the directive is lacking, and that the anti-discrimination legislation does not cover the entry and residence of foreigners, including EU citizens (European Commission 2007). The government presented a draft anti-discrimination law, the Act on Equal Treatment and Legal Means of Protection Against Discrimination and on Amendments of Some Acts, to the parliament on 12 July 2007. By October 2007, however, this law had yet to be passed.

Explanatory factors

In the early 1990s, Czech foreign policy supported the establishment of the institution of the OSCE High Commissioner on National Minorities. However, between 1992 and 1997, regional cooperation was limited to ambitious economic projects, and the emphasis on Czech exceptionality favoured orientation towards the EU and the West in general, to the detriment of regional cooperation with Hungary, Slovakia or Poland (Pehe 2002: 113–118). One colourful American report described the Czech foreign policy at the time as 'ethnocentric' and 'provincial', if not 'nationalist' (Blank 1996). Between 1992 and 1997, international human and minority rights had very little resonance in domestic policies towards minorities. Even after the scandalous Citizenship Law had been adopted, it took a long time before the Czech government admitted that discrimination of Roma was a major problem.

As a result of the dissolution of Czechoslovakia, two issues gained prominence in Czech foreign policy. The first was the re-negotiation of the association agreement with the EU, which was achieved in 1993. The second issue was that the country had to re-apply for membership in the Council of Europe and the OSCE, both of which it achieved in 1993. The worsening human rights situation of the Roma was in both cases ignored, despite the fact that the state of human rights in the Czech Republic had been documented in the German, French, British, US and Canadian press, as well as by human rights NGOs, such as Amnesty International and Helsinki Watch.

In the years after 1993, the Czech Republic was criticized by international actors mainly for its treatment of the Roma minority. Yet, the government was able to downplay the seriousness of anti-Roma racism, and the provincial superiority of the Czech Republic declared by the Klaus cabinets closed the country to outside influences (Vachudová 2001: 333). Although criticism by Czech NGOs and their lobbying with international organizations, such as the Council of Europe and the OSCE, resulted in significant pressure on the Czech Republic to amend its Citizenship Law, this law has only been partially amended and the final amendment took place as late as 1999. While the situation of the Roma was highlighted by a number of major international actors, including the OSCE, the Council of Europe, the US Commission on Security and Cooperation in Europe, and the EU, not enough pressure was exerted on the government to initiate change.

The lack of pressure in this stage was due to several factors: an excellent image of the Czech Republic abroad, strong governmental denial of human rights abuses, the lack of reliable NGO information on compliance with human rights standards, and the fact that the Czech Republic's renewed membership in the Council of Europe, the OSCE, the United Nations (UN), and the International Monetary Fund (IMF) was not tied to adherence to international human rights norms. The Czech state oscillated between an attempt to return to Europe and Czech provincialism, which exacerbated nationalist tendencies (Pehe 1995). Transition was viewed in purely economic parameters and did not include human rights norms and values. Within this period, Roma policy stagnated, and majority views on the Roma remained unchallenged (Vodičková 1996).

The NGOs dealing with human rights issues in the early 1990s, which were mostly chaired by former dissidents, focused mainly on the implementation of existing legal provisions (Zoon 1997: 3). However, after adoption of the Citizenship Law, human rights activists started to campaign for legislative change. In particular, the Helsinki Citizens Assembly, the Foundation Tolerance, and the Movement for Civic Solidarity and Tolerance understood that human rights work requires monitoring, reporting, lobbying and networking at the international level.

At the Human Dimension meeting of the OSCE in September 1994, the American representative, ambassador Norman Anderson, called the situation surrounding the Czech Citizenship Law a 'humanitarian crisis in the heart of Europe', while the Deputy Secretary General of the Council of Europe, Peter Leuprecht, referred to a 'dangerous precedent' for further east-lying countries (Sobotka 2004: 195). Furthermore, during the OSCE Review Conference in 1994, the OSCE High Commissioner on National Minorities urged the Czech government to consider the 'clearly negative impact of such legislation and urged appropriate changes be made' (Zoon 1997: 5; van der Stoel 2003). Similar concerns were expressed by the US delegation, the EU, and many NGOs. Criticism of the Commission on Security and Cooperation in Europe of the US Congress followed in the autumn of 1994. Prime minister Klaus, however, responded that the government saw no reason why the Citizenship Law should be amended (Sobotka 2004: 209).

In relation to countries in Central and Eastern Europe, the EU began to use conditionality only after the debacle of the Bosnian war. The first agreements with Czechoslovakia, Poland and Hungary, signed in December 1991, did not contain any conditionality. Between 1992 and 1997, the EU gradually developed the tools to identify the problems plaguing democratic consolidation in the Czech Republic. In particular the political conditionality of EU membership based on the 1993 Copenhagen criteria has been crucial in influencing minority policies in the Czech Republic (Cameron 2001). International human rights norms on their own had very little effect in facilitating domestic change. This changed when the immediate interests of the Czech Republic were challenged in the process of EU accession. The Czech case demonstrates how the fear of suffering rejection in the EU accession process can result in changes in minority policies (Vachudová 2001: 325, 361).

Conclusions

It can be concluded that the EU exercised the greatest leverage in changing minority policy in the Czech Republic, while the OSCE as a political process helped to frame the situation of Roma in human rights terms and provided a direction for further discussions at the national level. Domestic NGOs could then use these reference points to shame the Czech government over its failure to implement international human rights standards. Within the OSCE, the US has traditionally devoted the greatest attention to the situation of the Roma. Although the EU only gradually developed the tools necessary to compel reform in those areas where the Czech project was eventually revealed to have fundamental flaws, towards the end of the 1990s, it played an important role in triggering policy change. In its 1997 Opinion on the Czech Republic's application for EU membership (European Commission 1997), the Commission strongly criticized the treatment of the Roma and placed significant emphasis on their integration into Czech society as a condition for membership.

Despite a number of positive developments, there is still room for improvement in fields such as the use of minority languages in the public sphere, the teaching of and in minority languages, and the participation of minorities in public affairs, particularly at the local level. Recent comments of the UN Committee on the Elimination of Racial Discrimination pointed out a number of flaws that should be a matter of concern for policy-makers (CERD 2007). Media access for persons belonging to minorities and education reflecting their culture and traditions also require increased efforts. Furthermore, the public perception of Roma remains problematic.

The case of the Czech Republic shows that conditionality has worked, when compliance with human and minority rights standards was taken seriously by international actors. While conditionality has helped to improve the situation of minorities, in particular the Roma, there are still many issues that remain unresolved, such as continued discrimination and exclusion. The EU Race Equality Directive remains poorly transposed into domestic legislation, and violations of human rights by local governments continue in the areas of housing, employment, education, and access to health care, mainly affecting Roma. This question concerns all EU member states and points to the need to define and ensure compliance with human rights standards at the level of the EU. A particular issue in the Czech Republic will remain the definition of 'national minorities' in the Minority Law, which only includes citizens. This might be too narrowly crafted and expose some groups, such as the increasing number of residents with Vietnamese ethnic origin, to discriminatory treatment.

Notes

1 While in the 1991 census the declaration of ethnicity was obligatory, in the 2001 census it was optional. As a result, the numbers of some minorities dropped (Roma, Moravians etc.), while the number of "undeclared" grew substantially.
2 For a discussion about the role of the CDP, its ideological profile and party politics, see Hanley 2004a, 2004b.
3 For a discussion of Czech resentment of external influences, see Fawn (2002) and Sobotka (2004).
4 While the author would have preferred the term Racial Equality Directive, the term Race Equality Directive was used to maintain a uniform terminology throughout the book.

References

Blank, S. (1996) *Prague, NATO and European Security*, Carlisle Barracks, PA: Strategic Studies Institute.

Cameron, F. (2001) *The Impact of the EU on Human and Minority Rights: Central and Eastern Europe and the Newly Independent States*, Washington: Woodrow Wilson Research Center for Scholars.

CERD (2007) Concluding observations of the Committee on the Elimination of Racial Discrimination, Seventieth session, 19 February – 9 March 2007, Geneva: Committee on the Elimination of Racial Discrimination (CERD). Online, available at: http://daccessdds.un.org/doc/UNDOC/GEN/G07/417/12/PDF/ G0741712.pdf?OpenElement (accessed 12 November 2007).

Czech Republic (2001) *Law on the Rights of Members of National Minorities, entry into force on 2 August 2001*.

Czech Statistical Office (2007) Basic final results of the Population and Housing Census 2001 (from Statistical Yearbook of the CR 2002). Online, available at: www.czso.cz/eng/redakce.nsf/i/basic_final_results_of_the_population_and_housing_census_2001 (accessed 7 January 2008).

Czech Television 1 (1993) 'Debata, Beseda se zajímavými osobnostmi [Debate, Discussion with interesting personalities]', broadcast on 10 January 1993 at 12:50.

Dengler, R. and Kovařík, J. (1993) 'Klaus: Nehodláme připustit, aby uprchlický problém sklouzl na nás [Klaus: We will not let the immigration problem slide at us]', *Rudé Právo*, 5 February 1993.

European Commission (1997) Agenda 2000 – Commission Opinion on the Czech Republic's Application for Membership in the European Union, Brussels: European Commission. Online, available at: http://ec.europa.eu/enlargement/ archives/pdf/dwn/opinions/czech/cz-op_en.pdf (accessed 12 November 2007).

—— (2007) *Press release, Race and Ethnic Origin Directive: list of Member States to which a reasoned opinion will be sent*, Brussels: European Commission. Online, available at: http://europa.eu/rapid/pressReleasesAction.do?reference=MEMO/ 07/263&for mat=HTML&aged=0&language=EN&guiLanguage=en (accessed 11 November 2007).

Fawn, R. (2002) 'The Press between Conflict and Consensus in Czech-Romani Affairs', *Journal of European Area Studies*, 10 (1): 71–89.

Government of the Czech Republic (1999) *Concept of Governmental Policy Towards Members of the Roma Community Supporting Their Integration into Society; approved by government decree No. 279, 7 April 1999*.

Hala, N. (1995) 'Citizens Turned Aliens: Roma Victims of Czech Citizenship Law', *Peace & Democracy*, 8 (2): 21–23.

Hanley S. (2004a) 'Getting the Right right: redefining the centre-right in post-communist Europe', *Journal of Communist Studies and Transition Politics*, 20 (3): 9–27.

Hanley, S. (2004b) 'Blue velvet: the rise and decline of the new Czech Right', *Journal of Communist Studies and Transition Politics*, 20(3): 28–54.

Kovařík, J. (1993) 'Ministr Kinkel jednal v Praze o azylantech z Německa [Minister Kinkel discussed in Prague asylum seekers from Germany]', *Rudé Právo*, 8 February 1993.

Landergott, J. (1992) 'K "cikánské otázce" [On the "question of the Gypsies"]', *Metropolitní Telegraf*, 29 December 1992.

Lidové noviny (1993) 'Vláda jednala o romské problematice [The government discussed the Roma issues]', *Lidové noviny*, 29 April 1993.

—— (1996) 'Do Johannahofu Romové nesmějí [Roma are not allowed to enter Johannahof]', *Lidové Noviny*, 12 November 1996.

Mladý svět (1995) 'Domobrana [Home defense]', *Mladý svět*, 26 October 1995.

Open Society Institute (2002) *Monitoring the EU Accession Process: Minority Protection, Volume I, An Assessment of Selected Policies in Candidate States*, Budapest: Open Society Institute.

Pehe, J. (1995) 'Czech Foreign Policy: Return to Europe or provincialism?', Draft OMRI research paper, 24 May 1995.

—— (1998) 'Souvislosti domácí a zahraniční politiky [Connections of domestic and foreign policy]', *Mezinárodní Politika*, 12 (1): 6–7.

—— (2002) *Zahraniční politika: Souvislosti zahraniční a domácí politiky [Foreign policy: connections of foreign and domestic policy]*, Praha: Academia.

Rudé Právo (1993) 'Němci chtěli zaskočit Rumla [Germans wanted to surprise Ruml]', *Rudé Právo*, 8 February 1993.

Šídlo, J. (1993) 'Romům došla trpělivost – J. Rusenko: Jsme nuceni přistoupit k nátlakovým akcím [Roma lost their patience – J. Rusenko: We are forced to resort to pressure]', *Respekt*, 15–21 February 1993.

Sobotka, E. (2001) 'Crusts from the table: Policy formation towards Roma in the Czech Republic and Slovakia', *Roma Rights*, 2–3: 66–73.

—— (2003) 'Romani Migration in the 1990s: Perspectives on Dynamic, Interpretation and Policy', *Romani Studies*, 13 (2): 79–121.

—— (2004) 'Mobilising International Norms: Issue Actors, Roma and the State', unpublished PhD thesis, Lancaster University.

van der Stoel, M. (2003) Interview with the author, Skopje.

Sulitka, A. (1998) *Romové v České Republice [Roma in the Czech Republic]*, Praha: Socioklub.

Tichý, O. and Kastnerová, E. (1996) 'Averze k Vietnamcům v Železné Rudě narůstá, soudí starosta [Aversion against Vietnamese in Železná Ruda is on the rise]', *Mladá Fronta Dnes*, 14 August 1996.

Trojan, V. (1994) 'Laying the foundations for the future: dealing with the past in the post-Communist Europe', hCa Quarterly, 1 (4): 11–12.

Uhl, P. (1996a) 'Společnost bílých mužů', *Právo*, 5 September 1996.

—— (1996b) 'Nechat či nenechat se urážet od Sládka [Accept or not accept insults from Sladek]', *Právo*, 5 September 1996.

—— (1998) *Právo a nespravedlnost očima Petra Uhla [Law and injustice in the eyes of Petr Uhl]*, Praha: C.H. Beck.

UNICEF (2007) TransMONEE database.

US State Department (1994) *Czech Republic. Report of the US State Department*, Washington: US State Department.

Vachudová, M.A. (2001) 'The Czech Republic: The Unexpected Force of Institutional Constraints', in J. Zielonka and A. Pravda (eds.) *Democratic Consolidation in Eastern Europe: International and Transnational Factors*, Oxford: Oxford University Press: 325–362.

Vodičková, M. (1996) 'O snášenlivosti, rasismu a pseudohumanismu [About tolerance, racism and pseudohumanism]', *Mladá Fronta Dnes*, 3 September 1996.

World Bank (2007) World Development Indicators database.

Žák, V. (1996) 'Romové, restaurace a rasová nenávist [Roma, restaurants and racial hatred', *Právo*, 4 November 1996.

Zoon, I (1997) 'The positive effect of advocacy on legislation affecting minority rights: the Czech experience', paper presented at the Symposium on Legal Defence of the Rights of Roma, Budapest, 11–14 January 1997. Online, available at: www.errc.org/cikk.php?cikk=1763 (accessed 14 January 2008).

8 Estonia

Conditionality amidst a legal straightjacket

Vello Pettai and Kristina Kallas

Introduction

In international relations, conditionality is a variable phenomenon, with its forms and effectiveness differing, depending on the political strength players bring to the dispute at hand. Often, the country being conditioned will show its opposition to such efforts by foot-dragging or citing countervailing political principles such as state sovereignty.

Estonia represents a case where conditionality has been resisted on the basis of an elaborate international legal doctrine, which pre-determined a number of basic parameters of the minority situation before conditionality could even be applied. In this chapter we will show how at a preliminary point in time (in 1989–91), Estonia applied a special doctrine of 'legal restorationism' in terms of how it interpreted the very nature of its statehood. This in turn pre-defined a number of fundamental conditions relating to the country's large Russian-speaking minority, including citizenship and possible collective political recognition. As a consequence, later conditionality, be it from the Organization

Map 8.1 Estonia (source: http://maps.mygeo.info/maps_eu_ee.html – accessed 19 November, 2007).

for Security and Co-operation in Europe (OSCE), the Council of Europe, or the European Union (EU), was confronted with a legal straightjacket, which ultimately limited much of its effectiveness. International conditionality did succeed in altering certain details of minority policy, but in relation to major questions, such as citizenship rights and the political recognition of minorities, it was severely constrained by the legal doctrine already in place. The resulting minority rights regime has been one of ethnic control and the predominance of an ethnically understood Estonian nation-state.

Background

Estonia has often struck outside observers as an ideal candidate for consociationalism or at least ethnic federalism, primarily for three reasons. First, the population is comprised of two main ethnic groups, Estonians and Russian-speakers.[1] Second, in 1989 (shortly before the restoration of independence from the Soviet Union) the proportion between the two groups was roughly 62 per cent to 35 per cent (out of a total population of 1.5 million). This implied that the groups could form some kind of bi-national partnership. Third, approximately 35 per cent of the Russian-speaking population was concentrated in the north-eastern county of Ida-Virumaa, implying that even if full-scale consociationalism were not possible, some kind of separate status might be given to this region. (See also Table 8.1 for how these figures have changed up to 2006–07.)

Yet, two of the main characteristics of consociationalism are that the ethnic groups in question are historically indigenous populations and that there are relatively limited barriers to social communication and interaction (Bogaards 2000;

Table 8.1 Key indicators for Estonia

Total population (millions)[a]	1.34 (2006)
Urban population (% of total)[a]	69.1 (2006)
GDP per capita, PPP (US$)[a]	18,378 (2006)
Unemployment rate (%)[b]	5.9 (2006)
Ethnic composition (2007)[b]	Estonians: 68.6%
	Russians: 25.6%
	Ukrainians: 2.1%
	Belarusians: 1.2%
	Finns: 0.8%
	Tatars: 0.2%
	Latvians: 0.2%
	Poles: 0.2%
	Lithuanians: 0.2%
	Jews: 0.1%
	Germans: 0.1%
	Others: 0.7%

Sources: a World Bank 2007; b Statistics Estonia 2007.

Notes
PPP: purchasing power parity; unemployment rate is based on registered unemployment as a percentage of 15–74 year olds; GDP per capita is given in current international US$.

Andeweg 2000). Neither of these conditions obtained in Estonia during the late 1980s and early 1990s. The Russian-speaking population was largely a product of the Soviet rule in Estonia beginning in 1940. In 1945, the Russian-speaking population constituted only some 3 per cent of the population. In the following years, this proportion began to rise dramatically, as communist cadres were brought in from the rest of the Soviet Union and large-scale labour migration to Estonia was encouraged. Already by 1959, Russian-speakers represented over 22 per cent of the population, increasing to 35 per cent by 1989 (Taagepera 1993).

This rapid growth of the minority population was in no way tempered by efforts at inter-ethnic or social integration. Instead, the Soviet system privileged the use of Russian in most political and economic affairs, although it also allowed Estonian to be used. This led to extremely low levels of Estonian language knowledge among Russian-speakers and a high degree of social separation. The situation was compounded by considerable residential and economic segmentation (Kala 1992). In a word, Estonia's ethnopolitical situation was laden with disjunctures, all of which were of recent creation. Moreover, they were associated with a totalitarian regime, which had wreaked havoc on the ethnic Estonian population through mass deportations in 1941 and 1949, on top of stifling Sovietization throughout the post-war era.

In this context, consociationalism or ethnic federalism was difficult to envisage. Quite the contrary: the Estonian nationalist movement that sprung up under Mikhail Gorbachev's perestroika aimed explicitly at stemming this slide toward bi-nationhood. In November 1988, the Estonian Supreme Soviet (or local parliament) passed a declaration of political sovereignty within the Soviet Union; two months later a language law was adopted, declaring Estonian the official language, and additional measures were implemented to stem immigration from the rest of the Soviet Union. In 1989–90, the movement radicalized further when a group, known as the Citizens Committees, began to argue that Estonia had to see itself not as a Soviet republic, but as an independent state illegally occupied and annexed by the Soviet Union in 1940. By drawing attention to how Estonia had been taken over by Stalin (first through the Molotov–Ribbentrop Pact with Nazi Germany and thereafter through rigged elections which brought to power a communist government that 'requested' admission to the Soviet Union), the Committees maintained that Estonia had to also treat the entire post-war immigration of Russian-speakers as an illegal settler population. This meant that under any kind of restored independence, automatic citizenship could be accorded only to pre-war citizens and their descendants. Moreover, Soviet-era immigrants could only be naturalized, based on terms to be set by the restored Estonian state.

This principle of legal restorationism soon became the dominant political doctrine of the Estonian independence movement (Pettai 2004). Although the main proponent of this doctrine, the Citizens Committees movement, ebbed and flowed throughout 1990 and 1991, following the attempted coup in Moscow and Estonia's leap to independence in 1991, the restorationists were able to get their principle enshrined in the country's final independence declaration. As of that moment, Estonia began to see itself fundamentally as a state restored after illegal Soviet occupation. Already in November 1991, the Estonian Supreme Soviet adopted a resolution declaring that only pre-1940 citizens and their descendants would be eligible for automatic citizenship. In February 1992, again following a restorationist logic, the parliament reinstated Estonia's 1938 Law on Citizenship and formally enacted a set of residency and language requirements for the naturalization of non-citizens.[2] Lastly, when Estonia's first post-independence parliamentary elections were held in September 1992 under the new citizenship rules, the electorate became so biased ethnically (with ethnic Estonians constituting some 85 per cent) that not a single Russian party contested the elections and not a single non-Estonian was elected to the legislature. Estonia had been transformed from a Soviet republic teetering on bi-nationhood to an independent ethnic Estonian nation-state.

Estonian minority policy since 1992: from alienation to integration

Given the doctrine of legal restoration in which Estonia's minority situation had been cast, the scope for any policy change during the 1990s was severely limited. Moreover, the categorical nature of declaring roughly a quarter of the population 'non-citizens' entailed numerous practical challenges, some of which threatened to boil over into conflict. In 1993 the Estonian authorities proceeded to work out a procedure by which non-citizens would be issued new, Estonian, residency documents – especially since for many of these people their old Soviet passports were expiring or simply becoming anomalous. Yet, when a draft Aliens Act did not provide any guarantees that non-citizens in good standing would automatically receive a new residence permit, a number of protests took place in the mostly Russian towns of Narva and Sillamäe, eventually prompting local authorities in both cities to organize secessionist referenda in July 1993. The situation was made even tenser by the continued presence of some 25,000 former Soviet military personnel in Estonia. Moscow frequently threatened to delay the withdrawal of these troops as a way of pressuring Estonia into giving up its restorationist policy. Through the mediation of the OSCE High Commissioner on National Minorities, Max van der Stoel, as well as Western diplomats in Tallinn, a compromise was reached, in which the Estonian parliament amended the law to guarantee residence permits to more or less all Soviet-era residents, while the leaders of the Narva and Sillamäe secessionist referenda agreed to abide by a Supreme Court decision invalidating their polls.

The Aliens Act was the first indication that the centre-right government of Mart Laar at the time was not averse to encouraging a certain degree of uncertainty among the Russian-speaking population in the hope that some would leave Estonia for Russia. In addition to the denial of automatic citizenship for nearly 500,000 people (our calculations based on: Kodakondsus- ja Migratsiooniamet 2006: 13), as well as the complications over issuing permanent residence permits, the government did little to deter non-citizens from acquiring the citizenship of other former Soviet republics, mostly the Russian Federation. By the mid 1990s, some 100,000 non-citizens, roughly 13 per cent of the population, had taken advantage of Russia's simplified procedure for ex-Soviet citizens to obtain Russian Federation citizenship, the highest proportion of such applicants in any former Soviet republic. In the end, the government's stance to a certain degree paid off: during the period from 1990 to 1996, a net total of 80,000 people left Estonia,[3] the overwhelming majority to the East. This process was supported financially by the creation in 1992 of the Migration Foundation, which provided grants of up to 100,000 Estonian kroons for non-Estonians leaving for the former Soviet Union (Eesti Migratsioonifond 2006).

During the mid 1990s, the alienation process deepened through the adoption of another series of laws adversely affecting the Russian-speaking minority. In January 1995 the Estonian parliament adopted a new citizenship law, which tightened the naturalization requirements by extending the required residency period from two years to five and by introducing a civics examination (in Estonian) alongside the Estonian language exam. That same month, parliament also adopted a new Language Act, which declared Estonian the sole official language and termed all other languages spoken in Estonia 'foreign languages'. While the law represented a necessary update of Estonia's first, perestroika-era language law, it was also clearly designed to make the new ethnopolitical order even more unequivocal (Järve 2002). Lastly, in 1997 the parliament mandated a set of Estonian language requirements for electoral candidates at both the national and local level. Henceforth, candidates had to sign a written statement confirming that their level of Estonian was sufficient to take part in the work of legislative bodies. If it was not, the elected deputy could have his/her mandate stripped by a court. The president of Estonia, Lennart Meri, challenged the law in the Supreme Court, but while an initial version of the law was struck down on a technicality, the Court eventually deemed the law in compliance with constitutional norms. During the 1999 parliamentary and local elections the law was in effect.

Yet, alongside these restrictive trends, there were some elements of positive minority policy as well. In the new constitution, adopted in 1992, numerous minority rights were enshrined. First, Estonia took the bold step of according all permanent residents the right to vote at the municipal level (Article 156). This provision was already implemented during the 1993 local elections, leading to a surprisingly strong showing among Russian parties in the capital Tallinn and the north-east Ida-Viru county. Second, Estonia restored its much praised inter-war policy of cultural autonomy for minorities (Article 50). This constitutional provision was followed in 1993 by a Cultural Autonomy Act, which provided for the creation of minority voter rolls for the election of cultural autonomy boards. Third, in localities where at least half of the permanent residents belonged to an ethnic minority, the constitution provided the right to use that minority language in local government (Articles 51–52). Although not an explicit acknowledgement of the Russian character of Estonia's north-east, a majority of the 13 municipalities that ultimately qualified for this provision were in this region (Pärn and Veikat 1996). Lastly, in January 1997 Estonia became one of the first countries in Central and Eastern Europe to ratify the Council of Europe's Framework Convention for the Protection of National Minorities. Thereafter, Estonia went through two rounds of monitoring by the Council of Europe's Advisory Committee and was generally found to be compliant with the convention (see Chapter 4 on the Framework Convention).

Yet, each of these concessions on minority rights had its drawbacks. The municipal voting rights did not include the right for permanent residents to stand for local office, although the Council of Europe had encouraged Estonia to include this provision. With regard to cultural autonomy, a stipulation that only citizens could take part in this institution severely curtailed the usefulness and symbolic value of the scheme for most minority groups. Among ethnic Russians, only 40 per cent were Estonian citizens, while among Ukrainians and Belarusians, this ratio was just 29 and 23 per cent (Eesti Statistikaamet 2002). With regard to municipal language policy, the cities of Narva and Sillamäe applied four times between 1995 and 2004 for the right to use Estonian and Russian in parallel, but each time the government denied the request, insisting that the local governments had not yet fully ensured the use of Estonian in their affairs and therefore could not be allowed to add Russian (Tomusk 2004). Finally, when ratifying the Framework Convention, Estonia adopted a 'reservation', defining as minorities only those ethnically distinct people who were citizens of Estonia. The reservation thus removed a majority of Estonia's minority population from the protection afforded by the convention and has been criticized by both the Council of Europe and the European Commission (see European Commission 1997: 18).

By the late 1990s, Estonia's ethnopolitical regime could be described (based on the typology presented in the introduction to this volume) as one of 'individual civil rights without recognition of minorities'. It was clearly a regime without any major collective recognition of minorities, even in the case of cultural autonomy. Consociationalism had been definitely ruled out, and even some of the provisions for the local recognition of minorities declared in the constitution had proven hollow. Yet, this classification of Estonia is an understatement, since it masks the underpinning question of whether the minority effectively held citizenship within the country. Because of this additional division, some analysts have labelled Estonia an 'ethnic democracy' (Smith 1996; Pettai 1998; Järve 2000) or an 'ethnic control regime' (Pettai and Hallik 2002). The rationale here has been that ethnopolitical regimes can in fact be divided along two axes: whether they seek to preserve or eliminate ethnic diversity, and whether they do this democratically or not. In Estonia's case, the Estonian government was essentially preserving ethnic diversity, but doing so undemocratically through political marginalization.

By the late 1990s, Estonia was in what some prominent Estonian social scientists called a situation of societal 'separation' (Lauristin and Heidmets 2003: 15). According to the 2000 census, Estonia had a population of 1,370,052 people, of whom only 80 per cent had Estonian citizenship. A further 6.3 per cent were citizens of the Russian Federation and 12.4 per cent were people of 'undetermined citizenship', i.e. essentially stateless permanent residents (Eesti Statistikaamet 2002). Naturalization rates had fallen from a high of 22,773 in 1996 to 3,090 in 2001 (Kodakondsus- ja Migratsiooniamet 2006: 19). The labour market continued to be ethnically segmented (Hallik 1999) and a majority of non-Estonians believed that ethnic Estonians had an advantage over them in a range of societal spheres including getting jobs, promotions or greater pay (Pavelson 2000; Rose 2000: 35–38).

It was against this backdrop that the impulse began for the formation of a real minority integration policy. This began with the appointment in May 1997 of a Minister without Portfolio for Population Affairs whose task it was to deal (among other things) with ethnic integration. The first minister, Andra Veidemann, drew on the work done by the social scientists cited above and formulated an initial set of policy principles declaring minority integration a central political goal of Estonia. In 2000, under a new minister, Katrin Saks, a full-scale policy programme was completed and approved by the cabinet. The policy document defined the desired outcome of integration as 'an Estonian model of multicultural society that is characterized by the principles of cultural pluralism, the preservation and development of the Estonian cultural space, and a strong set of things in common' (Minister of Population Affairs 2000: 5). Despite criticism voiced by some minority representatives that the policy had assimilative tendencies and an overemphasis on Estonian language learning (Ernst & Young 2006), the emergence of the policy itself was a major change in the field of minority affairs. With a full-scale programme in place, the policy also attracted major financial support from the EU, the United Nations Development Programme, the Nordic countries (acting in concert), and the governments of Canada, the US and the Netherlands.

The role of the international community in Estonian minority policy and its implementation

Estonia's doctrine of legal restoration was to a large extent the product of political mobilization and discursive construction during the 1989–91 period. However, it also rested on objective legal tenets, such as the West's own policy of non-recognition of the occupation and annexation of the Baltic states in 1940 (Hough 1985). It was this dilemma that the international (Western) community struggled to deal with when the first expert commissions visited Estonia in order to assess allegations of minority rights violations. Fact-finding missions from different international organizations all expressed regret over the wide-scale consequences of Estonia's restorationist policy, but noted that the country was within the scope of international law, especially when one accepted the argument of Soviet occupation (European Bank for Reconstruction and Development 1992; Fall 1993; Parliamentary Assembly of the Council of Europe 1993; Birckenbach 1997).

During the first half of the 1990s, the most regular monitoring of minority rights in Estonia came from the OSCE and its High Commissioner on National Minorities, Max van der Stoel. Van der Stoel first visited Estonia in January

1993 and in April 1993 he issued a preliminary set of recommendations, calling on the Estonian government to disseminate more information about its laws (including in Russian) and to create a 'National Commissioner on Ethnic and Language Questions' (van der Stoel 1993).[4] Van der Stoel took pains to state that his intention was not to persuade Estonia to alter its fundamental policies, but rather to soften those pieces of legislation which might precipitate open conflict. Few of his recommendations, however, were immediately fulfilled; instead, the seven letters he wrote to the Estonian Minister of Foreign Affairs up to 1997 were generally met with a cool response. It was only during the 1993 Aliens Act crisis that van der Stoel played a critical role, travelling to the north-east of Estonia and talking to all sides (Zaagman 1999).

Meanwhile, the OSCE also set up (with agreement from the Estonian government) a long-term mission to the country, which monitored the situation on a day-to-day basis. The mission not only had an office in Tallinn, but also in the north-eastern towns Jõhvi and Narva. Although officially its mandate was never for more than six months, this was continually extended until January 2002, when the mission was closed.

In reality, however, it was only after the EU stood behind most of the OSCE's policy suggestions that Estonia took heed. While the OSCE mission played a key role in supplying steady information, it was only in tandem with the political muscle of the EU that changes were made. A clear example concerned the issue of stateless children. Under the UN Convention on the Rights of the Child, which Estonia ratified in 1991, states are obliged to offer automatic citizenship to such children if they remain otherwise stateless. Since this was an aspect of citizenship policy, which had been enshrined in 'hard' international law, Max van der Stoel took this up in his very first letter to Estonia. When Estonia tried to ignore this particular recommendation, the diplomatic pressure continued. Yet only when in 1997 the European Commission mentioned the issue in its Opinion on Estonia's application to join the EU (European Commission 1997: 19), did Estonian politicians realize that an amendment would be necessary. The Estonian parliament finally amended the law in December 1998.

Although the European Commission's 1997 report brought embarrassment in terms of stateless children, it was a victory for Estonia on the broader front of gaining acceptance for its legal restorationist doctrine. By including Estonia in its initial 'first wave' of EU accession countries, the Commission gave a clear signal that it was not going to make Estonia's citizenship and minority policy an issue of fundamental conditionality or demand a major liberalization of Estonia's policies.

Instead, the EU turned its main attention to its pre-accession financial instruments as the tool to influence policy in Estonia. From 1998 onwards, the EU channeled a total of €6.8 million to Estonia, mostly in support of Estonian language training programmes for non-Estonians; in exchange it had a seat on one of the programme's steering committees, thereby being able to monitor continually the spirit and practice of the policy.

The EU also continued its monitoring of particularly controversial aspects of Estonia's minority legislation. In 1999, it began criticizing the Estonian language requirement for electoral candidates as a violation of the UN's International Covenant on Civil and Political Rights. This pressure ultimately led to the requirements being repealed in November 2001. Also in 1999, the EU opposed a series of amendments to Estonia's language law, which were meant to enforce the use of Estonian in private business. On this score, the EU was able to bring in its own principles of open labour markets to argue that such restrictions would be illegal (European Commission 1999, 2000).

Assessing the impact of the EU

Assessments by different scholars of the effects of international conditionality on Estonia during the last 15 years have been varied. While some have considered European organizations to have been rather lax (Birckenbach 1997, 2000; Poleshchuk 2001; Poleshchuk and Tsilevich 2002/03: 304; Feldman 2003, 2005), others have claimed that Estonia has been subject to a level of scrutiny not applied to many Western countries (Ilves 2002; Ozolins 2003: 221–222; Johns 2003; Johnson 2006; see also Deets 2002). In her comparison of Estonia's relations with the OSCE, the Council of Europe and the EU, Judith Kelley concluded:

> while the OSCE relied mostly on persuasion, and the EU was the master of political conditionality, the CoE [Council of Europe] straddled the divide using persuasion at times, and conditionality at other times. However, often the organizations worked side-by-side exposing the governments to the interplay of persuasion and conditionality.
>
> (Kelley 2003: 36)

Our analysis largely corroborates this opinion, especially as regards the EU's ability to put real pressure on Estonia to rescind a number of measures clearly in violation of either international or EU law. Despite the OSCE's on-the-ground presence, it was rarely able to deter Estonia from adopting laws (such as the language requirements for electoral candidates), which would eventually require removal because of EU pressure. While the OSCE and the Council of Europe often helped facilitate the actual modalities of reaching a compromise on certain minority rights issues, either by dispatching a team of experts or providing behind-the-scenes diplomacy, the political muscle in each case was exerted by the EU and its conditionality in terms of future accession (see also Kelley 2004). By stating, for example, that some of Estonia's language policy restrictions could engender 'non-compliance by Estonia of the political criteria for membership' (European Commission 1999: 15), the EU sent an unmistakable signal that accession itself was in play.

In this respect our view differs from the somewhat disparaging assessment given by Hughes and Sasse (2003) of the EU's role in promoting minority rights as part of enlargement. Whereas they see the EU as 'groping for international benchmarks that do not exist' and characterize the EU's cooperation with other international organizations as an attempt 'to shift responsibility from its own monitoring process by internationalizing the benchmarking of the [candidate countries] with respect to minority protection' (Hughes and Sasse 2003: 17, 19), we see the EU as having had clearly defined goals, even if these were limited.

Moreover, whereas Hughes and Sasse rely exclusively on the EU's monitoring reports to assess conditionality, a much more valid indicator of the EU's political intent can be found in the Accession Partnership guidelines issued by the European Council. Although in the public eye the monitoring reports received a lot of attention, in reality they tended to represent a post hoc assessment of the situation. By contrast, the Accession Partnership agreements were a set of prescriptive goals to be achieved during a period of time in the future. For example, in the 1998 Accession Partnership guidelines, the European Council noted that '[t]hose listed under the short-term have been selected on the basis that it is realistic to expect that Estonia can complete or take them substantially forward by the end of 1998' (European Council 1998: 27). If ever there was a statement of policy demands, this was it.

Already in its first guidelines from March 1998, the Council stated that Estonia should 'take measures to facilitate the naturalisation process and to better integrate non-citizens including Stateless children [and] to enhance Estonian language training for non-Estonian speakers' (European Council 1998: 28). Indeed, these were the only goals the Council set concerning Estonia's compliance with the political part of the Copenhagen criteria.

In December 1999, the Council issued a revised set of guidelines. Because by this date Estonia had come into hot water with the EU for its adoption of new Estonian language requirements for the public and private sector, the Council added these concerns to its demands for Estonia as part of the next stage of accession. The Council mandated that Estonia 'align the language legislation with international standards and the Europe Agreement [and] implement concrete measures for the integration of non-citizens including language training and provide necessary financial support' (European Council 1999: 37).

By February 2002, when the Council issued its final partnership document, the message was 'steady as she goes' to the extent that Estonia had already begun implementing its large-scale integration programme and the language law issue had begun to fade. The Council called on Estonia to

> continue the integration of non-citizens by implementing concrete measures, including language training for non-Estonian speakers; [to] provide necessary financial support for the implementation of these measures, [and to] ensure that the implementation of language legislation is in line with both international standards and the Europe Agreement and respects the principles of justified public interest and proportionality.
>
> (European Council 2002: 31)

These bottom-line political statements by the Council highlight two things about how the EU's conditionality process worked. First, it is important to acknowledge how early the EU explicitly declared that Estonia would have to take measures 'to facilitate the naturalisation process and to better integrate non-citizens'. These words, first used in March 1998, were in fact well ahead of Estonian policy in this area. Although an expert group had been formed by Population Affairs Minister Andra Veidemann in July 1997 to prepare a set of initial policy principles on integration, this three-page document received preliminary approval from the cabinet only on 10 February 1998 and would be endorsed by the parliament only on 10 June 1998. It is true that the EU was not a trend-setter in terms of defining what 'naturalisation' or 'integration' would be. But it was very astute in picking up on an endogenous process already going on in Estonia and in clearly showing its desire to keep Estonia on this track. By bringing Estonia's own catchphrase of 'integration' into one of its first binding political documents, the EU actually helped to make this process irreversible. It created a kind of undergirding for the policy, without which it would have probably been politically unsustainable. If one adds to this the money the EU pledged through its aid programme – and only the EU could pledge such money among European organizations – one sees how the EU's conditionality played a role in moderating Estonia's ethnopolitical situation. Estonia did not become an explicitly binational or even multicultural state, but its degree of 'ethnic control' or ethnopolitical imbalances was reduced.

Conclusions

In 2007, three years after Estonia's accession to the EU, the future of majority-minority relations seemed promising. The government was completing the initial 2000–07 time span of its integration policy and was busy preparing a new cycle for 2008–13. International financing for a range of integration projects had subsided, but Estonia itself was willing to set aside part of its EU structural funds to maintain work in this field. Naturalizations per year had risen above 7,000 and the number of stateless persons had fallen to around 130,000 (Kodakondsus- ja Migratsiooniamet 2006:18–19). Among ethnic Russians, the number of people who claimed a 'good' knowledge of Estonian had reached 42 per cent; moreover, among Russians aged 15–29, only 8 per cent reported not knowing any Estonian (Proos 2005: 22). Estonia's economy continued to boom and socio-economic disparities between Estonians and non-Estonians seem to be decreasing.

It was against these positive developments that the riots in Tallinn on 26–27 April 2007 took so many people by surprise. Prime minister Andrus Ansip's determination to relocate a Soviet-era memorial known as the Bronze Soldier from a location in downtown Tallinn to a more distant military cemetery brought to the surface an issue that neither Estonia's integration programme nor any international organizations had dealt with sufficiently: history. While Estonians saw the monument – erected to commemorate the Soviets' recapture of Tallinn in 1944 – as a painful reminder of the Soviet occupation of their country, Russian-speakers generally viewed the statue as an essential element of their historical identity – the Soviet Union's victory in the Second World War. To the extent that Russia also interfered in the crisis in early May 2007 by allowing activists from the pro-Putin *Nashi* movement to besiege the Estonian embassy in Moscow, the controversy only added to many Estonians' preconceptions that the Kremlin was behind the disturbances. At the same time, although polls among Russian-speakers showed that almost 80 per cent believed the decision to move the Bronze Soldier was wrong, nearly 70 per cent said that they still considered themselves a part of Estonian society (Maasalu 2007).

The crisis also engendered intervention by the EU. German chancellor Angela Merkel, serving as the EU's rotating president, telephoned both prime minister Ansip and president Putin, urging them to exercise restraint. When the blockade of Estonia's Moscow embassy began to disrupt the staff's consular work, however, the EU turned sharply against the Kremlin, saying that the Russian government had an international obligation to safeguard diplomatic outposts. Still, the EU was very clearly in a new and difficult role. It now had to defend Estonia as a member state, despite the fact that Estonia itself was largely responsible for the crisis. The disturbances showed that the issue of minority relations in Estonia was far from over and that in many respects the EU was now in the same position that its European partners, the Council of Europe and the OSCE, were in during the 1990s. Following enlargement, its power of conditionality had vanished; all it had left was soft persuasion.

Notes

1 In this chapter we will stick to the relatively conventional term of 'Russian-speakers' to designate not only ethnic Russians but also those roughly 4 per cent of the population who may be of another ethnic origin (Ukrainian, Belarusian or other former Soviet nationality), but who live and work using the Russian language.
2 These requirements included a two-year residency period and the passage of an Estonian language examination, in which the applicant had to demonstrate a basic level of language proficiency, based on a number of practical tasks, such as filling out official forms or understanding a newspaper article.
3 These figures are estimates drawn from various yearbooks of the Statistical Office of Estonia. However, in recent years the office has declined to give definitive figures, citing the unreliability of data from this period.
4 A collection of the High Commissioner's letters to Estonian officials can be accessed on the Minority Electronic Resources website, www.minelres.lv and via the European Centre for Minority Issues, www.ecmi.de. See also Zaagman (1999) and Poleshchuk (2001).

References

Andeweg, R.B. (2000) 'Consociational Democracy', *Annual Review of Political Science*, 3: 509–536.
Birckenbach, H.-M. (1997) *Preventive Diplomacy through Fact-Finding: How international organisations review the conflict over citizenship in Estonia and Latvia*, Hamburg: LIT Verlag.
—— (2000) 'Half Full or Half Empty? The OSCE Mission to Estonia and its Balance

Sheet, 1993–1999', ECMI Working Paper No. 6, Flensburg: European Centre for Minority Issues.

Bogaards, M. (2000) 'The Uneasy Relationship Between Empirical and Normative Types in Consociational Theory', *Journal of Theoretical Politics*, 12: 395–423.

Deets, S. (2002) 'Reconsidering East European Minority Policy: Liberal Theory and European Norms', *East European Politics and Societies*, 16: 30–53.

Eesti Migratsioonifond (2006) *Migratsioonifondi vahendite kasutamine rändetoetusteks ränderegistri andmetel [Allocation of resources from the Migration Fund for migration support based on migration registry data]*, Tallinn: Eesti Migratsioonifond. Online, available at: www.migfond.ee/ee/pages.php?action= view&page_id=34 (accessed 19 November 2007).

Eesti Statistikaamet (2002) *Rahvaloendus 2000: RL226, Rahvastik rahvuse, võõr-keelte oskuse ja kodakondsuse järgi [Census 2000: RL226, Population by ethnicity, foreign language knowledge and citizenship]*. Online, available at: http://pub.stat.ee/px-web.2001/Database/Rahvaloendus/15Rahvus._Emakeel._ Veerkeelte_oskus/ 15Rahvus._Emakeel._Veerkeelte_oskus.asp (accessed 19 November 2007).

Ernst & Young (2006) *State integration programme 'Integration in Estonian society 2000–2007' mid-term appraisal report*, Tallinn: Ernst & Young.

European Bank for Reconstruction and Development (1992) *Human rights aspects of the citizenship issues in Estonia and Latvia, by Asbjorn Eide*, London: European Bank for Reconstruction and Development.

European Commission (1997) *Agenda 2000 – Commission Opinion on Estonia's Application for Membership of the European Union*, Brussels: European Commission.

—— (1999) *Regular Report from the Commission on Estonia's Progress Towards Accession*, Brussels: European Commission.

—— (2000) *Regular Report from the Commission on Estonia's Progress Towards Accession*, Brussels: European Commission.

European Council (1998) 'Council Decision on the principles, priorities, intermediate objectives and conditions contained in the accession partnership with the Republic of Estonia', *Official Journal of the European Communities*, L 121: 26–30.

—— (1999) 'Council Decision on the principles, priorities, intermediate objectives and conditions contained in the accession partnership with the Republic of Estonia', *Official Journal of the European Communities*, L 335: 35–40.

—— (2002) 'Council Decision on the principles, priorities, intermediate objectives and conditions contained in the accession partnership with the Republic of Estonia', *Official Journal of the European Communities*, L 44: 29–36.

Fall, I. (1993) *Allegations of Discriminatory Practices against Minorities in Estonia: Report on a fact-finding mission to Estonia from 7–11 February and to the Russian Federation on 12 February 1993*, New York: United Nations.

Feldman, G. (2003) 'Stabilizing Estonia: The International Dimension of State Security and Ethnic Integration Policy', *Demokratizatsiya*, 11: 555–572.

—— (2005) 'Culture, state, and security in Europe: the case of citizenship and integration policy in Estonia', *American Ethnologist*, 32: 676–694.

Hallik, K. (1999) 'Ethnically divided Estonia', in R. Vetik (ed.) *Estonian Human Development Report 1999*, Tallinn: United Nations Development Programme.

Hough, W.J.H.I. (1985) 'The Annexation of the Baltic States and Its Effect on the Development of Law Prohibiting Forcible Seizure of Territory', *New York Law School Journal of International and Comparative Law*, 6: 301–533.

Hughes, J. and Sasse, G. (2003) 'Monitoring the Monitors: EU Enlargement Conditionality and Minority Protection in the CEECs', *Journal on Ethnopolitics and Minority Issues in Europe*, 1: 1–38.

Ilves, T.H. (2002) 'The OSCE Mission in Estonia', *Helsinki Monitor*, 13: 320–325.

Johns, M. (2003) ' "Do As I Say, Not As I Do": The European Union, Eastern Europe and Minority Rights', *East European Politics & Societies*, 17: 682–99.

Johnson, C. (2006) 'The Use and Abuse of Minority Rights: Assessing Past and Future EU Policies towards Accession Countries of Central, Eastern and South-Eastern Europe', *International Journal on Minority & Group Rights*, 13: 27–51.

Järve, P. (2000) 'Ethnic democracy and Estonia: application of Smooha's model', ECMI Working Paper 7, Flensburg: European Centre for Minority Issues.

—— (2002) 'Two waves of language laws in the Baltic states: Changes of rationale?', *Journal of Baltic Studies*, 33: 78–110.

Kala, K. (1992) 'Eesti rahvuslikust koosseisust pärast Teist Maailmasõda [On the ethnic composition of Estonia after the Second World War]', *Akadeemia*, 3: 508–535.

Kelley, J. (2003) 'Does Domestic Politics Limit the Influence of External Actors on Ethnic Politics?', *Human Rights Review*, 4: 35–54.

—— (2004) *Ethnic Politics in Europe: The Power of Norms and Incentives.* Princeton: Princeton University Press.

Kodakondsus- ja Migratsiooniamet (2006) *Kodakondsus- ja Migratsiooniamet 2006 [Citizenship and Migration Board 2006]*, Tallinn: Kodakondsus- ja Migratsiooniamet.

Lauristin, M. and Heidmets, M. (eds.) (2003) *The Challenge of the Russian Minority: Emerging Multiculturalism in Estonia*, Tartu: Tartu University Press.

Maasalu, S. (2007) 'Uuring: eestlaste eelarvamused venelaste kohta on suurenenud [Study: Estonians' biases toward Russians have increased]', *Postimees*, 9 August.

Minister of Population Affairs (2000) *State Programme. Integration in Estonian Society 2000–2007*, Tallinn: Office of the Minister of Population Affairs.

Ozolins, U. (2003) 'The Impact of European Accession upon Language Policy in the Baltic States', *Language Policy*, 2: 217–238.

Parliamentary Assembly of the Council of Europe (1993) *Report on the Application of the Republic of Estonia for Membership of the Council of Europe, by Mr Bratinka*, Strasbourg: Parliamentary Assembly of the Council of Europe.

Pettai, V. (1998) 'Emerging ethnic democracy in Estonia and Latvia' in M. Opalski (ed.) *Managing Diversity in Plural Societies: Minorities, Migration and Nation-Building in Post-Communist Europe*, Nepean, Ontario: Forum Eastern Europe, 15–32.

—— (2004) 'Framing the Past as Future: The Power of Legal Restorationism in Estonia', PhD dissertation, Department of Political Science, Columbia University.

Pettai, V. and Hallik, K. (2002) 'Understanding processes of ethnic control: Segmentation, dependency and cooptation in post-communist Estonia', *Nations and Nationalism*, 8: 505–529.

Pavelson, M. (2000) 'Sotsiaal-majanduslik integratsioon: tööhõive ja sissetulekud [Socio-economic integration: employment and incomes]' in M. Lauristin and R. Vetik (eds.) *Integratsioon Eesti ühiskonnas. Monitooring 2000 [Integration in Estonian Society. Monitor 2000]*, Tallinn: TPÜ Rahvusvaheliste ja Sotsiaaluuringute Instituut: 22–27.

Poleshchuk, V. (2001) *Advice not Welcomed. Recommendations of the OSCE High Commissioner to Estonia and Latvia and the Response*, Münster: LIT Verlag.

Poleschchuk, V. and Tsilevich, B. (2002/2003) 'The Baltic States before EU Accession: Recent Developments in Minority Protection', *European Yearbook of Minority Issues*, 2: 283–305.

Proos, I. (2005) 'Eestivenelaste keeleoskus ja suhtumine 2007. aasta gümnaasiumire-formi [Language abilities among Estonian Russians and their attitude toward the 2007 secondary school reform]' in R. Vetik (ed.) *Uuringu 'Integratiooni monitooring 2005' aruanne [Final report of the study 'Integration Monitor 2005']*, Tallinn: TPÜ Rahvus-vaheliste ja Sotsiaaluuringute Instituut, 20–32.

Pärn, H. and Veikat, U. (1996) 'Volikogu liikmete riigikeeleoskusest [On local council members' knowledge of the state language]', *Eesti Päevaleht*, 14 May.

Rose, R. (2000) 'New Baltic Barometer IV: A Survey Study, Studies in Public Policy', Working Paper 338, Centre for the Study of Public Policy, University of Strathclyde.

Smith, G. (1996) 'The ethnic democracy thesis and the citizenship question in Estonia and Latvia', *Nationalities Papers*, 24: 199–216.

Statistics Estonia (2007) *PO0222: Population by Sex, Ethnic Nationality and County, 1 January.* Online, available at: http://pub.stat.ee/px-web.2001/Dialog/ varval.asp?ma=P O0222&ti=POPULATION+BY+SEX%2C+ETHNIC+NATIONALITY+AND+COUN TY%2C+1+JANUARY&path=../I_Databas/Population/01Population_indicators_and_ composition/04Population_figure_and_composition/&lang=1 (accessed 28 December 2007).

van der Stoel, M. (1993) 'Letter to Trivimi Velliste, Minister of Foreign Affairs, Republic of Estonia', 6 April.

Taagepera, R. (1993) *Estonia: Return to Independence*, Boulder: Westview Press.

Tomusk, I. (2004) 'Vaidlused kohaliku omavalitsuse asjaajamiskeele üle Narvas ja Sil-lamäel' ['Debates over local government language use in Narva and Sillamäe'], *Õigus-keel*, 10: 19–27.

World Bank (2007) World Development Indicators database.

Zaagman, R. (1999) 'Conflict Prevention in the Baltic States: The OSCE High Commis-sioner on National Minorities in Estonia, Latvia and Lithuania', Working Paper, Mono-graph Series No. 1, Flensburg: European Centre for Minority Issues.

9 Hungary

A model with lasting problems

Balázs Vizi

Introduction

Regarding the ethnic composition of Central and Eastern Europe, Hungary occupies a particularly important position: the fact that relatively large and politically active Hungarian minority groups live in neighbouring states puts the country at the crossroads for regional stability.[1] Furthermore, Hungary is not a homogenous state itself, even if its minority communities are much smaller and have been largely assimilated linguistically.

In the nineteenth century, Hungary was among the first states in Europe to elaborate a coherent legal framework for minority protection. Following the establishment of Austria-Hungary, the Hungarian parliament adopted the Act on Nationalities in 1868. While this law offered cultural autonomy for minorities, it was not consistently implemented and especially in the first decades of the twentieth century the Hungarian government pursued strong assimilatory policies.

The territorial settlement after the First World War raised awareness in Hungarian politics on minority issues. The new borders meant that Hungary lost two

Map 9.1 Hungary (source: htp://maps.mygeo.ifo/maps_eu_hu.html – accessed 22 December, 2007).

Table 9.1 Key indicators for Hungary

Total population (millions)[a]	10.1 (2006)
Urban population (% of total)[a]	66.7 (2006)
GDP per capita, PPP (US$)[a]	19,585 (2006)
Unemployment rate (%)[b]	7.2 (2005)
Ethnic composition (2001 census)[c]	Hungarians: 92.3%
	Did not answer: 5.3%
	Roma: 1.9%
	German: 0.6%
	Unknown: 0.3%
	Slovakian: 0.2%
	Croatian: 0.2%
	Rumanian: 0.1%

Sources: a World Bank 2007; b UNICEF 2007; c Hungarian Central Statistical Office 2007.

Notes
PPP: purchasing power parity; unemployment rate is based on registered unemployment as a percentage of 15–59 year olds; GDP per capita is given in current international US$; the categories for 'nationality' add up to more than 100 per cent, as respondents could declare more than one nationality.

thirds of its former territory and one third of its Hungarian population (Romsics 1999: 119–123), while Hungary became an ethnically rather homogenous state. Between the two World Wars, Hungarian political life was largely determined by territorial revisionism, and concerns about the situation of Hungarian minorities in neighbouring states overshadowed the question of minorities living in Hungary. Following the Second World War, Hungary became even more homogenous: a population exchange took place between Hungary and Czechoslovakia, and almost the entire German minority was expelled from the country in 1945–47.

In the communist period, the question of minorities (especially that of Hungarian minorities living in neighbouring states) became a political taboo, which, as a result of glasnost and perestroika, started to fall in 1987–88. Not only among the nascent opposition movement, but also within the ruling communist party, a new interest in minority issues emerged, partly fuelled by the immigration of Hungarians fleeing from Ceauşescu's extreme nationalist dictatorship in Romania in the late 1980s (Mák 2000; Kende 1995: 480–488).

Historical experience and concerns over the situation of Hungarian minorities in neighbouring countries led the Hungarian political elite in the 1990s to introduce a coherent approach, based on a large public consensus. The promotion of legal guarantees for the protection of minority rights has become the main instrument for addressing problems related to minorities in both the domestic and international sphere (Győri-Szabó 1998; Pataki 2002; Schöpflin 2000: 378–409; Valki 2001: 296–301). The basic principles of minority policy in Hungary have been outlined in the 1989 constitution:

1   The national and ethnic minorities living in the Republic of Hungary participate in the sovereign power of the people: they represent a constituent part of the state.

2 The Republic of Hungary shall provide for the protection of national and ethnic minorities and ensure their collective participation in public affairs, the fostering of their cultures, the use of their native languages, education in their native languages and the use of names in their native languages.

3 The laws of the Republic of Hungary shall ensure representation for the national and ethnic minorities living within the country.

4 National and ethnic minorities shall have the right to form local and national bodies for self-government.

5 A majority of two-thirds of the votes of the members of parliament present is required to pass the law on the rights of national and ethnic minorities.

(Republic of Hungary 1989)

The Act on the Rights of National and Ethnic Minorities (Minority Law), adopted on 7 July 1993, elaborated on these principles by establishing a coherent minority rights system, based on cultural autonomy and the free choice of identity. It listed 13 recognized minorities: Armenians, Bulgarians, Croats, Germans, Greeks, Poles, Roma, Romanians, Ruthenians, Serbs, Slovaks, Slovenes, and Ukrainians.

At the time of the adoption of the Minority Law, at the international level mainly the legally non-binding documents of the Organisation for Security and Co-operation in Europe (OSCE, named Conference for Security and Co-operation in Europe, CSCE, until 1994) offered guidelines for the Hungarian legislator. However, the role of international organizations in shaping Hungary's legislation was not as influential as later in some other countries in Central and Eastern Europe. In the early 1990s, Hungary was already an active promoter of international minority protection instruments. Representatives of Hungary actively participated in the *travaux preparatoires* (preparatory work) of the Council of Europe for the European Charter for Regional or Minority Languages and the Framework Convention for the Protection of National Minorities. Furthermore, Hungary strongly supported the 1992 United Nations Declaration on the Rights of Persons Belonging to National or Ethnic, Religious, and Linguistic Minorities and relevant OSCE documents (the 1990 Copenhagen Document, the 1990 Charter of Paris for a New Europe, and the 1992 Helsinki Document), and was one of the main promoters of the 1991 OSCE Meeting of Experts on National Minorities. Indeed, besides domestic and foreign policy interests, the desire to fulfil Hungary's international obligations was a strong motivation for the adoption of a specific law on minority rights.

Specific regulations on minority rights were also included in bilateral agreements with neighbouring states. Hungary's policy in this field was aimed at extending the legal protection of minorities, largely by incorporating existing international standards into bilateral treaties and, more recently, by extending domestic legislation on the support of its kin-minorities (the 2001 Law on Hungarians Living in Neighbouring Countries, or 'Status Law'). While the 'external' minority protection policy of Hungary raised much more concern at the international level than the situation of minorities living in Hungary (see e.g. Vizi 2006: 185–221), this chapter focuses on the legal and political developments regarding the protection of minorities living in Hungary.

New legislation after 1989

Regulating minority rights in a separate law was of great political importance at the beginning of the 1990s. Hungary, by adopting the Minority Law in 1993, was among the first states in Central and Eastern Europe to offer a consistent legal regulation of minority rights. Besides providing an institutional structure for minorities in Hungary, by adopting the Minority Law Hungary also wanted to provide a political justification for its support of Hungarian minorities in neighbouring countries (Schöpflin 2000: 375). The importance of keeping the Minority Law in line with international standards and of offering a 'good example' for other countries of the region was emphasized by all political sides in the parliamentary debate on the bill (National Assembly 1992). Not only the adoption, but also the content of the law were partly motivated by concerns for the situation of Hungarian minorities in neighbouring countries.

Among the Hungarian political elite, despite the significant differences in their rhetoric, there was a strong consensus on the conceptual approach towards minority issues: politicians, intellectuals and experts shaping the official Hungarian minority policy have continuously formulated the main policy goals in terms of the legal protection of minorities. The responsibility felt for Hungarian minorities living abroad has usually been articulated as political support for specific minority rights. This means that the arguments and goals formulated in domestic and foreign policy have been rather coherent.

A main intention behind the constitutional regulations and the Minority Law was to find a solution for the situation of a large number of small, scattered and in large part assimilated minorities in Hungary and for the significant Roma community that is dispersed throughout the country.[2] The demographic position of minorities in Hungary (except the Roma) is rather fragile, due to their small size and strong assimilatory pressures in the past (Government of Hungary 1997). While all other minorities are well integrated into society, the Roma often live in socially marginalized communities in suburban areas and face discrimination in everyday life. This was one area not addressed by the Minority Law. Instead, the primary goal was to establish institutional structures for guaranteeing the survival of minority identities, cultures, and languages and for assuring their political participation (Government of Hungary 1999). As far as the aim of minority policy was to make up for past assimilation, it can be described as 'cultural differentiation' (Vermeersch 2003: 12) or dissimilatory policy.

The Minority Law reflects an 'autonomist' concept of minority protection. The drafters of the law argued that without appropriate, legally defined self-government structures, minorities would be too weak and divided to establish effective institutional structures (Bíró 1995: 36–43). While the constitution did not specify the possibility of territorial autonomy, the 'autonomist' concept of granting cultural autonomy received unanimous political support and the Minority Law was adopted by the parliament with a majority of 96.5 per cent. Besides the Minority Law, the 1993 Act on Public Education, the 1996 Media Act and other minor laws contain specific minority provisions – but all these provisions are mainly based on the regulations of the Minority Law. The minority protection system designed by the Minority Law was completed with the establishment of the position of a Parliamentary Ombudsman for the Rights of National and Ethnic Minorities (hereafter Minority Ombudsman). This position was established in 1993 to provide an advocate institution for the full enjoyment of minority rights. The Minority Ombudsman is charged with calling attention to abuses of minority rights.

The minority law – law and practice

A very important feature of the Hungarian minority protection system is that it is only addressed at 'historical minorities' or 'native ethnic groups'. The Minority Law defines 'historical minorities' as minorities whose members hold Hungarian citizenship and have lived on the territory of Hungary for at least one century. With regard to the personal scope of the law, the Minority Law notes that belonging to a minority is a matter of individual choice.

The Minority Law further specifies the right to equal opportunity in politics and cultural life, the right to choose and use personal names in minority languages, and the right to use minority languages in private, as well as in public and in education. The law further covers the right to preserve minority languages and traditions, to organize feasts and events, and to preserve the architectural, cultural and religious heritage of minorities. The Minority Law also guarantees minorities the right to the establishment of a national network of educational, cultural and scientific institutions, as well as access to radio and television programmes in their mother tongue.

The explicit aim of the Minority Law was the establishment of person-based, non-territorial cultural autonomy. The essence of the entire regulation is a system of minority self-governments endowed with legal status. The parliament integrated minority self-governments into the system of local governments and modelled minority representation on the regulations for local governments. As a result of the territorial dispersion of minorities in Hungary, the principle of territorial autonomy could only be applied at the local level. Many minority communities live in small villages and for them the village is the only territorial setting in which they constitute the majority of the population. At the local level, the administrative self-government, if as a result of the elections the local council decides so, may transform itself into a minority self-government. If a minority does not represent the majority of the local population of a village or settlement, it is entitled to create local minority self-governments based on the personal principle.

Until amendments of the Minority Law in 2005, the system of minority self-governments consisted of two levels, the local and the national. After 2005 – in full coherence with the system of local governments in Hungary – an intermediate level, the regional minority self-governments, were introduced at county level.

The Minority Law makes it possible for local and regional minority self-governments to integrate at the national level: each minority group can establish a national minority self-government or national assembly. Today, all 13 minorities recognized in the Minority Law have their own national self-government. These self-governments can establish and maintain different types of national institutions (libraries, theatres, museums, publishing companies, secondary and higher education institutions) and also function as political representation of minorities.

Critical issues in Hungary's minority protection system

Despite the broad range of rights guaranteed under the constitution and the Minority Law, discrepancies still exist between the law and how it works in practice. One of the main problems of the Hungarian minority protection system is rooted in the financial conditions of the operation of minority self-governments. Minority self-governments receive financial assistance from the central budget, although this is variable from year to year. Other potential sources of financing are local governments, civil organizations, and minority kin-states, although so far only the German, Croatian and Slovenian minorities have received sustained support from their kin-states.

Sustainable funding is indispensable for the effective implementation of autonomous self-government structures (Vaillancourt and Grin 2002). The Minority Ombudsman continuously called attention to these financing problems. The implementation of minority autonomy was from the very beginning rather difficult because of the problematic financial regulations. Furthermore, the competencies between the different levels and types of self-governments were not clearly defined. Under the terms of the Minority Law, the functioning of autonomous political bodies largely delimits the exercise of other important rights of minorities, such as the right to education in their mother tongue, and their cultural and political rights. If minority self-governments do not work appropriately, minorities cannot have effective control over the functioning of institutions and public activities relevant for them. The Minority Ombudsman noted that these weaknesses of the minority self-government system could impede the original goal of the law, i.e. preserving minority identities and cultures (Minority Ombudsman 2001). Many scholars and politicians examining the functioning of Hungary's minority protection system arrived at similar conclusions (see Eiler and Kovács 2002; Eiler 2004; Szabó 2004).

A more theoretical, but similarly important problem of the minority protection system in Hungary is the so-called 'trap of free identity choice', causing representation problems in the functioning of minority self-government institutions. The free choice of identity and the objection of minority representatives to any form of registration of people belonging to minorities resulted in a controversial electoral system for minority self-governments. Independently of their ethnic belonging, all Hungarian citizens had a right to vote and stand for candidacy at elections for minority self-governments. In 1998, the Minority Ombudsman called attention to this 'business-like' phenomenon (Minority Ombudsman 1998). Similarly, after the 2002 elections, the national Slovak minority self-government claimed that the election of Slovak minority self-governments in Inánc, Jákfalva, Perkupa, Putnok and Szendrölád in Borsod county seems to be problematic, as no Slovak community was living there (Pap 2003). The phenomenon was also mentioned in the first Resolution of the Committee of Ministers of the Council of Europe on the implementation of the Framework Convention for the Protection of National Minorities (Committee of Ministers 2001). One of the main reasons why parliamentary parties started to work on a modification of the Minority Law was indeed the problem of minority self-government elections (Szabó 2004: 198–205).

Another problem associated with the minority protection system is that it does not address the parliamentary representation of minorities. This problem is not exclusively of a political, but also of a legal character: parliamentary representation of minorities was envisaged by the Minority Law, stating that '[m]inorities have the right – as determined in a separate Act – to be represented in the National Assembly' (Republic of Hungary 1993). However, by 2007, this separate law was still lacking. In 1992 and 1994, the Constitutional Court declared the absence of this law to be anti-constitutional. Several proposals have been prepared in the years since then to accommodate the legal obligation of granting parliamentary representation to minorities (Project on Ethnic Relations 2000), but no viable solution has yet emerged. An obstacle to realizing parliamentary representation of minorities is that the constitution prescribes a two-third majority of votes in parliament for any decision relating to the rights of minorities and in Hungary's politically divided society granting seats to minorities is too sensitive an issue to reach a viable compromise between opposition and governing parties. Furthermore, because people belonging to minorities form small communities, their right to parliamentary representation can only be ensured through positive discrimination.

The constitution and the Minority Law state that minority status requires Hungarian citizenship, and the 2005 modification of the Minority Law limits voting rights for minority self-governments to citizens. This approach generated enduring problems for the application of the Minority Law. Already in 1993, the Venice Commission expressed its doubts on the application of a historical time limit for the recognition of minority groups and also with regard to the exclusion of non-citizen residents from the benefits of the law (Venice Commission 1993). According to Hungary's definition of the term, non-citizens are not legally considered as being part of a minority and minorities need to have lived in Hungary for at least a century. Both these provisions are contrary to the United Nations Human Rights Committee's interpretation of the term 'minority' (Human Rights Committee 1994). Presumably, the requirement of citizenship and century-long residence were influenced by Resolution 1201 of the Parliamentary Assembly of the Council of Europe, which was adopted a few months before Hungary's

Minority Law. The definition of minorities provided by the 1201 Resolution explicitly refers to persons who are citizens of the state and who 'maintain long-standing, firm and lasting ties with that state' (PACE 1993). The definition offered by the Minority Law fulfils both conditions.

The present legislation contradicts the general provisions for local self-government elections, in which non-citizens are allowed to vote, if they have residence in Hungary and are citizens of another EU member state or are acknowledged refugees or immigrants. The limited personal scope of the Minority Law also contradicts the prohibition of discrimination between EU citizens on the basis of their nationality. However, the European Commission did not mention this matter in its monitoring reports and, as a Commission official told the author, it has not found the question to be of relevance to Hungary's EU membership.[3]

In the EU accession process, the European Commission did not specify domestic legal instruments for minority protection. The EU could not build on existing minority rights in EU law, this issue was not a political priority within the Union, and minority norms and their implementation are often disputed at the international level (Sasse 2004: 65). In the case of Hungary, the European Commission was not capable of providing a consistent and thorough analysis of the existing system of minority protection. In the Regular Reports and the Accession Partnerships, the Commission remained silent on the question of reforming the Minority Law, although officials in the European Commission were aware of respective endeavours of the Hungarian government.[4]

The shortcomings of Hungary's minority protection system became clear even in the first years of its implementation (Minority Ombudsman 1995). However, for a long time the Hungarian parliament remained reluctant to modify the Minority Law. Because of the strong mistrust between the political sides in Hungary, every question requiring a consensual decision in the parliament (like a two-third majority of the votes) was problematic. Moreover, from the mid 1990s, domestic minority issues almost disappeared from the political agenda (Szabó 2004). The Minority Law was finally modified on 13 June 2005, when, after long debates, the parliament with an overwhelming (95 per cent) majority adopted the Act on the Elections of Members of Minority Self-government and on the Modification of Certain Acts Relating to National and Ethnic Minorities.

The 2005 modification of the Minority Law established a registry of voters entitled to participate in the elections of minority self-governments. This registry is administered by the head of the local electoral office. The request for registration is optional and is based on self-declaration, without any further objective requirement. While this solution may not resolve all problems related to 'ethno-business', passive voting rights can be exercised exclusively on the recommendation of a minority organization. It might be more reasonable to introduce objective criteria both for passive and active voting rights, as proposed by Majtényi (2006).

International actors in the development of Hungary's minority protection system

Already from the dawn of political transition in Hungary, the new minority policy was shaped by multiple variables, including domestic and foreign policy goals. Moreover, Hungary's minority policy emerged in the context of European integration, one of the main foreign policy goals of post-communist Hungary. Already in the early 1990s, the Hungarian government was keen to design minority rights legislation in full compliance with existing international standards. International standards on minority rights at the time were mostly formulated in legally non-binding political documents, except for Article 27 of the International Covenant on Civil and Political Rights. In 1991 and 1992, Hungary started to enter bilateral treaties on good neighbourly relations with its newly emerging neighbouring states (Croatia, Slovenia, Ukraine; no treaty was agreed with the Federal Republic of Yugoslavia, but in 2003 a bilateral agreement was signed with Serbia and Montenegro) in which references to the mutual protection of minorities were included. These bilateral treaties reinforced the contracting parties' relevant OSCE commitments by turning them into legal obligations.

When preparing the Minority Law, international experts were consulted, including from the Council of Europe. The Council of Europe European Commission for Democracy through Law (Venice Commission) noted that the 'Hungarian proposal for comprehensive legislation in this field [i.e. the rights of minorities] is without known precedent' (Venice Commission 1993). The Minority Law was also praised by the Council of Europe Parliamentary Assembly's Commission on Legal Affairs and Human Rights and by the OSCE High Commissioner on National Minorities.

In its 1997 Opinion on Hungary's application for EU membership, the European Commission acknowledged the international legal obligations undertaken by Hungary (Hungary had signed the Framework Convention for the Protection of National Minorities in 1995 and had also subscribed to Recommendation 1201 of the Parliamentary Assembly of the Council of Europe). The Commission further praised the adoption of the Minority Law and concluded that '[t]he rights of minorities are guaranteed and protected' (European Commission 1997: 19).

Despite the lack of a consistent conditionality with regard to minority rights, the EU was rather powerful in influencing the political discourse on minority issues in Hungary and in motivating policy changes. This influence had observable implications in the modifications of policy strategies regarding the Roma and in the adoption of a law on anti-discrimination. During the accession process, different perceptions of 'minority protection' became apparent. While the EU raised attention with regard to the situation of the Roma and shortages in anti-discrimination legislation, it did not mention problems related to the effectiveness of the existing Minority Law. The weak political and legal background of EU conditionality and the low weight of minority issues in the accession process could not really provide a direct policy- or norm-transfer (Vermeersch 2003;

Sasse 2004). The implications of EU conditionality for Hungarian minority policy are visible in the timing of new domestic policies and legislation (i.e. anticipating or following EU recommendations) and in the reproduction of 'EU arguments' in domestic political discourse (Vermeersch 2003, Sasse 2004). In part, EU accession also shaped government priorities in minority policy. In the first half of the 1990s, the improvement of specific minority rights and their effective implementation was at the forefront of minority policy; in the period of accession negotiations, government policies focused much more on the integration of the Roma.

The Roma

In the late 1990s, the European Commission started to pay specific attention to the situation of the Roma. Decision-makers within the EU started to realize that there was a large Roma population in Central and Eastern Europe in a socially marginalized position, with the risk of an unwanted mass migration after EU accession. In 1997, the Hungarian government recognized that the integration of the Roma requires 'the implementation of measures which are different from those of traditional minority policy' (Government of Hungary 1997), as the cultural autonomy offered by the Minority Law did not sufficiently address the situation of the Roma (EÖKIK 2000: 79–81). The European Commission, however, did not pay attention to the potential tension between the protection of minority identity and the more complex needs of the Roma for – as the Commission labelled it – social integration. The Commission focused exclusively on the problem of widespread discrimination against the Roma and the need to integrate them into mainstream society. The main issues related to the Roma recurrently mentioned in the Regular Reports and in the resolutions of the European Parliament on enlargement were the social integration of the Roma, the fight against discrimination, and abuse by the police and other state authorities.

Until 1997, the specific minority question of the Roma was scarcely formulated by politicians in Hungary. Most policy documents addressing the situation of the Roma appeared in the period of EU accession negotiations, i.e. after 1997. The political pressure by the EU was clearly an important factor; however, it was also the period when the problems related to the implementation of the Minority Law became more apparent. The Hungarian government adopted various plans on Roma integration. The first sign of a more differentiated approach was the adoption of a Roma integration programme in 1995. This programme set out a medium- and a long-term plan to promote equal opportunities and social integration. The essence of the programme was the establishment of a government agency for cooperation between different ministries and other government bodies. In 1997, the first real action plan was launched, in which the government made an attempt to comprehensively assess and delineate the tasks necessary for the social integration of the Roma. After the socialist-liberal coalition was defeated at the 1998 parliamentary elections, the new right-wing cabinet led by FIDESZ (Alliance of Young Democrats) adopted a revised medium-term action plan in 1999, giving priority to education and culture. However, the 1999 integration programme was not fully implemented.

Following the 2002 elections, the socialist-liberal coalition replaced the FIDESZ cabinet and the new government redesigned once more the medium-term action plan, giving more weight to a policy of equal opportunities. The last modification of the medium-term action plan was made only two months before Hungary's Accession Treaty entered into force on 1 May 2004. The 2004 programme was based on earlier guidelines, but underpinned the need to establish effective instruments in the areas of education, employment and anti-discrimination. Overall, the modification of action plans in the years after 1997 largely depended on changes in government and the concerns formulated by the European Commission and by minority advocates in Hungary.

Implementation in practice has been hindered by several factors. Government bodies tasked with coordinating implementation were not invested with appropriate authority to oblige ministries to fulfil their obligations (European Commission 2001: 22). Furthermore, the government did not assign a separate budget for the Roma programme. In many cases, it was difficult to establish to what extent funds had been used for Roma, as officials sometimes deliberately blurred the distinction between policies targeting Roma and those addressing general poverty (Open Society Institute 2001: 217). Finally, spending on minorities was allocated in different departments and it was impossible to control actual spending (EÖKIK 2000: 85).

The European Commission and the European Parliament called attention to these obstacles of implementing the medium-term action plan (European Parliament 1999; European Commission 1999: 16). The 1999 Accession Partnership defined the provision of necessary financial support for the implementation of the action plan as a short-term priority to be fulfilled by 2000 (DG Enlargement 1999). The Hungarian government made an attempt to remedy the problems of financing and specific, separate budgetary sources (about €19 million) were made available for the implementation of the medium-term programme in 2000. This was acknowledged by the Commission as 'an important step forward' (European Commission 2000: 19) and as meeting the priority of the 1999 Accession Partnership (European Commission 2000: 84). A further increase of financial resources was welcomed by the Commission in the following Regular Report (European Commission 2001: 22). Regarding the implementation of the medium-term action plan, this positive view was also reflected in 2002 (European Commission 2002: 33). The 2001 Accession Partnership defined the efficient implementation of the medium-term action plan as an 'intermediate priority' and the Commission continued to pay attention to its implementation and provided financial assistance to the programmes of the action plan through the Poland and Hungary: Assistance for Restructuring their Economies (PHARE) funds (see Vizi 2005).

Anti-discrimination legislation

Another issue closely related to the social problems of the Roma minority was the question of reinforcing anti-discrimination legislation. While the European Commission highlighted discrimination against the Roma since 1997, it only asked Hungary to revise its anti-discrimination legislation in 2001, following adoption of the Race Equality Directive in 2000. The Hungarian constitution prohibits all forms of discrimination, including discrimination based on racial or ethnic origin, and envisages 'strict punishment' for acts of discrimination. The Minority Law expressively prohibits all discrimination against national minorities. This prohibition was implemented in various specific laws (such as the Act on Labour and the Act on Public Education). However, these provisions were dispersed in various laws, did not cover all areas of discrimination, and failed to be implemented in practice.

The experts participating in the preparatory consultations on the 1997 action plan for Roma integration argued for the adoption of a general codex on discrimination and an effective sanctioning system for its implementation (Kadar 2001). Despite these recommendations, the medium-term action plan did not include any commitments for the elaboration of an anti-discrimination law.

The Act on Equal Treatment and the Promotion of Equal Opportunities was finally adopted on 22 December 2003, more than one year after the conclusion of EU accession negotiations. By and large, the adoption of the anti-discrimination law was a successful transposition of the EU directive. The only two major problematic differences to the Race Equality Directive are the definition of the spheres of application, as the Hungarian law in the scope of application does not fully cover the public sphere, and the status of the Equal Treatment Authority, which is affiliated with the Ministry of Social Affairs and Labour. Since the adoption of the anti-discrimination law, the overwhelming majority of complaints against discrimination based on ethnic or national origin are submitted by persons belonging to the Roma minority. In many cases, however, the Authority could not detect the ethnic motivation behind presumed discriminatory acts.[5]

Conclusions

Overall, in the Hungarian case the EU did not decisively influence the development of domestic minority rights. The domestic debates surrounding the implementation of the Minority Law and the deficiencies in the functioning of cultural autonomy in Hungary did not raise specific concern in the EU. Apparently, the EU was not willing to formulate legal recommendations for the improvement of the situation of minorities. As the Deputy Head of the Mission of the Hungarian Representation to the EU put it:

the fact that the Commission never formulated legally relevant arguments on the situation of minorities, was as bad as good for us: they did not raise issues, which could be sensitive in the debates over the reform of minority protection legislation; but on the other hand they regularly formulated concerns, especially on the situation of the Roma, that could not be resolved solely by legal instruments.[6]

The almost exclusive attention of the EU to the situation of the Roma, however, was prompting the Hungarian governments to tackle this problem separately from the legal protection of minorities. The adoption and the modifications of the medium-term action plan for Roma integration reflected this increasing commitment. Moreover, each government was keen to present its own proposals for the integration of the Roma. Nevertheless, no breakthrough was achieved in the past 15 years in the living conditions and social integration of the Roma. While the success of direct financial assistance provided through the PHARE programme was limited, the Commission enhanced awareness of the matter, and this was an important achievement of the monitoring procedure. By welcoming the adoption and regular adjustment of government programmes for improving the situation of the Roma, the EU supported domestic policy initiatives in this area. Moreover, the adoption of a separate law on combating discrimination was largely motivated by the need to comply with EU accession requirements.

Notes

1 The number of Hungarians in neighbouring countries according to official censuses is: Austria 25,884; Croatia 15,595; Romania (Transylvania) 1,447,544; Serbia (Vojvodina) 290,207; Slovakia 520,528; Slovenia 6,243; Ukraine (Sub-Carpathia) 152,000. Source: Official census data quoted in 'Reports on Hungarians living abroad', Government Office for Hungarian Minorities Abroad. www.hhrf.org/htmh/?menuid= 060201, accessed 11 January 2008.
2 The Roma community in Hungary is composed of three main groups, according to their mother tongue, the Hungarian-speaking Romungro (89.6 per cent), the Romani-speaking Gypsy (4.7 per cent) and the Romanian-speaking Boyash (5.7 per cent) groups (Kállai 2002).
3 Interview of the author with an official working at Directorate-General Enlargement, Brussels, 5 August 2003.
4 Interview of the author with an official working at the Hungary Desk, Directorate-General Enlargement, Brussels, 3 August 2003.
5 For a summary of typical cases see: www.egyenlobanasmod.hu/index.php?g =cases. htm, accessed 11 January 2008.
6 Interview of the author with the Deputy Head of the Mission of the Hungarian Representation to the EU, Brussels, 5 August 2003.

References

Bíró, G. (1995) *Az identitásválasztás szabadsága [The free choice of identity]*, Budapest: Századvég.

Committee of Ministers (2001) *Resolution ResCMN(2001)4 on the implementation of the Framework Convention for the Protection of National Minorities by Hungary*, Strasbourg: Council of Europe.

DG Enlargement (1999) *Accession Partnership 1999: Hungary*, Brussels: Directorate-General Enlargement.

Eiler, F. (2004) 'Törekvések a kisebbségi önkormányzati választások reformjára [Aspirations for the reform of minority self-government elections]', in L. Szarka *et al.* (eds.) *Tér és terep III. [3rd Yearbook of the Institute for Minority Studies of the Hungarian Academy of Sciences]*, Budapest: Akadémiai Kiadó, 209–226.

Eiler, F. and Kovács, N. (2002) 'Minority Self-Governments in Hungary' in K. Gál (ed.) *Minority Governance – Concepts at the Threshold of the 21st Century*, Budapest: LGI-ECMI, 171–197.

EÖKIK (2000) *A Roma's Life in Hungary. Report*, Budapest: Public Foundation for European Comparative Minority Research.

European Commission (1997) *Commission Opinion on Hungary's Application for Membership of the European Union*, Brussels: European Commission.

—— (1999) *Regular Report on Hungary's Progress Towards Accession*, Brussels: European Commission.

—— (2000) *Regular Report on Hungary's Progress Towards Accession*, Brussels: European Commission.

—— (2001) *Regular Report on Hungary's Progress Towards Accession*, Brussels: European Commission.

—— (2002) *Regular Report on Hungary's Progress Towards Accession*, Brussels: European Commission.

European Parliament (1999) *Resolution on the Regular Report from the Commission on Hungary's progress towards accession*, Strasbourg: European Parliament.

Government of Hungary (1997) *Report of the Government of Hungary to the Parliament on the Situation of the National and Ethnic Minorities Living in the Republic of Hungary (J/3670 Report)*, Budapest: Government of Hungary.

—— (1999) *Report submitted by Hungary pursuant to Article 25, paragraph 1 of the Framework Convention for the Protection of National Minorities*, Strasbourg: Council of Europe.

Győri-Szabó, R. (1998) *Kisebbségpolitikai rendszerváltás Magyarországon [Transition in minority policy in Hungary]*, Budapest: Osiris.

Human Rights Committee (1994) *General Comment No. 23: The rights of minorities (Art. 27)*, Geneva: Office of the High Commissioner for Human Rights.

Hungarian Central Statistical Office 2007 *Population by nationality and main age groups, 1941, 1980–2001.* Online, available at: www.nepszamlalas.hu/eng/ volumes/18/tables/ load1_30_1.html (accessed 22 December 2007).

Kadar, A. (2001) 'A magyar diszkrimináció-ellenes jogi szabályozás a faji megkülönböztetés tilalmáról szóló EU irányelv tükrében [Hungarian anti-discrimination legislation in the light of the EU Race Directive]', International symposium on human rights, Budapest, 6 December 2001. Online, available at: www.helsinki.hu/docs/kaltenbach-diszkrimi.pdf (accessed 28 December 2007).

Kállai, E. (2002) 'The Hungarian Roma Population During the Last Half-Century', in E. Kállai (ed.) *The Gypsies/the Roma in Hungarian Society*, Budapest: Teleki László Foundation, 35–51.

Kende, P. (1995) 'The Trianon Syndrome: Hungarians and their neighbours', in B. Király (ed.) *Lawful Revolution in Hungary 1989–1994*, Boulder Co.: Social Science Monographs, 475–490.

Majtényi, B. (2006) 'What Has Happened to Our Model Child? The Creation and Evolution of the Hungarian Minority Act', *European Yearbook of Minority Issues* (5).

Mák, F. (2000) 'Az új nemzeti politika és a Határon Túli Magyarok Hivatala (1989–1999) [The new national policy and the Government Office for Hungarian Minorities Abroad (1989–1999)]', *Magyar Kisebbség* (3).

Minority Ombudsman (1995) *Annual Report*, Budapest: Office of the Parliamentary Commissioner for the Rights of National and Ethnic Minorities.

—— (1998) *Annual Report*, Budapest: Office of the Parliamentary Commissioner for the Rights of National and Ethnic Minorities.

—— (2001) *Annual Report*, Budapest: Office of the Parliamentary Commissioner for the Rights of National and Ethnic Minorities.

National Assembly (1992) *Official Records of the Hungarian National Assembly, 29 September 1992, 229th session*. Online, available at: www.mkogy.hu (accessed 11 January 2008).

Open Society Institute (2001) *Monitoring the EU Accession Process: Minority Protection*, Budapest and New York: Central European University Press.

PACE (1993) Recommendation 1201 on an additional protocol on the rights of national minorities to the European Convention on Human Rights, Strasbourg: Parliamentary Assembly of the Council of Europe

Pap, A.L. (2003) 'Etnikai-nemzetiségi identitás és választójogi korrupció [Ethnic-national identity and electoral corruption]', in I. Halász and B. Majtényi (eds.) *Regisztrálható-e az identitás? [Is it possible to register identity?]*, Budapest: Gondolat, 250–262.

Pataki, G.Z. (2002) 'Overview of Proposals for Minority Self-Governments of Hungarian Minorities in Central Europe', in K. Gál (ed.) *Minority Governance – Concepts at the Threshold of the 21st Century*, Budapest: LGI-ECMI, 245–272.

Project on Ethnic Relations (2000) *Parliamentary Representation of Minorities in Hungary: Legal and Political Issues*, Princeton: Project on Ethnic Relations.

Republic of Hungary (1989) *Act XX of 1949 The Constitution of the Republic of Hungary as modified by the Act XXXI of 1989 and Act XL of 1990, Amendment of the Constitution of the Republic of Hungary*. Online, available at www.mkab.hu/en/enpage5.htm (accessed 25 January 2008).

—— (1993) *Act on the Rights of National and Ethnic Minorities*, Budapest: Republic of Hungary.

Romsics, I. (1999) *Hungary in the Twentieth Century*, Budapest: Osiris.

Sasse, G. (2004) 'Minority Rights and EU Enlargement: Normative Overstretch or Effective Conditionality?', in G. Toggenburg (ed.) *Minority Protection and the Enlarged European Union: The Way Forward*, Budapest: OSI LGI, 59–85.

Schöpflin, G. (2000) *Nations, Identity, Power: the New Politics of Europe*, London: Hurst.

Szabó, O. (2004) 'Reform vagy módosítás? [Reform or modification?]', in L. Szarka et al. (eds.) *Tér és terep III. [3rd Yearbook of the Institute for Minority Studies of the Hungarian Academy of Sciences]*, Budapest: Akadémiai Kiadó.

UNICEF (2007) TransMONEE database.

Valki, L. (2001) 'Hungary: Understanding Western Messages', in J. Zielonka (ed.) *Democratic Consolidation in Eastern Europe*, Oxford: Oxford University Press, 281–310.

Vaillancourt, F. and Grin, F. (2002) 'Minority Self-Governance in Economic Perspective', in K. Gál (ed.) *Minority Governance – Concepts at the Threshold of the 21st Century*, Budapest: LGI-ECMI, 73–86.

Venice Commission (1993) *Opinion on the Hungarian Bill No. 5190 on the Rights of National and Ethnic Minorities approved by the Commission during its 14th meeting (Venice, 5–6 February 1993)*, Venice: European Commission for Democracy through Law.

Vermeersch, P. (2003) 'EU Enlargement and Minority Rights Policies in Central Europe: Explaining Policy Shifts in the Czech Republic, Hungary and Poland', *Journal on Ethnopolitics and Minority Issues in Europe*, 1.

Vizi, B. (2005) 'The EU and the Situation of Roma in Hungary in the Accession Process', *Central European Political Science Review*, 6 (20): 66–91.

—— (2006) 'Hungarian Minority Policies and European Union Membership – an interpretation of minority protection conditionality in EU enlargement', unpublished PhD thesis, Leuven: Katholieke Universiteit Leuven.

World Bank (2007) World Development Indicators database.

10 Latvia

Managing post-imperial minorities

David J. Galbreath and Nils Muižnieks

Introduction

Latvia's progress from a former Soviet republic to a European Union (EU) member state illustrates an amazing willingness to overcome authoritarianism, Sovietization, and Russification for democratization, marketization, and Westernization. One of the most important issues troubling this journey towards European integration has been coping with large Slavic minorities, many of whose members are remnants of a lost empire, the Soviet Union.

The impact of European integration on minority policies in Latvia has been well documented (see Jubulis 1996; Gelazis 2003; Muižnieks and Brands Kehris 2003; Tesser 2003; Galbreath 2005, 2006), but little has been written about the situation of minorities in Latvia since enlargement. With citizenship, language and education policies recognized by the EU, the Council of Europe and the Organization for Security and Co-operation in Europe (OSCE, until 1994 the Conference for Security and Co-operation in Europe, or CSCE), these organizations have tended to turn their attention elsewhere. This chapter brings the reader up to date on the condition of state-minority relations in Latvia following

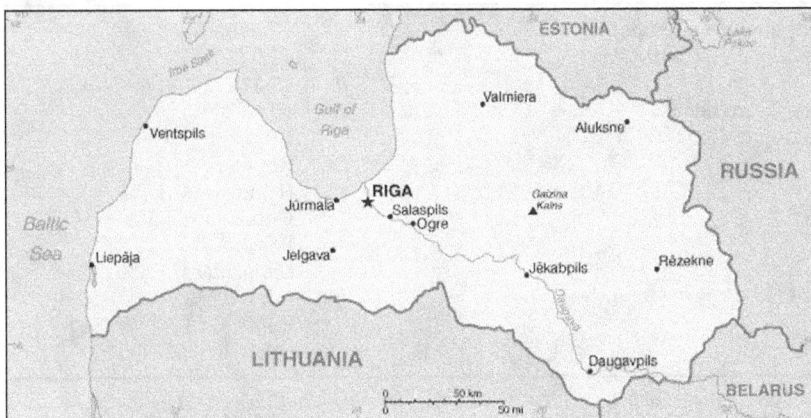

Map 10.1 Latvia (source: http://maps.mygeo.info/maps_eu_lv.html – accessed 4 October, 2007).

enlargement in 2004. We find that European institutions no longer condition minority policies as they did in the pre-accession period, but that they continue to influence the legal space in state-minority relations.

Historical and statistical background on minorities

In what is now Latvia, minorities have been living for centuries. This includes proto-Russian (*Krivichi*) settlements in the south-east, Russian old believers from the seventeenth and eighteenth centuries, as well as Baltic Germans beginning in the days of the Hanseatic League, not to mention the Finno-Ugric *Livs* along the Baltic Sea coast (see Kolstø 1995). Prior to the Second World War and the Soviet annexation of Latvia in 1944, the Russian-speaking community constituted approximately 11 per cent of the population (as cited in Smith 1996: 7). Once Latvia had forcibly become part of the Soviet Union, Soviet authorities used mass migration of Slavs into Latvia to promote stabilization, industrialization, and Russification. By the end of the Soviet period, the percentage of Russian-speakers had more than tripled to 40 per cent (with Russians constituting 34 per cent), leaving Latvia with more Slavs numerically and proportionally than either Estonia or Lithuania. Following independence, Latvia had not only a Slavic community that intended to remain in the country, but a lingering Soviet/ Russian military presence. By August 1994, after considerable international pressure, over 28,000 military personal had left Latvia (Galbreath 2005: 195–196). According to the Latvian Statistical Bureau, Russians constituted 28.3 per cent of the population in 2007, with smaller communities of Belarusians, Ukrainians, Poles and Lithuanians (see Table 10.1).

Table 10.2 shows the percentage of Russians in the country's cities and regions in 2007. Daugavpils, Rezekne, and Riga, the capital, are the cities with

Table 10.1 Key indicators for Latvia

Total population (millions)[a]	2.3 (2006)
Urban population (% of total)[a]	67.9 (2006)
GDP per capita, PPP (US$)[a]	15,878 (2006)
Unemployment rate (%)[b]	10.4 (2004)
Ethnic composition (2007)[c]	Latvians: 59.0%
	Russians: 28.3%
	Belarusians: 3.7%
	Ukrainians: 2.5%
	Poles: 2.4%
	Lithuanians: 1.4%
	Jews: 0.5%
	Roma: 0.4%
	Other: 1.8%

Sources: a World Bank 2007; b UNICEF 2007; c Latvian Statistical Bureau 2007a.

Notes
PPP: purchasing power parity; unemployment rate is based on registered unemployment as a percentage of 15–59 year olds; GDP per capita is given in current international US$.

Table 10.2 Percentage of Russians in Latvia's cities and regions in 2007

Cities	%	Regions	%
Daugavpils	53.3	Latgale	39.6
Rezekne	48.5	Pieriga	20.1
Riga	42.1	Zemgale	18.9
Jurmala	35.9	Kurzeme	15.7
Liepaja	32.9	Vidzeme	10.2
Ventspils	29.8		
Jelgava	29.6		

Source: Latvian Statistical Bureau 2007b.

the largest share of ethnic Russians. Among the country's regions, Riga and Latgale have the highest ratio of Russians. In Latgale region, a traditional Russian community has existed for hundreds of years, and the region is also notable for having a rural Russian community, whereas in the rest of the country Russians tend to be urban dwellers.

With such a large proportion of Russians and Russian-speakers (most Ukrainians and Belarusians use Russian as a native language) in Latvia, the first post-Soviet governments were keen to strengthen the state's independence, as well as to overcome the consequences of Soviet policies of Russification. Prompted by fears of post-Soviet Russian imperial ambitions and of becoming a minority within their own state, Latvian politicians instituted a restorationist policy of nation-building. The restorationist logic was an extension of the claim that Latvia had been illegally occupied by the Soviet Union, and thus still existed despite having lost its sovereignty for nearly 60 years. The restorationist logic affected Latvian politics and political institutions extensively, since it reinstalled the 1922 constitution and pre-war citizenship.

All residents who had hereditary links to Latvian citizens before the Second World War automatically received citizenship, while other residents now needed to pass a language and civic history examination before becoming citizens. In the early stages of independence, there was considerable overlap between ethnicity and the citizen/non-citizen divide. This divide was reinforced by the new language policy, which strengthened the position of Latvian as the sole state language at the expense of Russian, which had been the *lingua franca* in the Soviet Union, but was gradually reduced to the status of a minority language in Latvia.

The state also began a policy of promoting bilingualism among Russian-speakers, a policy reinforced in the minority school curriculum (see Galbreath and Galvin 2005; Silova 2006; Hogan-Brun 2006). In 1998, the Latvian parliament passed an education law calling for Latvian to become the primary language of instruction in all state-funded secondary schools. In 2003 this law was amended and since then minority language schools follow a 60:40 proportional split between Latvian and the minority language.[1]

Impact of Western conditionality

The international community was an active participant in shaping Latvian minority policy throughout the 1990s and early 2000s, focusing largely, but not exclusively, on legislation and policy pertaining to citizenship and language. Much of this involvement, in the form of official visits, monitoring reports, evaluations of draft legislation, and recommendations by officials from the United Nations (UN), the OSCE, the Council of Europe, the Council of the Baltic Sea States, the EU and others, has been well documented.[2]

International involvement began soon after the restoration of independence in 1991 and continued until Latvia's accession to the EU and the North Atlantic Treaty Organization (NATO) in 2004, after which it tapered off rapidly in both intensity and impact. While the OSCE and the Council of Europe played a prominent role in the early to mid 1990s, EU conditionality was critical in the latter part of the 1990s until accession. Membership in the Council of Europe was viewed by many both within Latvia and outside as a necessary intermediate station on the road to EU membership. At the same time, the OSCE High Commissioner on National Minorities (HCNM) served as a 'gate-keeper' to membership in the EU (Kemp 2001: 7) for Latvia and many other accession countries. The EU, for its part, frequently echoed and publicly supported the recommendations of the HCNM. In practice, representatives of all three organizations often worked side by side in joint expert groups, while officials coordinated public statements (Muižnieks and Brands Kehris 2003).

Conditionality was a critical part of this international involvement and operated primarily through the threat of non-membership, first in the Council of Europe, and then in the EU (and NATO). However, international involvement took other forms as well, such as providing funding for language training and social integration programmes, which was particularly relevant in the case of the United Nations Development Programme (UNDP) (Sīmane and Muižnieks 2005: 64–72) and the EU (Open Society Institute 2002: 319–321). At the same time, representatives of international and regional organizations frequently engaged in direct lobbying, provided advice on draft legislation, and attempted to persuade Latvian officials to liberalize minority policy.

It is clear that the threat of non-membership in the Council of Europe was absolutely critical in convincing the Latvian president to veto the initial version of a Law on Citizenship in 1994 which did not take into account the opinions of OSCE and Council of Europe experts. Thereafter, the desire to join the Council of Europe was critical in convincing Latvian lawmakers to adopt a revised law (Morris 2003: 5–6; Muižnieks and Brands Kehris 2003: 35–36; Dorodnova 2003: 34). At the same time, lawmakers ignored a number of recommendations made by the OSCE HCNM by opting for a more drawn-out naturalization schedule than he had suggested and by not granting citizenship automatically to all children born in Latvia. Here, as was often the case, the outcome represented what Dorodnova has termed a 'normative compromise' (2003: 41, 141).

As naturalization in subsequent years was quite slow, international organizations soon renewed pressure on Latvia to liberalize the Law on Citizenship. They focused on the need to rescind the naturalization timetable or 'windows', thereby allowing all eligible candidates to apply, and granting citizenship automatically to stateless children born in Latvia since independence. A key turning point was publication of the European Commission's Opinion on Latvia in July 1997, which included a number of recommendations to facilitate naturalization (European Commission 1997). While the Opinion did not call specifically for the law to be amended, EU officials, representatives of influential member states, and the OSCE all exerted intense pressure on Latvia over the following year to amend the law and its implementing regulations, threatening both directly and indirectly with non-admission to the EU (Muižnieks and Brands Kehris 2003: 39–42). While this conditionality prompted lawmakers to amend the law, parliamentary resistance was sufficiently strong to block promulgation of the amended law and to convoke a referendum. In October 1998, the electorate approved the liberalizing changes by a vote of 53 per cent in favour and 45 per cent against.

The international community invoked conditionality once again when Latvian parliamentarians sought to adopt a new law providing for extensive regulation of Latvian language use in both the public and the private sector in 1999. Representatives of the OSCE, the Council of Europe, and the European Commission coordinated their efforts at persuasion, arguing that human rights norms as well as EU standards required limited state intervention to prop up the state language and few, if any, restrictions on the use of minority languages. Persuasion was bolstered by the threat of non-membership in the EU, voiced by numerous foreign dignitaries and echoed by the president of Latvia, who argued that failure to follow OSCE recommendations could jeopardize Latvia's EU bid (Muižnieks and Brands Kehris 2003: 46). When the parliament ignored this and similar warnings and adopted a problematic law, the threats continued and the president vetoed the law in July 1999. Subsequently, after continued pressure and threats, the parliament adopted an amended law in December 1999 deemed by the HCNM to be 'essentially in conformity with Latvia's international obligations and commitments' (OSCE HCNM 1999). After a careful review of the involvement of the OSCE HCNM and his impact, Dorodnova concluded that 'political arguments linked to EU accession negotiations proved more effective than the reference to international human rights norms' (2003: 127).

There is a broad consensus among most scholars that the role of conditionality was quite significant in influencing Latvian minority policy. While Morris has stressed that 'Latvia's desire to join the EU has been crucial in the reform of citizenship legislation' (2003: 28), Galbreath argued that 'European institutions such as the OSCE, EU and the Council of Europe have had a significant influence over amendments to minority policy' (2006: 84). Elsuwege goes further and claims that

[t]he EU preaccession conditionality has – together with the efforts of other international organizations such the UN, the Council of Europe, NATO and

the OSCE – resulted in a number of amendments to laws on education, language and the status of non-citizens, efforts which can be praised as largely eliminating the possibility of ethnic violence.

(Elsuwege 2004: 54–55)

Muižnieks and Brands Kehris concur, concluding that 'conditionality related to EU membership was clearly essential in convincing Latvian politicians that concessions had to be made' (Muižnieks and Brands Kehris 2003: 50).

Analysts differ, however, over whether the impact of conditionality and the international minority rights regime was significant enough to be called 'successful'. Gelazis has termed conditionality in Estonia and Latvia a 'great success' (2003: 69), while Hughes has argued regarding both Estonia and Latvia that '[i]t is difficult to reconcile claims of successful international intervention with an outcome which has left some 700,000 persons stateless and without fundamental political and economic rights' (Hughes 2005: 752). While Dorodnova calls the impact of the HCNM on Latvian minority policy 'very significant' in terms of operational, normative and substantive effectiveness, she still judges the situation of Russian-speakers to be 'rather unsatisfactory' (Dorodnova 2003: 149–150). Muižnieks and Brands Kehris, finally, point out that 'sensitive legislation was liberalized in conformity with European standards' (Muižnieks and Brands Kehris 2003: 50), which was no mean feat.

Latvian minorities after enlargement

The state of Latvia's minorities has changed little since the country became an EU member in May 2004. There have been no wholescale changes in the state-minority relationship, nor has there been unrest in the same way that we have witnessed in Estonia in April 2007.[3] Latvia has only seen largely peaceful social protest over the education reforms described earlier that came into force in September 2004. While Latvia faces considerable challenges over its large Russian-speaking community, social integration in Latvia seems to be a long-term objective bolstered by EU membership.

Within the context of minorities in Central and Eastern Europe, Latvia, like its Baltic neighbours, does not fit easily into the minority rights scheme established in the introduction to this book. Unlike the traditional minorities in Bulgaria, Romania, Serbia, or Slovakia, most persons belonging to minorities in Latvia are relative newcomers, having arrived in the early Soviet period as part of a policy of colonization and industrialization. Thus, Latvia's situation can be more easily compared to that of France, Germany, and the United Kingdom with their recent immigrant populations, than with its Central and East European counterparts. This specific context of minorities in Latvia has had a large impact on minority policy, where successive governments have encouraged social integration, a half-way point between policies of assimilation and policies of autonomy. The following issue areas should be seen within this context.

Naturalization

In a referendum in 1998, Latvia rescinded the naturalization timetable or 'windows system' and permitted all who so desired to take naturalization exams. At the same time, the Latvian government established a 'social integration' project, which encouraged acquisition of Latvian as a second language among minorities and naturalization among those who arrived after the Second World War. As of December 2007, 12 years after the Latvian state began accepting citizenship applications, the Naturalization Board had received naturalization applications concerning 138,074 persons. Of these, 127,786 individuals, including 13,572 underage children, had been granted Latvian citizenship (see Figure 10.1).

As can be seen in Figure 10.1, the number of new citizens per year increased drastically after the changes in the citizenship law in 1998, which also came near the time when Latvia was named a forthcoming EU member state. The rate of naturalization initially peaked in 2000, which is likely due to an initial drive by non-citizens to gain what would become EU citizenship and also falls in the initial phase of the previously mentioned social integration project (see Zepa 2001). Naturalization numbers were lower between 2001 and 2004, rose again after Latvia became part of the EU, and declined dramatically in 2007.

It can be assumed that EU membership resulted in a new incentive to apply for citizenship. With enlargement came an opportunity for Latvian citizens to work abroad in those states that had opened their labour markets to new EU members; initially Ireland, Sweden, and the United Kingdom. Non-citizens did not have this automatic right to work abroad. The resulting restriction on the mobility of non-citizens suited the Latvian state and fit within the logic of the social integration project. Labour mobility acted as an incentive to naturalize,

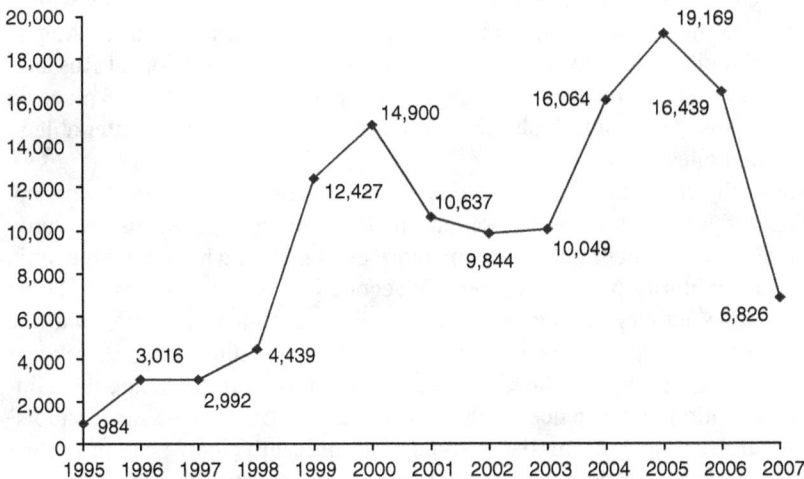

Figure 10.1 Naturalization in Latvia, 1995–2007 (source: data available from the Naturalization Board of the Republic of Latvia).

while at the same time requiring applicants to learn the Latvian language sufficiently to pass the language part of the naturalization examination.

In 2007, there were only 6,826 naturalizations. Apparently, those who were already inclined to become citizens likely did so shortly before and after enlargement. In addition, since January 2007 the labour markets of many EU member states have been opened to Latvia's non-citizens, eliminating a powerful economic incentive for naturalization. This leaves a large number of non-citizens who may never wish to naturalize. However, several factors also work in the opposite direction. For example, previously, an important disincentive for many young non-citizen males to naturalize was the requirement to do obligatory military service. As of 2006, Latvia has shifted to a professional military, which could affect the naturalization calculus of some. Currently, a discussion is under way within the government and the parliament that the citizenship law should be amended to allow for easier dual citizenship for children of labour migrants born abroad. If the law is amended, certain other liberalizing changes are also likely. Overall, though, non-citizens remain very passive and alienated, which suggests the need for caution in predictions about their future behaviour. In 2007, 362,902 of the ethnic Russians in the country were citizens of Latvia, 278,213 were non-citizens, and 22,115 were citizens of Russia (Naturalization Board of the Republic of Latvia 2008).

Education reform

In 1998 the Latvian parliament passed a new education law that called for a transition to a primarily Latvian language curriculum in all state-funded schools. If Latvian was already being taught in state-funded schools, why was there a perceived need to make it the dominant language in the curriculum of minority children? The answer lies primarily in the amendments to the citizenship law which, among other things, allowed non-citizen parents of children born after August 1991 to claim citizenship for their children. For the next generation of Russian-speakers, the battle for social and linguistic integration would take place in Latvia's schools. At no other point in their lives would the state be better able to achieve social integration.

The minority community's response to education reform was slow to develop. While the education law was adopted in 1998, organized opposition only occurred after the October 2002 parliamentary elections, in which the three main left-wing pro-minority parties received the second highest share of votes. These were the now defunct 'People's Harmony Party', 'Equal Rights', and the 'Latvian Socialist Party'. Opposition peaked in 2003 and 2004, when there were weekend protests in parks in the city centre of Riga, as well as outside the Ministry for Education and Science, with banners saying 'SOS: Save our Schools' and 'Latvian-Russian not Russian-Latvian'. Significantly, however, protesters did not demand to end the teaching of Latvian in minority schools. When the reforms were implemented at the beginning of the new school year in September 2004, protesters answered with rallies, sit-ins, walkouts and other protest methods, but the opposition quickly lost ground as the school year progressed and then disappeared completely.

Non-discrimination

Many Russian activists in Latvia, the government of the Russian Federation, and some Western observers have claimed that the Latvian government has discriminated against minorities. This section examines perceptions of discrimination, complaints, court cases, and the legal framework for combating discrimination.

Throughout the 1990s, the results of sociological surveys suggested that Russian-speakers expected similar treatment compared to ethnic Latvians from employers and service providers in the spheres of police, health, housing, and social security (Rose 1995: 39–40, 1997: 36–37, 2000: 46–47). More recently, the National Human Rights Office (NHRO), a government body charged with reviewing complaints and promoting human rights, has commissioned surveys on human rights and more general perceptions of discrimination. When asked in 2006 whether they had experienced human rights violations or discrimination over the previous three years, 13 per cent of non-Latvians answered in the affirmative, as compared to 9 per cent of Latvians. This marks a considerable improvement from a previous survey in 2000, when the corresponding figures were 31 per cent for non-Latvians and 18 per cent for Latvians (Baltijas Sociālo Zinātņu institūts [Baltic Institute for Social Science] 2006: 29).

In recent years, very few persons have gone to court or filed discrimination complaints to the NHRO (or, since its establishment in 2007, to the Ombudsman institution) or other agencies. In 2005, for example, the NHRO received five written complaints on racial or ethnic discrimination, one on linguistic discrimination, and gave 16 oral consultations (Valsts Cilvēktiesību birojs [NHRO] 2006: 62). In 2006, in the first court case of ethnic discrimination, the court awarded compensation to a Roma woman who was denied employment on account of her ethnicity (European Union Agency for Fundamental Rights 2007: 28). Regarding incidents of harassment, the most common victims have been Roma and visually different minorities, such as blacks and Asians (Lukumiete 2005: 13).

Much international attention has been devoted to two alleged categories of discrimination: differences in rights between citizens and non-citizens and various language requirements. While differences in political rights between citizens and non-citizens have not evoked much criticism, the same is not true for restrictions in private sector employment. Only citizens have been able to practice as attorneys, notaries, notary assistants, heads of detective agencies, and security guard managers (Mitrofanovs *et al.* 2006: 79–83). The government has claimed that these restrictions are reasonable and justified, as attorneys and notaries are inextricably tied to the judiciary, while managing detectives and security guards can impinge on public safety. However, both the UN Human Rights Committee and the Parliamentary Assembly of the Council of Europe have expressed concern and called on Latvia to review these requirements (Human Rights Committee 2003; Parliamentary Assembly of the Council of Europe 2006).

Another area in which Latvia has been accused of discrimination has been in language policy, where there is often limited international case law and the point at which language requirements become discriminatory is unclear. When Ingrida Podkolzina, a plaintiff from Latvia, challenged the language requirement for standing for public office before the European Court of Human Rights, the Court found in 2002 that 'requirements of that kind pursued a legitimate aim', although the plaintiff's procedural rights had been violated (European Court of Human Rights 2002). The Latvian authorities subsequently rescinded the language requirements for political reasons linked to Latvia's bid to join the EU and NATO. In the following years, Latvia's Constitutional Court ruled that certain language restrictions were discriminatory. The first case, in 2003, concerned a law restricting the use of languages other than Latvian in private radio and TV broadcasting. The second case, in 2005, concerned a law that allowed the state to subsidize only those private schools with Latvian as the language of instruction (Latvijas Republikas Satversmes Tiesa [Constitutional Court of the Republic of Latvia] 2003; Latvijas Republikas Satversmes Tiesa 2005).

Whereas Latvia is likely to face further legal challenges to certain language requirements in the public and private sector, the most immediate legal difficulties are connected with European Commission infringement procedures against Latvia for incomplete transposition of the Race Equality Directive. As the European Union Agency for Fundamental Rights recently noted, 'Malta and Latvia have been very slow in adopting the necessary legislation in compliance with the directive' (European Union Agency for Fundamental Rights 2007: 20).

Impact of the Framework Convention

Latvia had signed the Council of Europe's Framework Convention for the Protection of National Minorities (FCNM) already in 1995, but did not ratify it for more than ten years, despite repeated appeals by international and regional organizations and periodic efforts by the parliamentary opposition. Doubts about the compatibility of Latvian language legislation with the FCNM, as well as disagreements about a minority definition, long hindered ratification.

However, on 26 May 2005, Latvia finally ratified the FCNM, mainly due to a different domestic constellation and the realization that the convention leaves states a large measure of discretion. Latvia defined national minorities as:

> citizens of Latvia who differ from Latvians in terms of their culture, religion or language, who have traditionally lived in Latvia for generations and consider themselves to belong to the State and society of Latvia, who wish to preserve and develop their culture, religion or language. Persons who are not citizens of Latvia or another State but who permanently and legally reside in the Republic of Latvia, who do not belong to a national minority within the meaning of the Framework Convention for the Protection of National Minorities as defined in this declaration, but who identify themselves with a national minority that meets the definition contained in this

declaration, shall enjoy the rights prescribed in the Framework Convention, unless specific exceptions are prescribed by law.

(Council of Europe 2007)

While this minority definition denies non-citizens the symbolic gratification of recognition as minorities, it does extend them the protection of the FCNM. Latvia also attached declarations to two substantive articles of the FCNM, a step few countries have taken. Latvia declared that it would apply the provisions of Article 10, paragraph 2 (regarding the use of minority languages before local authorities) and Article 11, paragraph 2 (regarding minority language signs) 'without prejudice to the Satversme (Constitution) of the Republic of Latvia and the legislative acts governing the use of the State language that are currently into force' (Council of Europe 2007). While the Parliamentary Assembly of the Council of Europe has not criticized the minority definition, it has urged Latvia to consider withdrawing the two other declarations (Parliamentary Assembly of the Council of Europe 2006). Latvia submitted its first State Report in October 2006, but at the time of writing (October 2007), the Advisory Committee had not yet published its opinion on Latvia, which makes it difficult to make a more nuanced assessment of the impact of the Framework Convention.

Since ratification, no laws or regulations have been amended to implement the FCNM. However, several, more subtle, changes have taken place. According to the authors' interviews with responsible officials in the Secretariat of the Special Assignments Minister for Social Integration Affairs, ratification helped them to lobby successfully for additional government funds to be allocated for national minority NGOs, which increased from 98,694 Latvian Lats (€140,988)

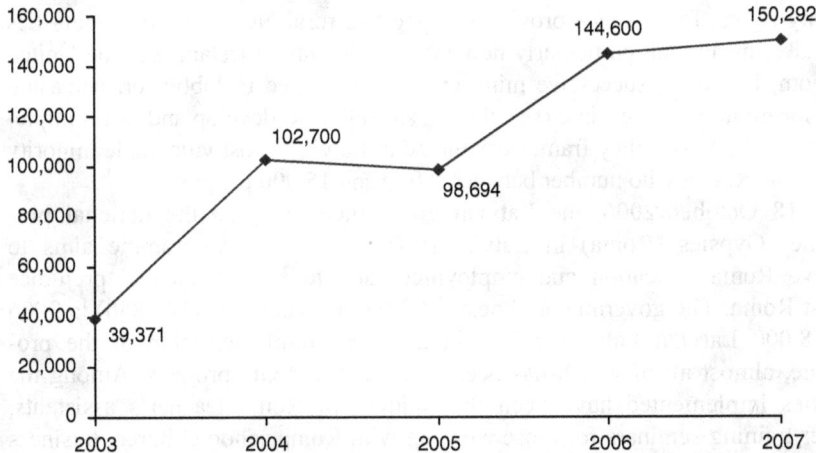

Figure 10.2 Government subsidies to national minority NGOs allocated by the Secretariat of the Special Assignments Minister for Social Integration Affairs, 2003–07 (in Latvian Lats) (source: Secretariat of the Special Assignments Minister for Social Integration Affairs, personal communication, 2007).

in 2005 to 150,292 Latvian Lats (€214,700) in 2007 (see Figure 10.2). After ratification, the secretariat also organized a number of awareness-raising seminars for minorities, state and municipal officials, and created a new dialogue mechanism – a 'participation council' – with representatives of minority groups nominated by NGOs themselves.

The Integration Ministry

In order to gauge the prospects for minority rights in Latvia, it is useful to examine the work of the Secretariat of the Special Assignments Minister for Social Integration Affairs, which holds primary responsibility for implementing minority rights. The secretariat was created immediately after the 2002 elections and has acquired the following functions:

* coordination of social integration policy;
* promoting national minority protection;
* combating racial discrimination;
* promoting the rights of Latvia's indigenous people (the *Livs*);
* promoting the development of civil society;
* supporting Latvians abroad.

The focus of the secretariat's work has evolved over time, depending on the priorities of the office holder and the overall political situation in the country. The first minister (2002–04) developed the office from scratch, helped to contain the unrest surrounding opposition to minority education reform, and sought to promote the registration of non-citizen children through a direct mail campaign (Government of Latvia 2006: 61). Subsequent ministers have often focused on issues other than minority rights, for instance providing support to rural NGOs or developing ties with Latvians abroad, particularly new labour migrants in Ireland and the United Kingdom. However, successive ministers have managed to lobby for increasing funds for minorities over time (see above), as well as to develop and begin implementation of a new policy framework aimed at Latvia's most vulnerable minority group – the Roma, who number between 9,000 and 15,000 people.

On 18 October 2006, the Latvian government adopted the national programme 'Gypsies (Roma) in Latvia, 2007–2009'. The programme aims to improve Roma education and employment and to reduce societal prejudice against Roma. The government allocated 30,000 Latvian Lats (€42,850) in 2006 and 18,000 Latvian Lats (€25,715) in 2007 for implementation of the programme, almost all of which has been dedicated to NGO projects. Among the activities implemented have been the training of Roma teacher's assistants, teacher training seminars for those working with Roma schoolchildren, business training seminars for Roma women, and various anti-discrimination and awareness raising events for the public and local officials (Government of Latvia 2006: 29–30; Īpašu uzdevumu ministra sabiedrības integrācijas lietās sekretariāts [Special Assignment Minister for Social Integration Affairs Secretariat] 2007).

While the staff and the budget of the secretariat have expanded considerably since its creation, its effectiveness has been hampered by several factors. Minority policy remains controversial and there is no consensus among the political elite on many important minority issues. Moreover, frequent changes in the governing coalition have led to instability and four different ministers occupied the post between 2002 and 2007. While a secretariat is essentially the same as a ministry and Special Assignments Ministers are full cabinet ministers, secretariats are ostensibly set up to address specific issues within a limited time period. The long-term fate of the office remains therefore uncertain.

Conclusions

Although Western conditionality had a significant impact on Latvian minority policy prior to EU accession, this external influence has waned in recent years, as political mechanisms have given way to legal battles over minority rights. Unresolved issues include the needs of a large non-citizen population, the transposition of the EU Race Equality Directive, and legal challenges to various restrictions on minority languages. The European Court of Human Rights and the Latvian Constitutional Court have ruled on a number of cases impinging on minority rights, primarily on issues dealing with language use. The problematic manner in which Latvia ratified the Framework Convention for the Protection of National Minorities is likely to result in an intense dialogue between Latvia and the Advisory Committee. While challenges remain, minority policy has become increasingly institutionalized and funding for the preservation and development of minority cultures has increased.

Notes

1 Minority language schools include Russian, Ukrainian and Belarusian, as well as other smaller language groups.
2 For collections of documents by international institutions on Latvian minority policy, the best sources are Birckenbach (1997) and two electronic libraries, one from Minority Electronic Resources www.minelres.lv/count/latvia.htm (accessed 6 October 2007), the other from the European Centre for Minority Issues www.ecmi.de/emap/download/Latvia_OSCE-HCNM_2005–04.pdf (accessed 6 October 2007).
3 See *Postimees*, 'Politsei on seoses vandalismiaktidega kontrollinud 500 isikut', 27 April 2007.

References

Baltijas Sociālo Zinātņu Institūts (2006) *Pētījums par Cilvēktiesībām Latvijā: Grafiku atskaite*, Riga: BSZI. [Baltic Institute for Social Science (2006) *Research on Human Rights in Latvia: A Report in Graphics*, Riga: BISS.]
Birckenbach, H.-M. (1997) *Preventive Diplomacy through Fact-Finding: How International Organizations Review the Conflict over Citizenship in Estonia and Latvia*, Hamburg: LitVerlag.
Council of Europe (2007) *Country specific information*, Strasbourg: Council of Europe.

148 *D.J. Galbreath and N. Muižnieks*

Online, available at: www.coe.int/t/e/human_rights/minorities/Country_specific_ eng. asp#P428_22391 (accessed 6 October 2007).

Dorodnova, J. (2003) *Challenging Ethnic Democracy: Implementation of the Recommendations of the OSCE High Commissioner on National Minorities to Latvia, 1993–2001*, Centre for OSCE Research Working Paper 10. Hamburg: Centre for OSCE Research.

Elsuwege, P. (2004) 'Russian-Speaking Minorities in Estonia and Latvia: Problems of Integration on the Threshold of the EU', *ECMI Working paper*, No. 20, April.

European Commission (1997) *Agenda 2000 – Commission Opinion on Latvia's Application for Membership in the European Union*, Brussels: European Commission.

European Court of Human Rights (2002) *Chamber Judgement in the case of Podkolzina v. Latvia. 9.4.2002, press release*. Online, available at: www.echr.coe.int/eng/ Press/2002/apr/PR%20Podkolzina%2009042002E.htm (accessed 6 October 2007).

European Union Agency for Fundamental Rights (2007) *Report on Racism and Xenophobia in the Member States of the EU*, Vienna: European Union Agency for Fundamental Rights.

Galbreath, D.J. (2005) *Nation-Building and Minority Politics in Post-Socialist States: Interests, Influence and Identities in Estonia and Latvia*, Stuttgart: Ibidem Verlag.

—— (2006) 'European Integration through Democratic Conditionality: Latvia in the context of minority rights', *Journal of Contemporary European Studies* 14 (1): 69–87.

Galbreath, D.J. and Galvin, M.E. (2005) 'The Titularization of Latvian Secondary Schools: the Historical Legacy of Soviet Policy Implementation', *Journal of Baltic Studies* 36 (4): 449–466.

Gelazis, N.M. (2003) 'The Effects of Conditionality on Citizenship Policies and the Protection of National Minorities in the Baltic States' in V. Pettai and J. Zielonka (eds.) *The Road to the European Union: Estonia, Latvia and Lithuania*, Manchester: Manchester University Press.

Government of Latvia (2006) *Report submitted by Latvia Pursuant to Article 25, Paragraph 1 of the Framework Convention for the Protection of National Minorities. Strasbourg, 11 October 2006. ACFC/SR (2006)001*, Strasbourg: Council of Europe.

Hogan-Brun, G. (2006) 'At the Interface of Language Ideology and Practice: The Public Discourse Surrounding the 2004 Education Reform in Latvia', *Language Policy* 5 (2): 69–73.

Hughes, J. (2005) ' "Exit" in Deeply Divided Societies: Regimes of Discrimination in Estonia and Latvia and the Potential for Russophone Migration', *Journal of Common Market Studies*, 43 (4): 739–762.

Human Rights Committee (2003) *Concluding Observations of the Human Rights Committee: Latvia 06/11/2003 CCPR/CO/79/LVA*, Geneva: Office of the High Commissioner for Human Rights.

Īpašu uzdevumu ministra sabiedrības integrācijas lietās sekretariāts (2007) Informatīvais ziņojums par valsts programmas 'Čigāni (romi) Latvijā' 2007–2009. gadam īstenošanu Riga: ĪUMSILS. [Special Assignment Minister for Social Integration Affairs Secretariat (2007) *Information Report on the Implementation of the State Programme 'Gypsies (Roma) in Latvia' 2007–2009*, Riga: SAMSIAS].

Jubulis, M.A. (1996) 'The External Dimension of Democratization in Latvia: The Impact of European Institutions', *International Relations* 13 (3): 59–73.

Kemp, W.A. (2001) *Quiet Diplomacy in Action: The OSCE High Commissioner on National Minorities*, The Hague: Kluwer Law International.

Kolstø, P. (1995) *Russians in the former Soviet Republics*, London: Hurst.

Latvian Statistical Bureau (2007a) *Resident population by ethnicity at the beginning of the year*, Riga: Latvian Statistical Bureau. Online, available at: http:// data.csb.gov.lv/ Dialog/varval.asp?ma=04–17a&ti=4%2D17%2E+RESIDENT+ POPULATION+BY+ ETHNICITY+AT+THE+BEGINNING+OF+THE+YEAR+++&path=../DATABA-SEEN/Iedzsoc/Annual%20statistical%20data/04.%20Population/&lang=1 (accessed 4 October 2007).

—— (2007b) *Resident population by ethnicity and by region, city and district at the beginning of the year*, Riga: Latvian Statistical Bureau. Online, available at: http://data. csb.gov.lv/Dialog/varval.asp?ma=04–19a&ti=4%2D19% 2E+RESIDENT+POPULAT ION+BY+ETHNICITY+AND+BY+REGION%2C+CITY+AND+DISTRICT+AT+T HE+BEGINNING+OF+THE+YEAR+++&path=../DATABASEEN/Iedzsoc/ Annual%20statistical%20data/04.%20Population/&lang=1 (accessed 4 October 2007).

Latvijas Republikas Satversmes Tiesa (2003) *Spriedums Latvijas Republikas vārdā: Rīgā 2003.gada 5.jūnijā Lietā Nr.2003–02–0106*, Riga: Latvijas Republikas Satversmes Tiesa. [Constitutional Court of the Republic of Latvia (2003) *Judgement in the name of the Latvian Republic: Riga, 5 June 2003,Case No. 2003–02–0106*, Riga: Constitutional Court of the Republic of Latvia.]

—— (2005) *Spriedums Latvijas Republikas vārdā Rīgā 2005. gada 14. septembrī Lietā Nr. 2005–02–0106*, Riga: Latvijas Republikas Satversmes Tiesa. [Constitutional Court of the Republic of Latvia (2005) *Judgement in the name of the Latvian Republic: Riga, 14 September 2005, Case Nr. 20032005–02–0106*, Riga: Constitutional Court of the Republic of Latvia.]

Lukumiete, D. (2005) *Racism in Latvia: ENAR Shadow Report 2005*, Brussels: European Network Against Racism. Online, available at: www.enar-eu.org/en/ national/latvia/ Latvia_2005.pdf (accessed 6 October 2007).

Mitrofanovs, M., Gamalejevs, A., Jolikins, V., Buzjevs, V., Dimitrovs, A., Ždanoka, T. (2006) *The Last Prisoners of the Cold War: The Stateless People of Latvia in their own Words*, Riga: Averti-R Ltd.

Morris, H.M. (2003) 'EU Enlargement and Latvian Citizenship Policy', Journal on Ethnopolitics and Minority Issues in Europe, 1.

Muižnieks, N. and Brands Kehris, I. (2003) 'The European Union, democratization, and minorities in Latvia', in P.J. Kubicek (ed.) *The European Union and Democratization*, London: Routledge, 30–55.

Naturalization Board of the Republic of Latvia (2008) *Statistics on naturalization*, Riga: Naturalization Board of the Republic of Latvia. Online, available at: www.np.gov.lv/ index.php?en=fakti_en&saite=statistic.htm (accessed 23 February 2008).

Open Society Institute (2002) *Monitoring the EU Accession Process: Minority Protection, Volume I, An Assessment of Selected Policies in Candidate States*, Budapest: Open Society Institute.

OSCE HCNM (1999) *High Commissioner Welcomes State Language Law in Latvia, press statement*, The Hague: OSCE HCNM, 9 December 1999. Online, available at: www.am.gov.lv/en/policy/4641/4642/4656/ (accessed 6 October 2007).

Parliamentary Assembly of the Council of Europe (2006) *Resolution 1527 (2006) Rights of National Minorities in Latvia*, Strasbourg: PACE.

Rose, R. (1995) *New Baltic Barometer II: A Survey Study*, Studies in Public Policy No. 251, Glasgow: University of Strathclyde.

—— (1997) *New Baltic Barometer III: A Survey Study*, Studies in Public Policy No. 284, Glasgow: University of Strathclyde.

—— (2000) *New Baltic Barometer IV: A Survey Study*, Studies in Public Policy No. 338, Glasgow: University of Strathclyde.

Silova, I. (2006) *From Sites of Occupation to Symbols of Multiculturalism: Re-conceptualizing Minority Education in Post-soviet Latvia*, Greenwich, CT: Information Age Publishing.

Sīmane, M. and Muižnieks, N. (eds.) (2005) *UNDP Latvia 1992–2005: Easing the Transition*, Riga: UNDP.

Smith, G. (1996) *The Baltic States: The National Self-determination of Estonia, Latvia, and Lithuania*, St. Martin's Press: New York.

Tesser, L.M. (2003) 'The Geopolitics of Tolerance: Minority Rights under EU Expansion in East-Central Europe', *East European Politics and Societies* 17 (3): 483–532.

UNICEF (2007) TransMONEE database.

Valsts Cilvēktiesību birojs (2006) *Valsts Cilvēktiesību biroja 2005. gada ziņojums*, Riga: Valsts Cilvēktiesību birojs. [National Human Rights Office (2006) *National Human Rights Office 2005 report*, Riga: National Human Rights Office.]

World Bank (2007) World Development Indicators database.

Zepa, B. (2001) *Towards a Civil Society – 2000*, Riga: Baltic Institute of Social Sciences.

11 Lithuania

Progressive legislation without popular support

Dovile Budryte and Vilana Pilinkaite-Sotirovic

Introduction

During the late 1980s and early 1990s, Lithuania developed a minority rights regime which offers cultural rights to traditional minorities. Most important policy decisions regarding the minority rights regime took place before Lithuania applied for European Union (EU) membership and the EU did not play a decisive role in this process. Lithuania's minority rights legislation, however, did not produce the cultural change necessary for the successful implementation of minority rights. Preserving the dominant ethnic identity (which is still perceived as endangered) remains one of the priorities in Lithuania's social and political life.

In contrast to the other Baltic states (Estonia and Latvia), Lithuania is one of the more ethnically homogenous post-Soviet states. According to the 2001 census, 6.74 per cent of Lithuania's residents identified themselves as Polish, 6.31 per cent as Russian, 1.23 per cent as Belarusian, and 1.2 per cent as Jewish (see Table 11.1). Approximately 2,571 (or 0.07 per cent of respondents)

Map 11.1 Lithuania (source: http://maps.mygeo.info/maps_eu_it.html – accessed 13 December, 2007).

Table 11.1 Key indicators for Lithuania

Total population (millions)[a]	3.4 (2006)
Urban population (% of total)[a]	66.6 (2006)
GDP per capita, PPP (US$)[a]	16,221 (2006)
Unemployment rate (%)[b]	8.3 (2005)
Ethnic composition (2001 census)[c]	Lithuanian: 83.4%
	Polish: 6.7%
	Russian: 6.3%
	Belarusian: 1.2%
	Jewish: 1.2%

Sources: a World Bank 2007; b UNICEF 2007; c Department of Statistics 2001.

Notes
PPP: purchasing power parity; unemployment rate is based on registered unemployment as a percentage of 15–59 year olds; GDP per capita is given in current international US$.

identified themselves as Roma, although the exact number may be slightly different (Department of Statistics 2001; Vaitiekus 1998: 14). In general, the ethnic self-identifications in the census correspond with the language spoken at home.

The country has a 'unipolar ethnic structure' (Bangura 2006: v) in which the Lithuanian majority is dominant, although this characteristic does not apply to south-eastern Lithuania which has a significant number of ethnic Poles and ethnic Russians. It is not surprising, therefore, that questions about minority rights and ethnic relations have been especially pertinent in that part of the country. In south-eastern Lithuania, half of the population is Lithuanian and a third Polish. Ethnic Poles constitute a majority (79 per cent) in the region of Salcininkai (10.4 per cent of the population there is Lithuanian and 5 per cent Russian) and the region around the capital, Vilnius (which comprises 61.3 per cent Poles, 22.4 per cent Lithuanians, and 8.4 per cent Russians). The town Visaginas is a unique place in so far as a nuclear power plant was built there in the 1970s that attracted a large number of labour migrants from all over the Soviet Union. As a result, Lithuanians constitute a minority in Visaginas (15 per cent) (Department of Statistics 2001).

Given the troubled history of the country, many ethnic Lithuanians still perceive their native language as endangered. As Timothy Snyder points out, 'the Lithuanian language had not been considered a language of politics for centuries' (Snyder 2003: 32). During the nineteenth century, in some peasant families (traditionally considered the 'core' of the Lithuanian nation), grandparents spoke Lithuanian, parents Belarusian, and children Polish (Snyder 2003: 32). Consequently, starting with the nineteenth century, when Polish- and Russian-speaking Lithuanian elites started to build the Lithuanian nation, they saw the need to 'strengthen' the Lithuanian language and 'defend' it from the influences of the Polish and Russian languages.

This perceived need to strengthen the Lithuanian language and ethnic identity continues to be an important variable in ethnic relations. Even the Soviet Lithuanian elites (the Lithuanian Communist party functionaries) felt that it was their 'duty' to 'Lithuanize' south-eastern Lithuania. In 1950, Mecislovas Gedvilas and Justas Paleckis, the Lithuanian Communist party leaders, suggested teaching Lithuanian instead of Polish in addition to Russian in the area. They argued that ethnic Poles in eastern Lithuania were in fact 'Polonized' Lithuanians and Belarusians. Similar attempts at 'Lithuanization' were disapproved by Moscow as nationalist, and Lithuania's Poles were able to preserve their right to speak and learn their language during the Soviet period (Kalnius 1998: 47). The Polish minority is currently Lithuania's most politically active and vocal minority, interested in preserving its cultural rights.

The Polish minority is remembered in Lithuania for the opposition by some of its members to the 1989 Language Law declaring Lithuanian the only state language. Although the law assured ethnic minorities residing in Lithuania that their constitutional rights would not be abridged and promised state support for the teaching of minority languages, due to the 'Lithuanization' campaigns in the 1950s, it prompted anxiety among the Polish minority in south-eastern Lithuania. In the late 1980s and early 1990s, the government made several attempts to 'appease' politically active members of the Polish minority in south-eastern Lithuania by extending cultural autonomy.

Arguably, the political activism of Lithuania's Polish minority strengthened the emerging minority rights regime in post-Soviet Lithuania. This regime offers limited cultural rights for traditional minorities (such as government support for education of ethnic minorities and language rights), but, by and large, cannot do much to address racism and intolerance towards 'new' minorities, such as the Chechens. Lithuania's minority rights regime is rooted in the Soviet nationalities policy which, despite several attempts at Russification, favoured Lithuania's 'titular nation' and allowed limited cultural rights to the two largest minority groups, ethnic Poles and ethnic Russians. Overall, the current minority rights policies follow this pattern, although recent reports by Western intergovernmental organizations, in particular the EU, highlighted the problems experienced by Lithuania's Roma and Jews and attempted to reframe the minority rights regime to address other minority rights issues, such as anti-Semitism and ethnic discrimination.

The burgeoning literature on 'Europeanization' has identified several mechanisms of EU influence during the accession process, including 'legislative and institutional templates' (incorporation of EU laws and norms), financial aid and assistance, monitoring, and advice on how to incorporate norms and laws (Grabbe 2002). At the same time, some scholars have questioned the influence of EU norms and rules on minority rights regimes, both during the process of accession and after it. For example, Merje Kuus described the 'ritual of listening to the foreigners' during the process of Estonia's EU accession. According to her argument, the importance of local actors, especially their power to interpret or ignore international norms, should not be underestimated (Kuus 2004). Her case studies suggest that local actors, not international interventions, were the crucial variables influencing the development of minority rights regimes in Central and Eastern Europe.

Interestingly, when analysing the development of the minority rights regime in Lithuania, the local elites rarely mention the influence of international actors. Their focus is on historical roots of the 'post-colonial' mentality, which makes ethnic and racial tolerance difficult (Donskis 2005). In 2007, a study conducted by leading Lithuanian scholars pointed out that a civic understanding of the Lithuanian 'nation' was lacking, making it difficult to establish a culture of tolerance, which could support anti-discrimination measures recommended by the EU. The study argued that attempts at preserving an 'archaic' ethnic identity, which is still perceived as being threatened, created a 'passive political culture' and impeded the development of a robust political community (Adomenas *et al.* 2007: 429). These observations give rise to the question of whether a post-Soviet society is capable of creating a culture supporting progressive legislation protecting minority rights.

The minority rights regime adopted after independence from the Soviet Union (1991–present)

During the early years of independence, Lithuanian politicians felt that it was necessary to convince the international community that the country had opted for democracy and peaceful coexistence with its neighbours. Legislation supporting minority rights was supported by international actors (including minority kin-states) and was viewed by Lithuanian elites as a necessary condition for eventual membership in EU and NATO.

The most important pieces of legislation adopted during this period include the 1989 Law on Ethnic Minorities that recognized the rights of minorities to cherish and foster their cultural traditions, history and language; the 1989 Law on Citizenship that extended the citizenship of Lithuania to those residing in Lithuania in 1990; and the 1991 Law on Education that granted access to minority language education and schools for Russian and Polish minority groups. The constitution of Lithuania adopted in 1992 guarantees cultural minority rights and prohibits discrimination based on ethnicity. It allows Lithuania's ethnic minorities to foster their language, culture and customs, and grants minorities the right to administer independently from the state the affairs of their ethnic culture, education, organizations and charities. These legal provisions bind Lithuania's state to support the rights of ethnic minorities. In addition, they help to make sure that Lithuania's traditional ethnic minorities are loyal to their host state.

Lithuania's legal framework for protecting minority rights has received positive evaluations from international actors, including the European Commission in the late 1990s, the UN Human Rights Committee overseeing implementation of the International Covenant on Civil and Political Rights, and the Council of Europe Advisory Committee on the Framework Convention for the Protection of National Minorities. Although Lithuania was not invited to start accession negotiations with the European Union in 1997, the 1997 Commission Opinion described the situation of minorities in Lithuania as 'satisfactory' and referred to the 1991 Law on Citizenship as a 'major contribution', since it granted citizen-

ship to all persons resident in Lithuania. The Opinion further noted that Lithuania's minorities had the right to manage their cultural and educational affairs,
and that 14.6 per cent of schoolchildren attended state-supported schools in
which all subjects were taught in minority languages. The Opinion also noted
that Lithuania's minorities had the right to use their languages for 'official communication' in the areas where they were in the majority (European Commission
1997). Overall, the Opinion confirmed the minority rights model embraced by
the Lithuanian government. The monitoring reports in the following years,
before the country became an EU member in 2004, maintained that Lithuania's
ethnic communities had 'well-established rights'.

Although Lithuania's minority rights regime supports cultural minority rights,
its functioning is affected by a very important variable: the historical legacy of
'ethnic insecurity' among the Lithuanian majority. Since the early 1990s, two
trends have been shaping Lithuania's minority rights regime. On the one hand,
in order to continue to please the international community and to maintain good
ethnic relations, the Lithuanian government continued to create minority-friendly
laws and programmes (such as transposing EU anti-discrimination directives).
On the other hand, several important laws (such as the language law or the dual
citizenship law) were passed to strengthen the Lithuanian 'ethnic core'. A closer
analysis of recent debates surrounding the revised Law on Citizenship (2002)
and the fate of the 1989 Law on Ethnic Minorities illustrates this point.

In 1989 the Law on Citizenship established the so-called 'zero-option' for
acquiring citizenship. Virtually all permanent residents of the country who
sought Lithuanian citizenship were offered it, irrespective of their nationality,
duration of residence in the country and knowledge of the state language. Pre-
1940 citizens and their descendants (that is, those who lived in Lithuania before
it was occupied by the Soviet Union) were also offered Lithuanian citizenship,
without having to renounce their current citizenship.

The Law on Citizenship was amended several times, in 1991, 1993 and 1996.
These revisions made it easier to restore Lithuanian citizenship for citizens of
Lithuania prior to the Second World War and their descendants. The 1996 revision allowed persons of 'Lithuanian origin' (i.e. ethnic Lithuanians) to retain
their citizenship, even if they had become permanent residents of other states. A
new Law on Citizenship adopted in 2002 included a similar provision. Given its
distinction between (ethnic) 'Lithuanians' and 'non-Lithuanians', this law has
been debated in Lithuania and abroad. Lithuania's Jewish community and Polish
organizations expressed their concerns about the discriminatory character of the
law. It did not allow ethnic Jews, Poles, Russians, Belarusians and members of
other minorities to retain their Lithuanian citizenship if they had decided to
become citizens of other states.

International actors also expressed their dissatisfaction with the law. In 2005,
the Council of Europe European Commission against Racism and Intolerance
recommended that the Lithuanian authorities ensure that the provisions regulating Lithuanian citizenship did not discriminate on the grounds of race, colour,
language, religion and ethnic origin (ECRI 2006: 8). In the following year,

Lithuania's Constitutional Court ruled that the 2002 Law on Citizenship was unconstitutional, arguing that any provision or amendment on double citizenship could not be adopted unless the constitution was changed by popular referendum.

This ruling attracted the attention of Lithuanians living abroad, including those who emigrated soon after the Second World War, as well as more recent economic migrants. It is difficult to underestimate the influence of this group which comprises approximately one million ethnic Lithuanians living outside Lithuania, most of whom are interested in keeping their Lithuanian citizenship. Many argued that changing the 2002 Citizenship Law would greatly weaken the 'ethnic' Lithuanian nation (Marcinkevičius 2007).

Their arguments were taken up by the Conservative Party, which was at the time in opposition. In 2007, this political party proposed to amend the Law on Citizenship one more time, retaining the discriminatory provisions regarding dual citizenship for ethnic Lithuanians. The ruling social democrats decided to support their opponents in this matter. Proposals to organize a referendum on dual citizenship were denounced as a 'threat to Lithuania's sovereignty'. The actions of Lithuania's leading political parties in the debate on the Citizenship Law suggest that the preservation of the ethnic Lithuanian 'nation' is considered a national interest by both left- and right-wing political forces, irrespective of the principle of non-discrimination proclaimed in the Lithuanian constitution. Political parties representing ethnic minorities, such as the Electoral Action for Lithuania's Poles, an ethnopolitical party which has two seats in Lithuania's 141-member parliament, have only a negligible influence on matters such as the Citizenship Law.

At the same time, according to the 1989 Law on Ethnic Minorities, Lithuania allows ethnic minorities to 'develop their culture freely', to expect financial support from the government for their cultural and educational activities, including teaching the official state language in minority schools. Revisions to the Law on Ethnic Minorities were initiated twice, in 1997 and 2002.

In the second half of the 1990s, it was debated in Lithuania what constitutes an 'ethnic minority' and whose rights should be protected by the Lithuanian state. Consequently, a new definition of 'ethnic minorities' was drawn up. However, politically active members of ethnic minorities resisted these revisions, as they were concerned that the government was not genuinely interested in protecting the interests of ethnic communities.

In 2002, a new working group was formed to amend the law one more time. The Department of National Minorities and Lithuanians Living Abroad, a government agency created in 1999 to support minority rights and the integration of minorities, prepared a new draft of the Law on Ethnic Minorities. According to this draft, individuals could freely decide whether they wanted to be treated as members of ethnic minorities. However, minority representatives expressed their concern that they had not been consulted in the preparation of the bill. At the end of 2007, no agreement between politicians and administrators working on the law and representatives of minority groups had been reached as to what the final draft of the bill should look like. While the leading political parties have not shown any political will to speed up the process, the representatives of minority groups remain frustrated and seemingly unable to communicate effectively with government representatives charged with protecting their rights.

International organizations and local non-governmental organizations (NGOs) have pointed out the absence of politically strong institutions able to formulate and implement minority rights policies in Lithuania. The Department of National Minorities and Lithuanians Living Abroad continues to focus on the cultural activities of Lithuania's ethnic minorities. In the past, the Department tried to play a more active role in shaping Lithuania's minority rights regime. It proposed a minority policy strategy which incorporated the provisions of relevant international documents, such as the European Charter on Regional or Minority Languages and the UNESCO Convention against Discrimination. However, this initiative was ignored by the Lithuanian parliament, and the activities of the Department now focus again on cultural issues. Its current activities include the organization of Lithuanian language courses and support for cultural programmes pursued by ethnic minority groups. The number of individuals attending Lithuanian language courses and the number of cultural activities supported by the Department are used as ways to measure the 'integration' of ethnic minorities into Lithuanian society.

The nature of the activities pursued by the Department of National Minorities and Lithuanians Living Abroad points to a major flaw in the minority rights regime embraced by Lithuania. Extending limited cultural rights for traditional minorities may, in fact, redraw and re-enforce the boundaries between ethnic majority and ethnic minorities, creating an 'us' versus 'them' mentality. Furthermore, if minority rights are discussed only in terms of preserving the cultures and languages practiced by a small number of ethnic groups, then such a minority rights regime can do little to address ethnic intolerance and discrimination. Both issues are becoming more and more salient in Lithuanian society and politics.

Ethnic intolerance, responses from the Lithuanian government, and international interventions

Annual public opinion surveys conducted by human rights monitoring agencies and other organizations suggest that the Lithuanian society has become increasingly intolerant towards certain ethnic groups. The percentage of residents of Lithuania with anti-Roma attitudes increased from 59 per cent in 1990 to 75.4 per cent in 2006. Anti-Semitic attitudes increased from 18 per cent in 1990 to 25 per cent in 2006, and anti-Muslim attitudes from 34 per cent in 1990 to 58.2 per cent in 2006 (Table 11.2). In public opinion polls conducted in 2007, 68.7 per cent of respondents asserted that they were unwilling to live in the same neighbourhood with Roma, and 59.6 per cent of respondents were unwilling to live in the same neighbourhood with Muslims (Ethnic Research Centre 2007: 2). The latter finding is particularly interesting, as in the 2001 census only 0.08 per cent

Table 11.2 Ethnic groups towards which respondents expressed the most negative attitudes in opinion surveys (%)

	1990[a]	1999[a]	2005[a]	2006[b]
Roma	59	62	77	75.4
Muslims	34	31	51	58.2
Jews	18	21	31	25

Sources: a Leoncikas 2005: 7–21; b Ethnic Research Centre 2007.

of Lithuania's residents identified themselves as Muslims. Most of them are Lithuanian Tatars who are long-time residents of the country. The rise in anti-Muslim attitudes can be explained by the negative portrayal of Islam and of Muslims in the mass media after the terrorist attacks on the United States on 11 September 2001.

These results point to a particularly strong prejudice against the Roma. At least partially these attitudes are due to the way in which the Roma are portrayed by the mass media. There is a powerful stereotype linking the Roma to criminality, a stereotype often perpetuated by government officials. The actions of the Vilnius municipality in 2004 are a case in point. During this year, the municipality ordered the destruction of 'illegally' built houses inhabited by Roma residents in the Roma settlement in Kirtimai. The actions of the municipality were condemned by the Equal Opportunities Ombudsperson (an institution established in 1999 to protect human rights), the Ombudsman of the *Seimas* (the parliament), and the European Commission against Racism and Intolerance. On behalf of an individual whose house was destroyed, the Human Rights Monitoring Institute (a Lithuanian NGO) complained to the prosecutor's office of Vilnius district. Although the court acknowledged that the victim had experienced harm from the local government, as of 2007 the government officials responsible for the demolishing Roma houses had not been sanctioned.

Government actions against discrimination were prompted by the anti-discrimination directives issued by the EU. Responding to the Race Equality Directive, the Lithuanian authorities adopted the Law on Equal Opportunities in 2005 and expanded the mandate of the Ombudsperson for Equal Opportunities to cover all grounds of discrimination. According to Danguole Grigoloviciene, Adviser to the Ombudswoman for Equal Opportunities, in 2005 the Office of the Ombudsperson for Equal Opportunities received 18 complaints regarding racial or ethnic discrimination, 11 of which concerned members of the Roma community. 'The biggest resonance was caused by the demolition of Roma houses at the end of 2004. After thorough investigation we issued a warning to the mayor of Vilnius' (Delfi Report 2006b).

In 2006, 20 complaints were submitted to the Ombudsperson for Equal Opportunities. By and large, these complaints did not receive much attention from the authorities or the public. In 2007, the European Union Agency for Fundamental Rights criticized Lithuania for failing to adopt adequate measures in the fight against ethnic discrimination. It noted that, although Lithuania has created channels for victims of ethnic and racial discrimination to express their complaints, these complaints did not typically result in sanctions or compensation. Instead of using punitive measures, government institutions relied on ineffective 'recommendations' or moral pressure (ELTA Lithuanian News Agency 2007).

Lithuanian human rights experts have reached similar conclusions. They continue to criticize the incompetence of law enforcement officers when addressing cases involving anti-Semitism and racism. Such cases are classified by government authorities as 'hooliganism' or 'vandalism' and generally do not lead to prosecutions, despite the fact that Lithuania's criminal code prohibits incitements to hatred and violence against members of ethnic, religious, or sexual minorities. In 2004, Lithuania's courts started to investigate five cases related to incitement to hatred, a number decreasing to two cases in 2005, and increasing to 20 in 2006, with two sentences being passed in 2006. Apparently, international pressure from the UN Committee on the Elimination of Racial Discrimination and the European Commission against Racism and Intolerance made a difference. In 2006, recommendations of these two institutions were discussed in the office of the Prosecutor General, following which the Prosecutor General sent a letter to public prosecutors encouraging them to initiate proceedings even without formal complaints from victims of racial hatred. This explains the rise in the number of court cases in 2006 (Human Rights Monitoring Institute 2006; Ethnic Research Centre 2007: 11).

Adoption of the Law on Equal Opportunities was followed by the 'National Antidiscrimination Programme 2006–2008' which attempts to promote democracy based on ethnic diversity and non-discrimination. The programme was Lithuania's response to a call by the European Commission for national programmes promoting equal opportunities. Created and coordinated by the Lithuanian Ministry of Social Security and Labour, the Lithuanian programme stated that there was a pressing need for 'research, analysis and education for tolerance' (Lithuanian Ministry of Social Security and Labour 2007). Unfortunately, the initiative does not go beyond an evaluation of the situation. It fails to address the real issues related to ethnic intolerance and discrimination, such as the poverty experienced by ethnic minorities and discrimination in the marketplace. Similarly, the new 'Strategy of Development of Ethnic Minority Policies 2007–2015', approved by the government of Lithuania in October 2007, did not include any measures to reduce unemployment and social exclusion of ethnic minority groups, despite the fact that these issues were identified by the government as the main obstacles for the social integration of minorities (Government of Lithuania 2007a).

Recent sociological studies suggest that Lithuania's labour market is segregated along ethnic lines. Ethnic Lithuanians are more likely to be in the higher echelons of government and administration, while ethnic Poles and Russians are more likely to work as skilled or unskilled workers. Ethnic Poles and Russians report that they have to rely on their ethnic connections when looking for a job

(Kasatkina and Beresneviciute 2006: 43; Kasatkina and Leoncikas 2003: 106–108). These findings suggest the absence of equal opportunities in the labour market, but so far this issue has not received the attention of the Lithuanian government.

In 2006, the European Commission against Racism and Intolerance reported that in Lithuania cases of employment discrimination are 'extremely rare', due to 'progressive labour legislation' adopted following the EU directives on employment. However, the European Commission against Racism and Intolerance acknowledged that ethnic discrimination may be an explanation why different ethnic groups have different employment status (ECRI 2006: 8). According to 2003 data (in 2003 the Lithuanian Statistics Department discontinued the gathering of unemployment data based on ethnicity), the Roma community experienced some of the highest levels of unemployment. In the same year, 18.7 per cent of ethnic Russians were unemployed, compared to 11.7 per cent of ethnic Lithuanians (Poviliunas 2005: 5, 19).

The decision of the Lithuanian government to address the plight of the Roma was inspired by international actors and their willingness to cooperate with Lithuanian human rights NGOs. In 1997–98, the Lithuanian Human Rights Centre, in cooperation with the Lithuanian youth organization 'Transylvania' and a French ethnic minorities group, became engaged in a project sponsored by the Council of Europe. The goal of this project was to integrate ethnic minorities into Lithuanian society (Vaitiekus 1998: 9). The national government recognized the need to integrate Roma only in 2000, when it released the 'National Programme for the Integration of Roma into Lithuanian Society 2000–2004'. In practice, the focus of this programme was on preschool and artistic education of Roma children. The Lithuanian government seems to have launched this programme in the hope of joining the EU. The programme states that the 'desire of Lithuania to integrate faster into the European political, economic and security structures necessitates to make decisions regarding the social integration of Roma in a more timely fashion' (Government of Lithuania 2000).

The European Commission against Racism and Intolerance, the Open Society Fund Lithuania, and other organizations praised the efforts of the Lithuanian government to address the problems of the Roma, who are clearly the most marginalized group in society. However, the programme was not successful, as it had been prepared without effective consultation with the Roma community. The focus of the programme on artistic education did not meet the needs of the Roma community. In addition, the programme did not explicitly address the problem of discrimination which directly affects Roma in employment, housing, education, health and other spheres. Finally, as noted by international organizations, the Lithuanian government lacked the political will to take this programme seriously. According to the third report of the European Commission against Racism and Intolerance, published in 2006, the Lithuanian government did not provide sustainable funding for the measures outlined in the programme (ECRI 2006: 22–29). Furthermore, many initiatives developed very slowly. The Department of National Minorities and Lithuanians Living Abroad, which was made responsible to implement the programme, focused on offering Lithuanian language courses to members of the Roma minority and tried to help them to find employment. These strategies were not successful.

In 2006, the European Commission against Racism and Intolerance and the UN Committee on the Elimination of Racial Discrimination criticized the inadequate progress in addressing the problems experienced by Lithuania's Roma community. Both international organizations noted social problems: unemployment, place of residence, health care and education (ECRI 2006; CERD 2006).

Currently, Lithuania's politicians still lack the political will to come up with a strategy to address these issues. Only in 2007, responding to international pressure, did the Lithuanian government release another Roma 'integration' programme. At the end of 2007, the draft programme had not yet been approved by the government (Government of Lithuania 2007b; Savickaja 2007).

The new programme was released after public discussion of the 2006 report of the European Commission against Racism and Intolerance which was, as mentioned above, critical of Lithuania's ability to fight racism and anti-Semitism. The report also noted lack of awareness of discrimination in Lithuanian society. Henrikas Mickevicius, the Executive Director of the Human Rights Monitoring Institute, argued that 'it is essential to fully implement the provisions of the EU Race and Employment Directives of 2000 by creating a mechanism for the Roma population to obtain legal assistance' (Delfi 2006a). The discussions in Lithuania show how important local actors – human rights activists, defenders of minority rights and non-governmental organizations – are in interpreting and transferring international norms to a domestic context. These actors are able to link international norms to local 'traditions', making them legitimate. However, it is not easy to establish a convincing link between the traditional minority rights regime with its roots in the Soviet nationalities policy and the EU's anti-discrimination directives. Furthermore, human rights NGOs are relatively weak in post-Soviet Lithuania. Their internationalist agenda faces resistance not only from conservative political forces, but also from traditional minority communities.

Currently, there are approximately 300 ethnic minority NGOs registered in Lithuania. The main goal of their activities is to preserve the culture of ethnic minorities, protecting them from assimilation. At the same time, these NGOs promote networking based on belonging to the same ethnic group, creating an ethnically segmented civil society (Department of National Minorities and Lithuanians Living Abroad 2007). Even the Council of Ethnic Communities, which has an advisory role in the creation of ethnic policies in Lithuania, embraces cultural nationalism, hindering the development of cross-cultural civil society.

Resistance from traditional minorities to the EU anti-discrimination discourse is an unintended consequence of international involvement, which was meant to empower ethnic minorities. During a public discussion of the minority situation in Lithuania, organized by Laima Andrikiene, a member of the European Parliament, Vitalijus Karakorskis, Chairman of the Council of Ethnic Communities, argued that the interests of traditional ethnic minorities (ethnic Poles and ethnic Russians, among others) are often misrepresented, as because of the new EU directives, ethnic minorities are often discussed in the same context as gays or lesbians. 'We are rather conservative; we are interested in preserving traditions; thus, any association with the "other" minorities is unacceptable for us. Perhaps we should think about creating the position of an Ombudsman just for (traditional) ethnic minorities?', Karakorskis went on to express his scepticism regarding the EU's ability to cater to his community (Kilpys 2007).

This discourse raises an important question: are Lithuanians – the Lithuanian-speaking 'majority', traditional and 'non-traditional' (or, to be more precise, not readily accepted) minorities, and the government – willing to respond to international interventions and adopt effective strategies to combat intolerance? Prior to joining the EU, Lithuania's politicians were ready to go an extra mile to get into the Euro-Atlantic security space and to do whatever it takes to prove that their country belongs to the West. Currently, as an EU member, Lithuania has to comply with EU directives. However, EU member states are free to choose how the directives are implemented. In the case of minority rights, Lithuania's politicians have already realized that there is a lot of freedom for interpretation. Thus, some members of the Conservative Party in parliament argued against amendments to the Law on Equal Opportunities guaranteeing equal social and economic rights to sexual minorities. They argued that Lithuania is a 'unique' Catholic country and therefore should not be obliged to blindly follow 'unclear' EU directives (Parliament of Lithuania 2007).

The 2005 Law on Equal Opportunities and the 1999 Law on Equal Opportunities for Women and Men were adopted to prevent discrimination, and to at least partially comply with EU directives. The Ombudsperson of the Office of Equal Opportunities monitors the implementation of these laws. However, so far, not all regulations set out in EU anti-discrimination directives have been incorporated into Lithuania's legal system. In 2007, to better comply with the directives, the Ministry of Social Affairs and Labour proposed amendments to the Law on Equal Opportunities and the Law on Equal Opportunities for Women and Men. When presented with the proposed amendments, parliamentarians did not object to amending the Law on Equal Opportunities for Women and Men to make it fully compliant with EU directives. However, there was a lot of resistance to amending the Law on Equal Opportunities, because the amendments included references to sexual orientation. Apparently, the majority of Lithuania's parliamentarians were opposed to legislating equal rights for gays and lesbians. The bill with the proposed amendments was returned to the Ministry of Social Affairs and Labour, and it is unclear what will happen with it in the future (Parliament of Lithuania 2007).

This example illustrates the limits of the EU's influence on domestic minority rights regimes. International interventions can do little to overcome the sources of resistance to international norms, which, in this case, stem from the country's conservative social culture. In the early 1990s, led by the desire to return to the 'West', the Lithuanian political elite supported relatively progressive legislation which guaranteed support for minority rights. However, they were not able to develop proper implementation mechanisms. So far, the Lithuanian government has not been able or interested to create effective and fair sanctions for those who violate anti-discrimination norms. In addition, local human rights NGOs are not allowed to represent the victims of discrimination in court. Despite their obvious weaknesses, local human rights NGOs are probably the most enthusiastic supporters of international interventions aimed at fighting discrimination and promoting minority rights. Lithuanian NGOs, such as the Human Rights Monitoring Institute, are engaged in numerous activities fighting discrimination, such as 'shaming' campaigns, lobbying the government to adopt minority-friendly laws, or carefully monitoring legislation. Implementation of the EU's anti-discrimination directives may depend on the strength of civil society and its ability to transform the resistant conservative social culture.

Conclusions

Several conclusions can be drawn from the development of Lithuania's minority rights regime. First, our case study suggests that domestic variables (historical experiences and the orientation of Lithuania's elites during the late 1980s and early 1990s) were more important than international interventions in shaping Lithuania's minority rights regime. At the same time, international interventions in general and the EU's anti-discrimination directives in particular did matter, especially regarding the status of Lithuania's Roma's minority. Not only did the EU and other international actors increase the awareness about the despicable social conditions and outright discrimination experienced by the Roma in Lithuania, there is evidence suggesting that the 'National Programme for the Integration of Roma in Lithuanian Society 2000–2004' was created in direct response to international influences.

However, the power of international actors, including the EU, to influence the development of Lithuania's minority rights regime is limited. As the process of amending the Law on Equal Opportunities suggests, it is difficult to integrate EU norms into the national legal system if there is no social culture supporting such norms. Our case study suggests that there are domestic actors (for example human rights NGOs and the Lithuanian Ministry of Social Affairs and Labour) interested in transmitting the norms of ethnic and racial tolerance promoted by the EU and the Council of Europe. However, these domestic actors do not have enough power to re-shape the existing minority rights regime with its roots in the Soviet nationalities policy. This regime favours the so-called 'traditional' minorities (ethnic Poles and ethnic Russians, among others) and does not open avenues for the cultural change needed to support progressive legislation related to minority rights. Such a change can be expected if Lithuania's nascent civil society becomes stronger. In this case, anti-discrimination measures and genuine support for minority rights will become more than a polite ritual of 'listening to the foreigners'.

References

Adomenas, M., Augustinaitis, A., Janeliunas, T., Kuolys, D. and Motieka, E. (2007) *Lietuviu Tauta: Bukle ir raidos perspektyvos [The Lithuanian nation: its current status and its future]*, Vilnius: Versus Aureus.

Bangura, Y. (ed.) (2006) *Ethnic Inequalities and Public Sector Governance*, Houndmills: Palgrave MacMillan.

CERD (2006) *Concluding observations of the Committee on the Elimination of Racial Discrimination: Lithuania*, Geneva: Committee on the Elimination of Racial Discrimination.

Delfi (2006a) 'Human Rights Monitoring Institute introduces the latest report of the European Commission Against Racism and Intolerance (ECRI)', 24 February 2006. Online, available at: http://search.delfi.lt/cache.php?id= 96AD6E0B4E22B7C4&m=txt (accessed 6 December 2007).

—— (2006b) 'HRMI urges to take seriously the rising level of intolerance in Lithuanian society', 21 June 2006. Online, available at: http://search.delfi.lt/cache.php?id= 96AD6E0B4E22B7C4&m=txt (accessed 6 December 2007).

Department of National Minorities and Lithuanians Living Abroad (2007) Internet site. Online, available at: www.tmid.lt/index.php?page_id=308 (accessed 30 November 2007).

Department of Statistics (2001) *Data of the 2001 population census*, Vilnius: Department of Statistics.

Donskis, L. (2005) 'Pokolonijines samones grimasos [Expressions of post-colonial consciousness]', *Politika*, 20 June 2005. Online, available at: www.politika.lt/index. php?cid=9299&new_id=4558 (accessed 6 December 2007).

ECRI (2006) *Third report on Lithuania*, Strasbourg: European Commission against Racism and Intolerance. Online, available at: www.coe.int/t/e/human_rights/ ecri/1-ECRI/2-Country-by-country_approach/Lithuania/Lithuania_CBC_3.asp (accessed 6 December 2007).

ELTA Lithuanian News Agency (2007) 'Lietuvai – ES kritika del kovos su etnine diskriminacija [Lithuania is criticized by the EU because of racial discrimination]', 28 August 2007.

Ethnic Research Centre (2007) *Visuomenes nuomones apklausos rezultatai [Public opinion poll data]*. Online, available at: www.ces.lt/downloads/structure/files/ ETC%20 2007%2002%2005–19%20apklausa.pdf (accessed 6 December 2007).

European Commission (1997) Agenda 2000 – Commission Opinion on Lithuania's Application for Membership of the European Union, Brussels: European Commission. Online, available at: http://ec.europa.eu/enlargement/archives/ pdf/dwn/opinions/lithuania/li-op_en.pdf (accessed 13 December 2007).

Grabbe, H. (2002) 'Europeanization Goes East: Power and Uncertainty in the EU Accession Process', paper presented at the ECPR Joint Sessions of Workshops, Turin, 22–27 March 2002. Online, available at: www.cer.org.uk/pdf/grabbe_ ECPR.pdf (accessed 6 December 2007).

Government of Lithuania (2000) *Decision of the Government of Lithuania No. 759, 1 July 2000 on the Programme of Roma Integration into Lithuanian Society 2001–2004*. Online, available at: www.tmid.lt/images/default/source/attachments/ RIILVP_2000–2004.pdf (accessed 6 December 2007).

—— (2007a) *Decision No. 1132, 17 October 2007, on Approval of the Strategy of Development of Ethnic Minority Policies*. Online, available at: www.tmid.lt/ images/default/source/attachments/TMPPS_2015.pdf (accessed 6 December 2007).

—— (2007b) *Draft Programme on Roma Integration into Lithuanian Society 2007–2010*. Online, available at: www.tmid.lt//images/default/source/attachments/ Romu%20integracijos%20i%20Lietuvos%20visuomene%202007–2010%20metu%20programa.pdf (accessed 6 December 2007).

Human Rights Monitoring Institute (2006) *Zmogaus teisiu igyvendinimas Lietuvoje 2005 metu apzvalga [Implementation of human rights in Lithuania in 2005]*. Online, available at: www.hrmi.lt/images/img/Zmogaus_teises2006–2007_ maketas.pdf (accessed 6 December 2007).

Kalnius, P. (1998) *Etniniai Procesai Rytu Lietuvoje XX amziaus II-ojoje puseje [Ethnic processes in eastern Lithuania during the second half of the twentieth century]*, Vilnius: Zara.

Kasatkina, N. and Leoncikas, T. (2003) *Lietuvos etniniu grupiu adaptacija: kontekstas ir eiga [Adaptation of ethnic groups in Lithuania: Its context and process]*, Vilnius: Eugrimas.

Kilpys, V. (2007) 'Vilniuje diskutuota apie tautiniu mazumu padeti Lietuvoje [The situation of ethnic minorities in Lithuania discussed in Vilnius]', 1 June 2007. Online, available at: www.bernardinai.lt/index.php?url=articles/63088 (accessed 5 December 2007).

Kuus, M. (2004) '"Those Goody Goody Estonians": Toward Rethinking Security in the European Union Candidate States', *Society and Space*, 22: 191–207.

Leoncikas, T. (2005) 'Tolerancija visuomeneje: tyrimu duomenys [Public tolerance: research findings]' in: Zmogaus Teisiu Centras [Human Rights Monitoring Centre] *Tautiniu mazumu teises [Ethnic minority rights]*, Vilnius: Zmogaus Teisiu Centras.

Lithuanian Ministry of Social Security and Labour (2007) *2007-ieji paskelbti Europos lygiu galimybiu visiems metais [2007 was Designated as the Year for Equal Opportunities in Europe for Everyone]*. Online, available at: www.socmin.lt/ index.php?-1310876980 (accessed 6 December 2007).

Marcinkevičius, R. (2007) 'Dviguba pilietybe pastumetu antrajam sajudziui [Dual citizenship may lead to a second independence movement]', Portalas lrt.lt, 18 April 2007, Online, available at: www.ivaizdis.lt/res_zinpr_det.php?id=14456 (accessed 5 December 2007).

Parliament of Lithuania (2007) *Minutes of the sixth (327) parliamentary session, 18 September 2007*. Online, available at: http://www3.lrs.lt/pls/inter3/dokpaieska.showdoc_l?p_id=304466 (accessed 29 December 2007).

Poviliunas, A. (2005) *Regional and Local Implementation of NAP/inclusion: Lithuania, Third Report 2005*. Online, available at: http://ec.europa.eu/employment_social/social_inclusion/docs/4lt_report_en.pdf (accessed 6 December 2007).

Savickaja, G. (2007) telephone interview with the authors, 27 November 2007, Head of the Integration programme division at the Department of National Minorities and Lithuanians Living Abroad, Vilnius.

Snyder, T. (2003) *The Reconstruction of Nations: Poland, Ukraine, Belarus 1569–1999*, New Haven and London: Yale University Press.

UNICEF (2007) *TransMONEE database*, 2007 version.

Vaitiekus, S. (1998) *Cigonai [Gypsies]*, Vilnius: Tyto Alba.

World Bank (2007) *World Development Indicators*, Online database.

12 Poland

Minority policies in a homogenized state

Peter Vermeersch

Introduction

On 30 April 2004, one day before the official date of the eastward enlargement of the European Union (EU), the county governor of Strzelecki county in south-eastern Poland (*Opolskie voivodship*) ordered the removal of the Polish national emblem, a white silhouette of an eagle on a red background, from its usual place above the entrance door of the county house in the city of Strzelce Opolskie. He replaced it with a regional blue-yellow coat of arms bearing the name of Strzelecki county in two languages: Polish and German.

Was this a political statement? Or was it merely a badly timed but essentially innocent revision of local heraldic traditions? The responses were mixed. Although the move hardly created a big sensation in the Polish media, it was mentioned in several country-wide newspapers and some local politicians from across the political spectrum were severely alarmed.[1] In the view of the latter, the county governor, who had been appointed by a district council controlled by the German minority party, had meant to point out that the enlargement of the

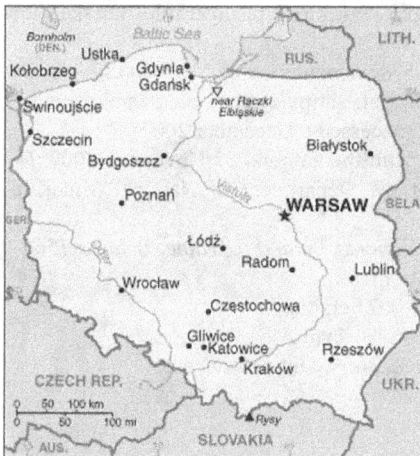

Map 12.1 Poland (source: http://maps.mygeo.info/maps_eu_pl.html – accessed 3 November, 2007).

Table 12.1 Key indicators for Poland

Total population (millions)[a]	38.1 (2006)
Urban population (% of total)[a]	62.2 (2006)
GDP per capita, PPP (US$)[a]	15,444 (2006)
Unemployment rate (%)[b]	18.5 (2005)
Ethnic composition (2002 census)[c]	Poles: 99.3%
	Germans: 0.4%
	Belarusians: 0.13%
	Ukrainians: 0.08%
	Roma: 0.03%
	Other: 0.06%

Sources: a World Bank 2007; b UNICEF 2007; c Główny Urząd Statystyczny 2003.

Notes
PPP: purchasing power parity; unemployment rate is based on registered unemployment as a percentage of 15–59 year olds; GDP per capita is given in current international US$.

EU had made it perfectly acceptable for minorities in Poland to distance themselves from the national symbols of the state in which they lived. Several of these indignant politicians argued that this case exemplified the high levels of latent national disloyalty among minority groups in Poland. Less than a week later, the county governor himself repudiated this interpretation before the press and apologized for what he claimed had simply been the mistake of the workers charged with the renovation of the building. German minority activists, in turn, were quick to condemn what had happened and emphasized that they had nothing to do with the failings of an otherwise good local public servant.

The event was trivial by many standards, and the fact that some politicians were so agitated over the matter seems puzzling. To be sure, there is a relatively large group of German minority citizens in Strzelecki county, as is the case in the entire Opolskie voivodship – according to the 2002 census, of the 152,897 self-declared Germans in the whole of Poland (including those without Polish citizenship) 71 per cent live in this voivodship (Adamczuk and Łodziński 2006: 105) and they are well represented in the local government structure (Cordell and Wolff 2005: 271). Some mainstream Polish politicians have been afraid that this group would form an even stronger linguistically defined political force in this region. Seen from a different angle, however, there seems little reason why Polish mainstream parties should fear political competition or claims for autonomy from German minority politicians. In proportion to the entire Polish population, the German minority is tiny (less than 0.4 per cent according to the census and only slightly over 1 per cent according to the most generous estimates), and the economy in Opolskie voivodship is to a great extent dependent on the rest of Poland. Moreover, the region is peaceful, and nobody anticipates growing tension between language groups: for many of the Polish-speaking inhabitants of Strzelce Opolskie, concern over the incident of the temporary removal of the Polish eagle, if it could be called an incident, evaporated quickly.

The story, however, did not disappear so quickly from the political scene. In the weeks following 30 April 2004, the news of what had happened continued to be of great concern to a number of politicians in Warsaw, who referred to it during parliamentary debates and used it in order to substantiate their demands for a fundamental change in the draft law about minority protection, which was at that point being discussed (Dziadul 2003). The draft law proposed to allow the official use of a minority language as a supplementary language in municipal institutions, if at least 8 per cent of the local population would be registered as belonging to a national minority. Alleging that the 8 per cent quota would threaten national loyalty in areas where large groups of minorities live, parliamentarians in the Sejm first proposed to raise this quota to 20 per cent and then to 50 per cent, which, had this quota been adopted, would have given such language rights to minorities only in five municipalities (Łodziński 2005: 162–173). The 50 per cent threshold was rejected by the senate, and in the final Law on National and Ethnic Minorities and Regional Language, adopted in January 2005 (and now also known as the Minorities Law), the quota remained at 20 per cent.[2] The discussion on quota, fuelled in part by media stories about instances of alleged national disloyalty among minority groups, prolonged what had already been a very long legislative process. Although the first proposals for a law on minority protection had been tabled in the beginning of the 1990s, Poland adopted the final law and officially recognized 13 minorities[3] only after the country had already become a member of the EU.

The above story raises a number of important questions. Why could small events, like the one in Strzelce Opolskie, turn parliamentarians cautious and concerned about a minority law that even in its most liberal form would only grant limited privileges to a relative small population? How can it be that in a country where there is not much ethnic diversity, and where, according to the 2002 census, the total number of national minorities is only slightly higher than 1 per cent of the population, mainstream politicians fear that a law to protect minorities would harm national unity? And why did it take so long for Poland to draft and adopt minority rights legislation even though minority protection was a requirement for EU accession?

In order to answer these questions, I will discuss three factors that have contributed to the complicated and uneven development of minority policies in Poland over the last decade and a half: first, the legacies of the Second World War and communism; second, the complicacy of current minority activism in Poland, which is in part a consequence of the different ways in which actors have tried to come to terms with history; and third, the EU's restrained evaluation of Poland's progress in the field of minority protection in the period before enlargement, as well as the role of other international actors.

Legacies: minority issues before 1989

To gain a certain sense of the historical controversy that has surrounded discussions on minority protection in Poland, it is useful to have a look at the results of the latest census. This census was held in 2002 and was of important symbolic significance because it allowed citizens, for the first time since the census of 1921, to indicate their ethnic nationality (*narodowość*). Some of the outcomes, however, were more than slightly puzzling. For example, while 3.26 per cent of the respondents (1,246,400 people) had indicated that they were not ethnically Polish, only 471,500 people (1.23 per cent of all respondents) gave an exact indication (i.e. a name accepted by the authorities) of the non-Polish ethnic group under which they wanted to be grouped. Moreover, both minority activists and academic experts agreed that for practically each minority the results were surprisingly low. Different reasons were mentioned. Roma activists argued, for example, that Roma had been suspicious of official registration because of traumatic experiences with government policies in the past. The Ukrainian activists argued that the result was inaccurate because Ukrainians have been secretive about their 'real' ethnic identity ever since the large-scale relocation and assimilation campaigns shortly after the Second World War. German activists, in turn, argued that many people who in daily life would consider themselves to be 'German' had wrongly registered as 'Silesians', a regional designation that perhaps sounded more neutral (173,153 people had registered as 'Silesians'). The latter result was doubly problematic because the Polish authorities did not consider the 'Silesians' to be a national minority. Kashubian activists, on the other hand, faced a different problem: although Kashubian activists vigorously lobbied to have the Kashubian language recognized and protected as a separate language, they did not want to be seen as an ethnic or a national minority. Such discussions increased the level of confusion regarding the extent of ethnic diversity in Poland, a fact that is perhaps most clearly illustrated by the discrepancy between the 2002 census figures and earlier estimates made by government officials and minority activists (Table 12.2).

Table 12.2 Size of minorities in Poland

Official minority categories	2002 census results[a]	2002 government estimates[b]	Estimates by minority organizations[c]
German	147,094	300,000–500,000	250,000–300,000
Belarusian	47,640	200,000–300,000	300,000–400,000
Ukrainian	27,172	200,000–300,000	250,000–300,000
Roma	12,731	20,000–30,000	30,000
Russian	3,244	10,000–15,000	–
Łemko	5,850	60,000–70,000	–
Lithuanian	5,639	20,000–25,000	25,000–30,000
Slovak	1,710	10,000–20,000	20,000–25,000
Jews	1,055	8,000–10,000	6,000–10,000
Armenians	262	5,000–8,000	–
Czech	386	2,000–3,000	–
Tatar	495	5,000	–
Karaites	45	200	–

Sources: a Official census results are taken from Główny Urząd Statystyczny (General Office of Government Statistics) (2003). The figures in this table only include census respondents with Polish citizenship. b Government estimates are cited from Poland's report submitted to the Council of Europe in 2002 (Government of Poland 2002); c Estimates by minority organizations are taken from Łodziński (2006: 189).

Minority activists have been sensitive about the census results, not only because they have realized that the official outcomes may decide in part on subsidies and other state benefits. Their concern has also been related to an acute awareness of the historical circumstances that have influenced current political decisions on minority issues. In particular, minority activists who have sought to achieve recognition (and sometimes compensation) for past injustices have argued that census results are an important tool for making their claims heard. This is especially so, they have argued, since mainstream Polish politicians are usually unwilling to listen to minority claims for their own particular historical reasons: they have often relied on historical narratives about the fragile position of Poland between large forces to justify their suspicion about the presence of minority populations (especially Russians and Germans) within the country. In response to the dominant narrative about the Polish nation as a victim of history, minority activists have sought to point out the fragility of the position of minorities in Poland. For that exact reason, issues of recognition are so important to them, and discussions about the past play a crucial role in the politics of the present.

Jewish–Polish relations in Poland today, for example, are not solely about the current political and social situation of the small Jewish minority but also, and perhaps even more, about issues of responsibility with regard to the role of Polish authorities and ordinary citizens during the Holocaust and in the post-war period. Unsurprisingly, Jewish minority leaders in Poland today demand protective measures and financial support for their culture, not only because they seek to maintain their position as a minority in the current political and social context, but also because they demand official recognition of and compensation for the past injustices inflicted on them or their families (see e.g. Gross 2001). Such reconciliation-seeking processes had been as good as impossible before the 1990s, because communist times had known their own instances of state-directed anti-Semitism.

For other ethnic minorities, too, the communist period has left a strong imprint on their current political action, a fact that is in part caused by the communists' strategies to maintain power. From the very beginning of the one-party rule, the Polish communists were active in constructing the idea that they had been the architects of the Polish national state. In reality, post-war rulers in Poland merely tried to benefit from a changed international environment and acted in accordance with the way the post-war European map had been redrawn as the result of a geopolitical decision by Churchill, Roosevelt and Stalin.

Polish ethnic homogeneity could also more easily be imagined in a greatly altered demographic context: not only had large parts of the Jewish and Roma populations been murdered during the Holocaust, after the war the Soviet Union also introduced a policy of national relocation, forcing about 780,000 Polish-speaking individuals from Soviet Ukraine to move to Poland. As a result of the Potsdam Conference, about three million Germans were removed from the new Polish territories in the West, leaving relatively small groups of Germans who were either allowed to stay as skilled workers in the indigent mining and metallurgical industries or who were seen as 'Germanized Poles' (Madajczyk 1998).

The Polish post-war rulers themselves actively helped the process of cultural, linguistic and ethnic homogenization of the new Polish state through actions of 'repolonization' (for example, while at first education in German was allowed under strict circumstances, later, in the 1960s, any use of German was illegal) and large-scale expulsion and forced resettlement operations. Belarusian, Łemko and Ukrainian populations were removed from the eastern parts of the new Poland and deported to areas outside the new borders. Up to 500,000 people were relocated from Poland to Ukraine in the period from September 1944 to June 1946. Moreover, in 1947, a large-scale forced resettlement operation replaced approximately 140,000 people identified as Ukrainians from the south-eastern border zone to the north and west of Poland, in order to assimilate them into the Polish-speaking population (*Ackja Wisła* or 'Operation Vistula').

In the post-war period, Polish communists tried to garner political support by building something that could be called 'ethnic communism' (see e.g. Snyder 2003: 202–214; Zaremba 2001). Although some communist minority policies may have looked minority-friendly on paper, especially when they included state support for minority organizations, in reality, they did not guarantee much genuine protection, nor did they prevent discrimination. The state-supported cultural organizations for minorities were often exclusively allowed to sustain folkloristic versions of their minority culture (a fact that may have further induced stereotypical perceptions of these groups), and simply served the state as control institutions.

Legal developments, policies and institutions after 1989: one law for very different demands

At the end of the 1980s, the time the party-state began to lose power, there was growing political debate in Poland about the rights of minority populations and about what policies and legal frameworks needed to be implemented in order to protect those rights sufficiently. For a large part, although not exclusively, the debate took place in the parliamentary commission on national and ethnic minorities (*Komisja Mniejszości Narodowych i Etnicznych*) of the Polish lower house, the Sejm, a commission already established in 1989. The long political discussion on the draft law for minority rights did not so much revolve around legal provisions to forbid discrimination, but on the forms of affirmative action that it envisaged. In May 2002, the government refused to adopt the draft law, although it admitted that the legal proposal was a legitimate response to Poland's ratification of the Council of Europe's Framework Convention for the Protection of National Minorities. According to the government, the proposal contained a number of fundamental problems. It was feared, for instance, that minority education would reinforce the isolation of minority pupils. Furthermore, there appeared to be no clarity on the circumstances that mandated a municipality to introduce special protection measures for the public use of minority languages. Most importantly, however, politicians from various political parties were totally abhorrent of the idea of offering language rights to minorities, because, as one of them argued, the Polish language was simply a crucial 'national value' (quoted in Łodziński 2005: 174). As one journalist observed, discussions on the Minorities Law provoked lawmakers to use 'xenophobic and nationalist rhetoric' (Kość 2004).

Meanwhile, government institutions had been created to implement and monitor government policies relating to the protection of minorities. In 1997, an Interdepartmental Group for National Minority Issues (*Międzyresortowy zespół do spraw mniejszości narodowych*) was established within the government administration. In 2000, the government founded the Division of National Minorities (*Wydział mniejszości narodowych*) at the Ministry of Interior and Administration. The Interdepartmental Group for National Minority Issues has included representatives of various governmental departments. Although it has not included minority representatives, it has organized dialogues and information sessions with prominent activists and representatives of officially recognized minority organizations. The Division of National Minorities, on the other hand, is a purely ministerial body aimed at raising the government's activities in the field of minority protection, without opening official meetings to minority activists. In 2005, when the new Minorities Law was adopted, the government also set up a Joint Commission of the Government and National and Ethnic Minorities (*Komisja Wspólna Rządu i Mniejszości Narodowych i Etnicznych*), which was designed to function as the main advisory body to the government on minority issues and includes minority representatives.[4] In terms of the taxonomy set out in the introductory chapter of this book, Poland now provides for limited cultural rights for traditional minorities.

Outside of this state framework, political participation of minority citizens was guaranteed through various legal provisions relating to elections to the Sejm. These provisions ensure easier procedures for minority parties to register and a lower electoral threshold. As a result, the German minority party has in recent years been represented in the Sejm by two parliamentarians, something that would not have been possible without these special provisions. Other minorities, however, found it more difficult to secure political representation (Łodziński 2005: 209–210).

Despite developments at the level of government institutions and electoral representation, minority rights protection in such fields as culture, education and language continued to be a topic of political discussion and controversy for about 15 years, before it resulted in a law that applied only to a very small proportion of the population. The reasons for such a prolonged discussion were not only related to the difficulty that politicians had with seeing the Polish nation as being ethnically diverse, but also with the technicalities of how a national or an ethnic minority should be defined and how minority entitlements should be delineated. Some of the delay was also related to the lack of political will among certain parties to push this law through; some parliamentarians found that there was no need for an extra law since, so they argued, minorities were already sufficiently protected by other laws.

Furthermore, the long discussion on the modalities of minority protection in Poland also revealed the very different agendas, concerns and demands of the different minority spokespersons. On par with the controversy among main-stream politicians, there was disagreement among minority activists about the usefulness of a special law, or at least a law in the form as it was discussed, dealing specifically with cultural entitlements such as language protection. For the Ukrainian minority activists, for example, the discussion on thresholds for allowing a minority language to be a supplementary language of communication at the level of the commune (*gmina*) was pointless. Whether the threshold was set at 50 per cent, 20 per cent or 8 per cent, for the Ukrainians it did not make much of a difference, as they had been dispersed and assimilated in the past. The number of people who could potentially register as belonging to the Ukrainian minority was nowhere higher than 20 per cent. Instead of demanding a change in the proposed law, Ukrainian minority activists pointed towards other issues and matters specific to their case, in order to show that their problems were different from those of other minorities, had to be treated differently, and justified the introduction of additional measures. They argued that even general minority regulations would have a disproportionate effect on the Ukrainians because of the consequences of policies in the past, such as Operation Vistula. Instead of focusing on general minority regulations, Ukrainian activists sought to achieve a discussion on the possibility of tailor-made measures for 'their' group (Vermeersch 2007). These were mainly issues related to past injustices: claims for the restitution of property that once had belonged to Ukrainian organizations, compensation for the people (and the families of the people) who had been imprisoned in the labour camp site in Jaworzno (a former Nazi concentration camp that from 1947 to 1949 was used by the Polish authorities as a detention camp for Ukrainians suspected of cooperation with the Ukrainian Insurgent Army, the UPA), and symbolic deeds of reconciliation, such as an official apology for Operation Vistula.

Another group of activists who were ambivalent about the value of the Minorities Law were those representing the Roma. Although the Roma have been officially recognized as an ethnic minority and were therefore considered to be protected by the Minorities Law, Roma activists frequently expressed concern about needs other than those for increased protection of the language and culture of their group; they demanded, among other things, material support for housing, measures on poverty alleviation, and anti-discrimination. In August 2003, the Polish government responded with a specific programme, a long-term policy aimed at addressing the socio-economic problems facing the Roma community.

Assessing the role of EU institutions and other international actors

Although some political parties framed EU conditionality as an infringement on Polish sovereignty, many minority activists could use references to Poland's EU membership aspirations when lobbying for policy changes. EU leverage can be considered a relatively important factor instigating domestic political interest in the development of domestic minority protection in Poland. Through the 1993 Copenhagen criteria, the EU provided politicians and activists a powerful tool for pressuring acceding countries into making minority protection a political priority.

Although the minority protection criterion was to some extent a vague and paradoxical element in the EU's membership conditionality strategy, among other things because its lack of a foundation in EU law (Sasse 2006), it did persuade acceding countries like Poland to adopt a number of international legal documents such as the Council of Europe's Framework Convention for the Protection of National Minorities and the European Charter for Regional or Minority Languages. Poland signed and ratified both documents before 2004. Indeed, since the European Commission had referred to the importance of the Framework Convention already in 1997, it can be speculated that Poland adopted it 'in time' in order to strengthen its reputation on minority protection issues vis-à-vis the European Commission. The domestic consequences were quite tangible and went beyond the issue of reputation. Politicians and activists who sought to advance the work on the new Polish law on minorities could now frame Poland's legislative work as a moral obligation springing from being a party to these international documents.

The EU's attempts to influence may have been tangible; in the case of Poland, they were largely rather low-key. This may have been due to the small size of the country's minorities and the fact that the potential for ethnic violence was considered to be minimal. In the 1999 progress report, the European Commission simply stated that '[i]n Poland, the respect for and protection of minorities continues to be assured' (European Commission 1999: 17). Subsequent reports, however, were sometimes more critical, especially when they pointed out the problems facing the Roma as an area of special concern.

The rather sudden reference to the Roma in the Commission's reporting can be read as evidence for the fact that the Commission in some particular areas sought to have more influence than in others. The attempt to make a difference in the area of policies towards the Roma turned out to be quite effective. Polish policy-makers most probably became concerned about the plight of the Polish Roma exactly because of the European Commission's growing concerns about the situation of that group, not only in Poland but also in other accession countries. As mentioned above, in 2003 Poland adopted a programme for Roma integration. Although there is no hard evidence that this programme was established as a *direct* result of EU pressure, the timing of its introduction suggests that the Polish initiative was in some ways related to growing international scrutiny. To be sure, EU leaders and the European Commission were mainly concerned about a possible influx of poor immigrants from new member states with large Roma populations, such as Bulgaria, the Czech Republic, Hungary, Romania, and Slovakia; and they were obviously less concerned about the situation in Poland, where there are only small groups of Roma. Yet the overall context of a growing European concern about the situation of Roma in Central and Eastern Europe was clearly taken into account by the Polish government when it first initiated a pilot programme in the Małopolska region (2001) and later (in 2003) expanded it to cover the entire country.

Since May 2004, however, the EU's leverage in the field of minority rights has declined substantially. The EU continues to have some limited influence in the sphere of anti-discrimination, but minority protection per se seems to have dropped out of sight. Poland transposed relevant anti-discrimination provisions into domestic legislation (Filipek and Pamula 2005), but it remains to be seen how far these will result in changes on the ground.

Other international organizations may have had less real power than the EU, but they were, on the whole, a lot more critical about Poland's legal, institutional and policy efforts in the area of minority protection. In its 2003 opinion on Poland, the Council of Europe's Advisory Committee on the Framework Convention argued that the Polish attempts to protect minorities lacked 'overall coherence' and contained 'important shortcomings'.

> This is particularly the case for the use of minority languages in relations with administrative authorities, as well as the display of traditional local names and other topographical indications in minority languages. In these areas, legislative guarantees are needed as a matter of priority.
>
> (Advisory Committee 2004: 30)

The Advisory Committee also criticized Poland's halting implementation efforts, especially with regard to protecting the Roma. According to the Committee, the Polish programme directed towards the Roma followed a problematic top-down approach and could therefore not achieve any long-lasting results in the areas where those results were most needed (equal opportunities and the fight against discrimination): 'Consultation with the Roma is crucial for the successful implementation of the newly adopted Programme together with further action to address acts of discrimination and ensure equal opportunities for access to education' (Advisory Committee 2004: 30). Other international monitoring bodies reached more or less similar conclusions about the situation of minorities in Poland in general, and the situation of the Roma in particular (see e.g. ECRI 2005).

The official response of the Polish government was partly conceding and partly defensive. In its comments submitted to the Council of Europe in 2004, for example, the government argued that it took the criticisms seriously, but it did not make clear how it planned to remedy some of the Advisory Committee's concerns about implementation of the Framework Convention. The government placed a lot of emphasis on the fact that it would sustain its efforts to get the Minorities Law approved by parliament. The points about the Roma were accepted, but the government did not specify how to address the implementation problems nor the lack of consultation and cooperation with Roma communities.

Particularly dismissive was the Polish response to the Advisory Committee's signalling of the problem of nationalist rhetoric and the argument that the authorities 'often stress the homogeneity of modern-day Poland' (Advisory Committee 2004: 14). 'This thesis is not true', the Polish government wrote. It is

> harmful for the Polish authorities and it is not supported by any evidence. It is contradicted even by the Polish legislation, in which the matter of protection of the rights of the national and ethnic minorities is given much consideration.
>
> (Government of Poland 2004: 7)

In light of that comment it is ironic that a year later independent international NGOs began to repeat the Advisory Committee's criticism more loudly than they had ever done before. In particular, NGOs became more critical of Polish attitudes towards minorities following the parliamentary and presidential elections of 2005, which had brought the ultraconservative Law and Justice party to power, a party that had relied on an electoral campaign emphasizing its faith in the value of a (morally, culturally, but perhaps also ethnically) homogeneous country. Minority rights monitors became especially wary of developments in Poland after the Law and Justice party had formed a government with Samoobrona (Self-defence), a party mainly known for its populism, and the League of Polish Families (LPR), a party representing the radical nationalist and extreme Catholic right. They argued that there were signs that, outside the realm of the institutional protection of minority rights in the fields of language and culture, there might be problems with minority protection, particularly in the field of anti-discrimination. One worrying indication, according to NGOs and observers inside and outside Poland, was the abolishment in November 2005 of the government commissioner for the Equal Status of Women and Men.[5]

This government decision was strongly criticized, among others, by the European Monitoring Centre on Racism and Xenophobia (now the European Union Agency for Fundamental Rights) in its 2006 annual report, noting that now 'there is no entity in Poland fulfilling the role of the Specialised Body under Art 13 Race Equality Directive' (European Monitoring Centre on Racism and Xenophobia 2006: 30).

The government was also criticized more broadly by a range of international actors for not taking the promotion of diversity and social inclusion to heart. In particular the nomination of Roman Giertych (from the League of Polish Families) in 2006 to the post of education minister raised fears inside and outside Poland of a strong moral view of Polish national identity gaining ground – a view in which those who do not conform to a certain moral image are not accepted as equal citizens and as members of the 'true' Polish nation.

In the summer of 2007, the governing coalition fell apart and as a result of the elections of October 2007, the Law and Justice party lost its position of power and had to make way for government formation initiatives by the winning right-wing liberal Citizen's Platform. It remains to be seen what this government change will mean for the further development of minority policies in Poland.

Conclusions

The enlargement of the EU created an opportunity for Polish minority activists to raise their demands for recognition and protection more forcefully than ever before. Polish policy-makers responded both positively and negatively. Some feared that minority activists would utilize the EU's concern for minority protection as an opportunity to antagonize the relationship between minority and majority populations; others believed that the EU enlargement process finally created the perfect opportunity for unburdening minorities of traumatic legacies and creating a brand new legal framework for minority-friendly policies in the future. Prior to 2004, the EU enlargement process was a relatively important factor influencing domestic political debates about minority protection, although it was clearly not the only contextual element of importance in this field.

In more recent times, the situation has become considerably different. In the current circumstances, the EU has obviously less power to steer Polish domestic law-making debates and policy decisions towards particular outcomes. International organizations, international monitoring bodies, and NGOs, however, continue to scrutinize developments in Poland, and since 2005 they have done so with more dedication and a growing sense of urgency. Although they have met with a positive response from many civil society organizations in Poland, they have also come to realize how difficult it is – in Poland as well as in many other EU countries – to make quick and substantial progress in fostering a genuine climate of ethnic diversity, equal opportunities, anti-discrimination, and social inclusion.

Notes

1 See, for example, the indignation voiced in an issue of *ZaPIS Śląski*, the newsletter of a regional branch of Lech and Jarosław Kaczyński's right-wing conservative Law and Justice party (PiS) (www.zapis.w.szu.pl/archiwum/2004/ZaPiS_05.04b.pdf, accessed 3 November 2007).
2 Law 141 'Ustawa o mniejszościach narodowych i etnicznych oraz o języku regionalnym' (Dziennik Ustaw nr. 17).
3 In 2003 the census report of the Polish statistical office had called groups such as the Germans, Belarusians and Ukrainians 'nationalities' (*narodowości*). Groups without an external homeland, such as the Silesians and the Roma, were defined as 'communities' (*społeczności*) (Główny Urząd Statystyczny 2003: 39). But while the official list of minorities published by the Ministry of the Interior included the Roma, it did not mention the Silesians (see www.mswia.gov.pl/index.php?dzial=61&id=37, accessed 3 November 2007). The 2005 Minorities Law followed this logic: the Roma, the Karaites and the Lemkos were recognized as 'ethnic' minorities (*mniejszości etniczne*), because they have no external homeland. Recognized groups with an external homeland were called national minorities (*mniejszości narodowe*). These are: the Germans, Belarusians, Ukrainians, Russians, Lithuanians, Slovaks, Jews, Armenians, Czechs, and Tatars. Despite protest from Silesian activists, the Silesians were neither recognized as a national nor as an ethnic minority.
4 Article 23 and 24 of Law 141 'Ustawa o mniejszościach narodowych i etnicznych oraz o języku regionalnym' [Law on national and ethnic minorities and the regional language], (Dziennik Ustaw nr. 17).

5 Decree of the Council of Ministers of 3 November 2005 regarding the abolition of the Government Commissioner for Equal Status of Women and Men, Dz.U. 2005/222/1913. See also Magdalena Kula, "Co z biurem ds. Równego statusu kobiet i mężczyzn?" [What with the Bureau for the Equal Status of Women and Men?], *Gazeta Wyborcza*, 25 October 2005.

References

Adamczuk, L. and S. Łodziński (eds) (2006) *Mniejszości narodowe w świetle narodowego spisu powszechnego z 2002 roku* [National minorities in light of the 2002 national census], Warszawa: WN Scholar.

Advisory Committee on the Framework Convention for the Protection of National Minorities (2004), *Opinion on Poland*, Strasbourg: Council of Europe.

Cordell, K. and S. Wolff (2005) 'Ethnic Germans in Poland and the Czech Republic: A Comparative Evaluation', *Nationalities Papers*, 33 (2): 255–276.

Dziadul, J. (2003) 'Droga przez Niemcy' [The road through Germany], *Tygodnik Powszechny*, 6 March 2005, Online, available at: http://tygodnik.onet.pl/1547, 1217827,1,dzial.html (accessed 2 October 2007).

ECRI (European Commission against Racism and Intolerance) (2005), *Third report on Poland (CRI (2005) 25). Adopted on 17 December 2004 and made public on 14 June 2005*. Strasbourg: Council of Europe.

European Commission (1999) *1999 Regular Report from the Commission on Poland's Progress towards Accession*, Brussels: European Commission. Online, available at: http://ec.europa.eu/enlargement/archives/pdf/key_documents/1999/Poland_en.pdf (accessed 2 October 2007).

European Monitoring Centre on Racism and Xenophobia (2006), "The Annual Report on the Situation Regarding Racism and Xenophobia in the Member States of the EU", Vienna: EUMC. Online, available at: http://eumc.europa.eu/eumc/material/ pub/ar06/ AR06-P2-EN.pdf (accessed 1 November 2007).

Filipek, P. and M. Pamula (2005) *Poland country report, executive summary*, Brussels: European Commission, January 2005.

Główny Urząd Statystyczny [General Office of Statistics] (2003) *Narodowy spis powszechny ludności i mieszkań. Raport z wyników* [General national population and housing census. Report of the results], Warszawa: Główny Urząd Statystyczny.

Government of Poland (2002) *Report submitted by Poland pursuant to Article 25, Paragraph 1 of the Framework Convention for the Protection of National Minorities*, Warsaw: Government of Poland.

—— (2004) *Comments of the Government of Poland on the Opinion of the Advisory Committee on the Implementation of the Framework Convention for the Protection of National Minorities in Poland*, Strasbourg: Council of Europe.

Gross, J. T. (2001) *Neighbors: The Destruction of the Jewish Community in Jedwabne, Poland*, Princeton: Princeton University Press.

Kość, W. (2004), 'The 1 Percent Solution' *Transitions Online*, 8 November 2004.

Łodziński, S. (2005) *Równość i różnica: mniejszości narodowe w porządku demokratycznym w Polsce po 1989 roku* [Equality and difference: national minorities in the Polish democratic order after 1989], Warszawa: WN Scholar.

—— (2006) 'Trauma i władz liczb: wybrane problemy społecznego odbioru pytania o 'narodowość' w narodowym spisie powszechnym z 2002 roku' [Trauma and the power of numbers: selected social problems with regard to the question about 'nationality' in the 2002 national census], in: Adamczuk, L. and S. Łodziński (eds.) (2006), *Mniejszości narodowe w świetle narodowego spisu powszechnego z 2002 roku* [National minorities in light of the 2002 national census], Warszawa: WN Scholar, 171–208.

Madajczyk, P. (1998) 'Niemcy' [The Germans], in: P. Madajczyk (ed.) *Mniejszości narodowe w Polsce* [National minorities in Poland], Warszawa: Instytut Studiów Politycznych Polskiej Akademia Nauk, 66–109.

Sasse, G. (2006) 'Gone with the wind? Minority Rights in Central and Eastern Europe before and after EU enlargement', working paper presented at the workshop *Ethnic Mobilization in the New Europe*, Brussels 21–22 April 2006.

Snyder, T. (2003) *The Reconstruction of Nations: Poland, Ukraine, Lithuania, Belarus, 1569–1999*, New Haven and London: Yale University Press.

UNICEF (2007) TransMONEE database.

Vermeersch, P. (2007) 'A Minority at the Border: EU enlargement and the Ukrainian Minority in Poland', *Eastern European Politics and Societies*, 21 (3), 475–502.

World Bank (2007) World Development Indicators database.

Zaremba, M. (2001) *Komunizm, legitymizacja, nacjonalizm: Nacjonalistyczna legitymizacja władzy komunistycznej w Polsce* [Communism, legitimacy, nationalism: nationalist legitimation of communist power in Poland], Warszawa: Wydawnictwo TRIO, Instytut Studiów Politycznych Polskiej Akademii Nauk.

13 Romania

From laggard to leader?

Melanie H. Ram

Introduction

In assessing the protection of minorities in Romania since the collapse of communism, it is useful to keep in mind the country's history and point of departure. Romania began its post-communist transition with a violent revolution, ending one of the most repressive regimes in the region under the almost 25-year rule of Nicolae Ceauşescu. When Romania applied for Council of Europe membership in 1990 (just three months after its revolution), it was put under exceptionally intense scrutiny because the committee reviewing its application felt Romania 'starts from the lowest possible base in the denial of human rights' (Council of Europe 1994). Romania was rated among the worst countries in the world in terms of civil and political rights and as one of the least promising for democratic consolidation. Regarding minorities in particular, the communist legacy Romania had to build on was one of forced assimilation and denial of minority rights.

For minorities, Romania's post-communist transition did not get off to a propitious beginning. Initial government overtures towards the Hungarian minority

Map 13.1 Romania (source: http://maps.mygeo.info/maps_eu_ro.html – accessed 19 October, 2007).

Table 13.1 Key indicators for Romania

Total population (millions)[a]	21.5 (2006)
Urban population (% of total)[a]	53.9 (2006)
GDP per capita, PPP (US$)[a]	10,091 (2006)
Unemployment rate (%)[b]	7.2 (2005)
Ethnic composition (2002 census)[c]	Romanians: 89.5%
	Hungarians: 6.6%
	Roma: 2.5%
	Germans: 0.3%
	Ukrainians: 0.3%
	Russian-Lipovans: 0.2%
	Turks: 0.2%
	Other: 2.9%

Sources: a World Bank 2007; b UNICEF 2007; c Institutul National de Statistica 2002.

Notes
PPP: purchasing power parity; unemployment rate is based on registered unemployment as a percentage of 15–59 year olds; GDP per capita is given in current international US$.

just after the revolution dissipated quickly, and scholars spoke about 'deep-seated ethnic conflicts' between ethnic Romanians and ethnic Hungarians in the Transylvania region (Calinescu and Tismăneanu 1991: 296). Violence between Romanians and Hungarians broke out in Tirgu Mureş in March 1990, making Romania the first place in post-communist Europe where inter-ethnic differences led to deadly conflict (Gallagher 1995: 88). Violence also emerged early on against the Roma in Romania, including attacks in the early 1990s that led to several deaths, the destruction of Roma houses, and entire Roma communities being driven from their hometowns. Attacks against Roma continued into the decade; as the European Commission noted in its Opinion on Romania in 1997, the Roma 'are quite often assaulted by police officers or members of the public, offences that go unpunished' (European Commission 1997: 18).

The Hungarians and the Roma are the largest minorities in Romania, and the subject of most of the discussions regarding minority rights in the country. According to the 2002 census, Hungarians number 1.4 million, or 6.6 per cent of Romania's total population of almost 21.7 million people, while the Roma number 535,000, or 2.5 per cent of the population. All other ethnic minorities in Romania, which include Germans, Russian-Lipovans, Turks, and Ukrainians, each constitute 0.3 per cent or less of the population (see Table 13.1). As is widely acknowledged, census data are particularly unreliable regarding the Roma, who often do not choose to identify themselves as such. The actual number of Roma in Romania is estimated to be between 1.4 million and 2.5 million, equivalent to 6.5–11.5 per cent of the population (Minority Rights Group data, as cited in European Commission 2004: 30). This makes Romania home to the largest absolute number of both Roma and Hungarians (outside of Hungary) in Europe. Due to low birth rates and emigration, however, the Hungarian population in Romania has been shrinking, decreasing from 7.1 per cent of the population in 1992 to 6.6 per cent in 2002. Given that dwindling population size could mean decreased political power and increased risk of assimilation, some consider this trend to be the 'toughest challenge' and the 'greatest and most burning problem' for the Hungarians in Romania today (Government Office for Hungarian Minorities Abroad 2006).

Key policy changes

The first important step towards minority rights in post-communist Romania was a constitutional guarantee in 1991 of a seat in parliament for all national minorities.[1] In the latest parliamentary elections in 2004, 18 different minorities gained a seat in parliament thanks to this rule. A Council for National Minorities was established in 1993 as an advisory body to the government consisting of representatives of ethnic minority organizations, with the mandate to follow up on problems of minorities in exercising their rights. Issues regarding the Hungarians received the most attention in the early 1990s (from both within and outside Romania), while the Roma gained more attention since the late 1990s. Despite initial policy changes, the first post-communist governments were allied with nationalist parties, and demands by the Hungarian minority during these years – including for cultural autonomy – were viewed as highly controversial.[2] It was only after the 1996 elections that key policy reforms began to be adopted, although often by emergency ordinance in order to bypass parliament. In terms of the taxonomy of state responses to minorities outlined in Chapter 1, Romania over the course of its post-communist transition has been increasingly 'accommodating diversity', although not without continued difficulty, substantial debate, and certain limits.

Hungarians

The situation of ethnic Hungarians in Romania changed significantly with the inclusion of the Hungarian minority party, the Democratic Alliance of Hungarians in Romania (DAHR), in the government coalition in 1996. The DAHR joined the coalition only after receiving assurances that the government programme would include reform of the public administration and education laws and restitution of Hungarian property (Csergo 2002). A member of the DAHR also became head of the Department for the Protection of National Minorities, established by government decree in 1997. Since 1996, cooperation has continued between successive governing parties and the Hungarian minority party. Although it did not join the new government coalition formed after the December 2000 elections, the DAHR signed annual cooperation agreements with the government. Following the 2004 elections, the DAHR again joined the government coalition and it currently holds four ministerial posts, including the post of deputy prime minister. DAHR members are also widely represented in the government as state secretaries and leaders of central institutions, including the National Council Against Discrimination, which was established in 2002 for the implementation of anti-discrimination legislation. Ten DAHR senators and 22

DAHR deputies were elected in 2004 to the Senate and the Chamber of Deputies respectively.

For Hungarians, language rights have been the predominant concern in post-communist politics in Romania, and the debate focused for some time on public administration and education laws. A 1991 law that allowed only the Romanian language to be used in public administration was eventually replaced by an emergency ordinance in May 1997 that declared the right to use minority languages in the public administration of areas where at least 20 per cent of the population belongs to this minority. Parliament continued to debate this contentious issue until 2001, when the DAHR, in its cooperation with the government, managed to get the provisions of the emergency ordinance adopted as the Public Administration Law, an achievement it considered an important victory. Another significant law was adopted in 1999 (Law No. 188) that required administrative areas with a minority population of over 20 per cent to employ individuals who can speak that minority language.

In the area of education, parliament adopted a new law in 1995 that Hungarians criticized for its restrictions on minority language education. A new version that was much more in line with Hungarian demands was adopted by emergency ordinance in July 1997. Finally, in 1999, a new law was adopted that guaranteed mother tongue education from the primary to university level. Language rights for minorities were further codified with an amendment to the Romanian constitution in 2003, which was approved by a referendum. Hungary's Government Office for Hungarian Minorities Abroad (2006) called this amendment 'the most significant event in the field of legislation in recent years', 'a breakthrough in the sphere of minority interest protection', and an action that has 'completed the codification of linguistic rights' by giving existing legislation constitutional status. Romania also signed the European Charter for Regional or Minority Languages in 1995, and over twelve years later ratified it, one of only fifteen European Union (EU) countries so far to have done so.

Apart from language rights, the restitution of property confiscated under communism has been a key concern of ethnic Hungarians. Since 2000, the government adopted several laws addressing this issue, although the restitution process remains slow and incomplete. Some other Hungarian demands remain unfulfilled, including long-term efforts to achieve adoption of a law on minorities that would define national minorities and endorse cultural autonomy.[3] Moreover, Hungarians have had no success in the re-establishment of a state-funded university with Hungarian as the language of instruction. So far, a private Hungarian university has been established with support from the government of Hungary, and Hungarian language education has been made available to a certain extent within existing state universities. While the situation remains unsatisfactory to a number of Hungarians, the OSCE High Commissioner on National Minorities recently called Babeş-Bolyai University 'a good example of a working solution', noting that 'there are no clear answers' as to the best approach for giving minorities access to higher education (Vollebaek 2008: 4).

Whether or not the rights extended to date to Hungarians in Romania meet the standards of other European states and liberal democracies depends on what 'standards' one chooses for comparison. Romania has gone beyond the standards of some countries by giving special rights to minorities. On the other hand, minorities in many countries in Western Europe have some degree of cultural or territorial autonomy, including the Catalans, the Swedes in Finland, the Welsh, and the South Tyroleans; Hungarian rights in Romania by comparison seem insufficient.[4] Yet granting ethnic Hungarians in Romania greater institutional autonomy continues to clash with a fear of the majority population of a 'fragmentation of state sovereignty' (Csergo 2002: 29). Hungary's adoption of the 2001 Status Law, which offered Romania's ethnic Hungarians a national identity card and certain benefits, and the debate over dual citizenship in Hungary only further exacerbated such concerns (see Kovács 2005). Two DAHR deputies recently decided to demonstrate that cultural or territorial autonomy is neither dangerous nor exceptional by weekly submitting in parliament examples from 11 EU countries that provide some form of autonomy for their minorities (Divers 2008b).

Roma

Those fighting for the rights of the Roma in Romania, as in other countries across Central and Eastern Europe (see Chapter 5), focus on quite different issues, namely poor socio-economic conditions, discrimination, and lack of political participation. In the socio-economic sphere, Romania has adopted good Roma-focused policies in education and health, but less so in employment and housing (Nicoara 2007). In the education sector, recent non-governmental organization (NGO) assessments rate Romania highly compared to its peers. The government adopted progressive affirmative action policies for Roma for vocational, university, and secondary education, including university scholarships, programmes to encourage primary and preschool attendance (such as free meals and transportation), and Roma language programmes at all levels of education. It also assigned an inspector of Roma education and Roma school mediators in each of Romania's 41 counties (Bercus and Radulescu 2007: 114–115). Roma school enrolment has been increasing, but remaining problems include school segregation (in part due to the geographical isolation of Roma communities), insufficient numbers of mediators, and poor conditions of schools with large numbers of Roma pupils (such as insufficient heating and sanitation) (Open Society Institute 2007: 25–35). On Roma health, DecadeWatch, a recent NGO assessment, credited Romania with 'substantial progress' in recent years, giving it the highest score of the nine countries participating in the Decade of Roma Inclusion initiative (Nicoara 2007: 27). This is especially due to the government's Roma health mediators programme (Nicoara 2007: 27, 43) and the Ministry of Health's ministerial commission and budget line dedicated to Roma (Bercus and Radulescu 2007: 117).

In the area of employment, on the other hand, Romania is ranked among the worst of the new EU member states that are part of the Roma Decade, although better than Macedonia and Montenegro. The government has no policies for actively promoting Roma employment outside of Roma job fairs, and the Ministry of Employment does not have any specific Roma strategy (Bercus and Radulescu 2007: 116). In the area of housing, the Ministry of Transportation, Constructions, and Tourism reported that it had delivered over 10,000 housing units and built water supply systems in 42 villages. But, according to local NGOs, 'the good intentions expressed by the national government are often at odds with the actions of local authorities', whose practices, including forced evictions and relocations, often aggravate segregation and unsatisfactory living conditions (Bercus and Radulescu 2007: 118).

Regarding discrimination, Romania quickly moved to transpose the EU's 2000 Race Equality Directive. Government ordinance No. 137 on preventing and punishing all forms of discrimination was adopted in 2000 and passed as Law No. 48 in 2002, and a National Council for Combating Discrimination (NCCD) was established in 2002. With this, Romania became the first EU accession country in Central and Eastern Europe to adopt comprehensive anti-discrimination legislation. In mid 2003, the European Commission reported that among the candidate countries only Romania's legislation protected against all aspects of discrimination on the grounds of racial or ethnic origin. Moreover, Romania was the only country that clearly had legislation prohibiting discrimination in housing, the only country with a special body for hearing discrimination cases, and the country that had gone furthest in terms of positive action, with quotas for universities to admit Roma students (European Commission 2003a). When the NCCD began operating with some delay at the end of 2002, Romania was the first candidate country to have 'a functioning equality body' (European Commission: 2003b: 79). After only about a year in operation, it had already received 450 petitions (over half from Roma), conducted 37 investigations, and applied sanctions in 31 cases (European Commission 2003b: 22, 30).

In 2001, Romania adopted a 'Governmental Strategy for Improving the Situation of the Roma', the country's 'first governmental initiative to take a comprehensive approach to addressing the problems facing the Roma' (Open Society Institute 2002: 478).[5] The Strategy reflected many of the concerns of Roma organizations, who were involved in its design and generally approved of its content (Open Society Institute 2002: 523). In 2004, Romania established by emergency ordinance a National Agency for Roma, succeeding other Roma offices established since 1997. Finally, in 2005, Romania became one of the nine countries participating in the Decade of Roma Inclusion.

Overall, these laws, institutions, strategies, and initiatives are important steps towards addressing the issues and concerns of the Roma. The overall impact of these policies, however, remains unclear and the poor living conditions of most Roma persist. Moreover, political representation of Roma in Romania remains low. The first Roma mayor was elected only in 2007, in a small town near Bucharest (Ganga and Zoltan 2007). At the national level, the Roma have only one deputy representing them in parliament, and this is only due to the constitutional guarantee of a seat for each minority. Between 2000 and 2004, one other

Rom was also in the Chamber of Deputies as a member of a non-Roma party. For a population whose size rivals, and probably exceeds, that of the Hungarians, the political representation of the Roma remains trivial.

Implementation obstacles

Legislation affecting ethnic Hungarians has often met with implementation obstacles at the local level, partly due to its initial adoption by emergency ordinance without parliament's approval or widespread support. Even when the parliament adopted the Public Administration Law in 2001, however, the nationalist mayor of Cluj vowed to prevent its enforcement (*Magyar Hirlap* 2001). Meanwhile, 71 deputies challenged certain provisions of the law as unconstitutional, a petition that was dismissed by the Constitutional Court in an April 2001 judgement. Some Hungarians continue to criticize the government for incomplete implementation of language and education rights.

Effective implementation of policies and programmes to improve the situation of the Roma met with three key obstacles: lack of funding, lack of capacity in local administrations, and continued prejudice. Most of the funding for Roma projects has come from the EU, but funding was insufficient and not enough reached people on the ground. The Romanian government has co-financed some projects, for example, through the Decade Trust Fund, but the government has not provided adequate funding for implementing the national Roma strategy (Open Society Foundation *et al.* 2006: 18). Another implementation obstacle lies with local administrations, which have limited experience, capacity, and financial resources to address Roma issues, and often exhibit continued prejudice.

Prejudice against Roma by the majority population, although certainly not unique to Romania, remains a direct impediment to effective implementation of legislation and policies. In a national survey by the Romanian government in 2006, for example, 60 per cent of respondents indicated that they would not hire someone who is Roma because 'most of them are lazy and steal' (Freedom House 2007). Even progressive employment or anti-discrimination legislation would find it difficult to overcome such opinions. Nonetheless, public attitudes towards minorities appear to have significantly improved. A 2006 survey, for example, found that 37 per cent of ethnic Romanian respondents did not want Roma as neighbours; while still high, this ratio represents a dramatic improvement when compared to a survey in 1993, in which 73 per cent of ethnic Romanians said they would not want Roma neighbours (Voicu 2007: 56).

The EU and other explanatory factors

Both domestic and international factors influenced the adoption of minority rights in Romania. For the Hungarians, changes can be best explained by the EU membership objective, the change of government in 1996, and advocacy by the DAHR and the Hungarian government. The limits to the reforms adopted can also be partly explained by the relative satisfaction of European institutions with the results achieved. For the Roma, changes can be attributed to the objective of EU membership, the funding and advocacy of international NGOs, and the involvement of domestic NGOs. Given the strong support for EU membership, criticism and requirements from the EU (and early on from the Council of Europe) were probably a necessary, although not always sufficient factor in effecting reforms on minority issues. The EU's ongoing assessments and critiques of specific policies and programs kept these issues on the agenda up until accession in 2007, while international and European human rights norms and EU conditions and expectations were used as advocacy tools by domestic and international NGOs and activists.

Council of Europe membership was the first hurdle Romania had to overcome to get the EU's stamp of approval on minority rights issues. Early on, Hungarians and kin-state Hungary made the Council of Europe an important advocacy target, as it was seen as a 'waiting room' for EU membership (Niculescu 2004). In order to get into the Council of Europe, the Romanian government was compelled to make certain commitments, including the ratification of the European Convention on Human Rights and a written agreement to protect minorities on the basis of the principles of Recommendation 1201 (Council of Europe 1993).[6] Romania signed and quickly ratified the human rights convention in 1994. It also signed the Framework Convention for the Protection of National Minorities in 1995 on the day it was opened for signatures and was the first country to ratify it.[7] In a statement on the occasion of the entry into force of Romania's Europe Agreement the same day, Romanian president Iliescu emphasized that Romania's quick signing of the Framework Convention was 'clear evidence' of the country's commitment to 'directly assimilating European standards' (Iliescu 1995: 50, my translation).

Although Romania joined the Council of Europe in 1993, it was subject to a monitoring procedure until early 1997, at which point the Council's Parliamentary Assembly observed that Romania 'made considerable progress towards the fulfilment of her obligations and commitments' (Council of Europe 1997). The remaining shortcomings noted by the Parliamentary Assembly were mostly unrelated to minority rights, although it requested Romania to reform legislation on the return of confiscated property (especially to churches), to promote an anti-racism campaign with a particular focus on the Roma, and to commit itself to protect minorities on the basis of Recommendation 1201 (Council of Europe 1997). Besides serving as a 'gatekeeper' to the EU on human rights issues and continuing to monitor Romania's progress on the Framework Convention for the Protection of National Minorities, the Council of Europe has also brought attention to violations of Roma rights through judgements by the European Court of Human Rights.

One of the first steps in resolving Hungarian minority rights issues was the adoption of a Hungarian–Romanian friendship treaty in 1995, which included Council of Europe Recommendation 1201. This controversial agreement took years to adopt and was directly influenced by both countries' EU and NATO membership goals (see Ram 2001). The inclusion of the DAHR in the new

Romanian government in 1996, which enabled significant subsequent reforms, was probably also in part the result of Romania's EU membership objective. At the very least, there was a clear desire to gain political capital with the EU from the decision to include the Hungarians in the government. As President Constantinescu stated at the time, 'the presence of the UDMR [DAHR] in the ruling coalition was brought about by the need to show Europe and the Hungarians a positive sign over the rights of minorities in Romania' (S.P.A. 1998: 3). Interestingly, the DAHR's leader criticized the Romanian government for using it as a 'showpiece' and emphasized that the coalition also needed his party's votes (S.P.A. 1998: 3). European aspirations may also have prevented the DAHR from leaving the coalition in the first few years, despite often bitter disputes and several threats to do so. The DAHR maintains that it was in constant, almost daily, contact with the delegation of the European Commission in Romania, for example to advocate for inclusion of specific information in the Commission's Regular Reports on Romania (Niculescu 2004). The Romanian government, at the same time, tried to gain acceptance of its legislative reforms by comparing them to other European laws or international treaties, even when the laws were rejected by the ethnic Hungarian population. As important EU membership decisions approached, Romania also reformed legislation criticized by the EU by adopting emergency ordinances. For example, the Education Law and the Public Administration Law were adopted this way just shortly before the EU was to complete its Opinion on Romania's eligibility for accession negotiations in July 1997 (see Ram 2003: 44–45).

The EU was also instrumental in bringing government attention to the situation of the Roma. As the executive director of one local Roma NGO indicated, the government was not so interested in the Roma, but made changes 'because the EU required them' (Duminica 2004). The changes were also facilitated by the EU's periodic assessments. As an NGO representative in Cluj described it, 'Regular Reports are like landmarks, and we can use the Reports to ask governments what they have done. Reports are good for this because they are from outside and are supposed to be objective' (Szakáts 2004). Even the development of a strategy to address the situation of the Roma was probably a result of the EU membership objective. As the president of the Roma NGO *Aven Amentza* stated, 'I'm sure there would have been no strategy from the government side without EU influence' (Grigore 2004). Finally, the EU has also been an important source of funding for Roma projects.

While the EU was likely a critical factor in the development of minority rights (see Ram 2001), interest representation organizations were also essential. For Hungarians, the DAHR, established in December 1989 as a body to represent the interests of Hungarians in Romania, played an important role in bringing about minority rights reforms. The DAHR has provided a continuous, elected, organized, and, until recent years, mostly unified[8] representation of the Hungarian minority. With support from the majority of ethnic Hungarians, the DAHR enabled the Hungarians to have direct representation in parliament beyond a single guaranteed minority seat. Hungarian interests in Romania were also directly supported by the government of Hungary's Office for Hungarian Minorities Abroad, established in 1992. Hungary made its concerns regarding ethnic Hungarians in Romania directly known to international institutions, such as the EU and the Council of Europe, although its criticism was tempered somewhat by its belief that Romanian membership in the EU would be beneficial for Romania's Hungarian population.

In sharp contrast, the Roma do not have a single leader, organization, or elected body in Romania to represent their interests. Nor do they have an external kin-state or an international Roma organization with widespread acceptance that supports them. They do have a handful of international NGOs that have often been vocal in defending Roma rights, and numerous local NGOs, usually established with support from either the EU or the Open Society Institute. The international NGOs have been influential in getting the Roma on the EU's agenda (Ram 2004), and some local Roma NGOs (independently and in coalitions) have been active in conveying Roma interests to the Romanian government. Nonetheless, these are unelected groups and it is not always clear who they represent.

The Roma Party, which has consistently attained the reserved Roma seat in parliament, likewise has only limited support among Roma. Many Roma NGOs are disappointed with the party's achievements and believe it does not incorporate their views. A recent NGO report states that the Roma deputy in parliament is relatively inactive and often absent, and that the Roma Party has publicly criticized the head of the National Agency for Roma (who is not a member of the party), highlighting political divisions among the Roma (Open Society Foundation *et al.* 2006: 19). A number of Roma NGOs recently created the Roma Civic Alliance as an alternative voice; a different group of Roma then established another coalition, the National Chamber of Romany Representatives (Roma Virtual Network 2007). While one cannot fault the Roma, a large and diverse community, for not having a unified agenda and a single voice, the lack of unity has been an obstacle to political representation and policy formulation and implementation.

Assessing the EU's role

The EU's different stance over time on the rights and situation of the Hungarians and Roma in Romania reflects the EU's position on minority rights more generally. Already by 1998, the European Commission did not see Hungarian minority issues as posing any major problems. As the 1998 Regular Report stated, 'in general terms, the protection of minorities in Romania remains satisfactory, with the major exception of the Roma' (European Commission 1998: 11). This assessment changed little in subsequent years (see for example European Commission 2004: 30), and no specific mention of Hungarians was made in the two monitoring reports in 2006, the final ones prior to accession in January 2007 (see European Commission 2006a, 2006b). The draft law on national minorities was mentioned in the 2006 reports, but the Commission only noted that it continued to be discussed in parliament and 'this legislative process needs to be followed closely' (European Commission 2006a: 40). The positive assessment of Hungarian rights can be partly attributed to the fact that the EU does not itself have common rules or standards regarding language rights or other minority rights. The Copenhagen criteria required new members to have 'stability of institutions [. . .] guaranteeing respect for and protection of minorities' (EU 1993: 1). But as long as no group is facing extreme forms of discrimination, laws are fairly well implemented, and concerns are addressed though the political process rather than through violence, minority rights do not seem to be an issue of concern to the EU.

On the other hand, the EU continued to find faults with the situation of the Roma up until Romania's accession date. The European Commission's September 2006 monitoring report on Romania noted some positive developments, such as a just-approved National Employment Plan with 'targeted action for minorities, including Roma', revisions to the anti-discrimination law regarding the independence of the National Council for Combating Discrimination to meet EU standards, and improvements in the administrative and project implementation capacity of the National Agency for Roma. The report described numerous remaining shortcomings, however, including slow implementation, inadequate living conditions, structural barriers to social inclusion, insufficient employment measures, continued toleration of racism by government authorities, police violence against Roma, forced evictions, limited knowledge of the national strategy for Roma at the local level, and limits to the effective participation of Roma in decision-making (European Commission 2006a). As it was little more than three months before Romania was to be admitted to the EU, the Commission only prescribed that 'Romania's preparations in this area should be stepped up immediately and continued after accession' (European Commission 2006a). No doubt, these problems remain today. In the case of the Roma, the EU's unfavourable assessment certainly reflected its concern about inheriting a large, poor, substantially unemployed population, some members of which had already tried to escape poverty and/or discrimination by seeking refuge in Western European countries.

Conclusions

Overall, the Romanian government has made significant strides in the adoption of minority rights, especially considering the point from which it began in 1989. The transition has been gradual and often contentious. Without the opportunity and objective of EU membership, the results may have been quite different. While some Hungarians still see 'major deficiencies' in the current state of affairs (see for example Hungarian Human Rights Foundation 2006), the Romanian government has fulfilled key demands of its ethnic Hungarian population. The government has also adopted strategies and projects to address the situation of the Roma, though the socio-economic conditions, discrimination, and social exclusion faced by the Roma cannot be resolved simply with legislation.

As Romania joined the EU only in January 2007, it is too early to say how the absence of conditionality will affect the situation of Romania's minorities, but the laws, initiatives, government institutions and monitoring bodies, minority parties, and NGOs already in place will probably prevent any major backtracking. In addition, while it seems unlikely that the EU will intervene in domestic debates, the EU remains a focus of Romania's ethnic minorities. Three ethnic Hungarians from Romania gained seats in the European Parliament, including two from the DAHR and the head of the National Council of Hungarians in Transylvania, Laszlo Tokes, as an independent. The split of the Hungarian minority representation, including recent registration of the Hungarian Civic Party to run in the 2008 elections in Romania, has made autonomy a key theme in political discourse. The ethnic Hungarians that are pushing hardest for more autonomy consider the EU and other European organizations a key target for their appeals (see for example Divers 2007a, 2007b). Tokes even planned to set up a lobby office in Brussels to represent the interests of ethnic Hungarians (Divers 2008a).

For the Roma, a number of previously adopted initiatives are continuing, including the National Strategy for Improving the Situation of the Roma (2001–10), the National Development Plan (2007–13), the Anti-Poverty Plan (2002–08), the Decade of Roma Inclusion (2005–15), and the Joint Memorandum on Social Exclusion signed with the EU (2005–10) (see Bumbu 2007). Roma-focused projects and programmes will continue with funding from the EU, the World Bank, and other sources, and individual EU member states will undoubtedly continue to pressure the Romanian government to improve the situation of the Roma in order to forestall Roma migration to their countries. The Romanian government is likely to continue its efforts, which will have a small gradual impact on the Roma, while many of the current problems will probably continue for years to come.

Notes

1 Each minority can be represented by only one organization and is guaranteed a seat if it does not meet the regular 5 per cent threshold for gaining seats in parliament, but achieves a lower threshold specified in the electoral law.
2 The objective of self-government and cultural autonomy has been a goal of the Hungarian minority party in Romania since its inception, but the Romanian government has always seen this as a challenge to the notion of a 'unitary national state' (Csergo 2002).
3 For an analysis of some of the difficulties in adopting the Draft Law on the Status of National Minorities, including the lack of support from some other national minorities, see Decker (2007).
4 Thank you to Zsuzsa Csergo and my anonymous reviewer for raising this point.
5 Modifications for implementation and completion of the strategy were adopted by the government in 2006 (government decision No. 522).
6 Recommendation 1201 included the right to use one's mother tongue in private and public and (in regions in which there is a large minority population) in contacts with administrative authorities, as well as the right to education in one's mother tongue.

7 Signing the Framework Convention was not without controversy. Romanian nationalist and president of the Romanian National Unity Party (PUNR) Gheorghe Funar criticized the convention as 'a document designed to create concrete conditions for making Transylvania autonomous and later annexing it to Hungary' (Radio Romania Network 1994).

8 There have been disagreements for a long time within the DAHR between those favouring a moderate approach and a smaller, more radical faction (see Mato 2000), but in 2003 there was a split in the representation of the Hungarian minority with the establishment of the National Council of Hungarians in Transylvania and the National Szeckler's Council, both of which want greater autonomy for Hungarians and do not believe the DAHR is doing enough to achieve this objective.

References

Bercus, C. and Radulescu, G. (2007) 'Romania' in M. Nicoara (ed.) *DecadeWatch: Roma Activists Assess the Progress of the Decade of Roma Inclusion 2005–2006*, Hungary: Open Society Institute. Online, available at: www.romadecade.org/ index. php?content=6 (accessed 7 September 2007).

Bumbu, G.I. (2007), President of National Agency for Roma, 'Statement on behalf of the Romanian Delegation in the Plenary Session 3', OSCE Conference on Combating Discrimination and Promoting Mutual Respect and Understanding, Bucharest, 7–8 June.

Calinescu, M. and Tismăneanu, T. (1991) 'The 1989 Revolution and the Collapse of Communism in Romania', in V. Georgescu (ed.) *The Romanians: A History*, Columbus: Ohio State University Press, 279–297.

Council of Europe (1993), Parliamentary Assembly, Opinion No. 176 on the application by Romania for membership of the Council of Europe.

—— (1994) Parliamentary Assembly, 'Forty-Fourth Ordinary session (Seventh Part) 27 September–1 October 1993' in *Official Report of Debates*, Vol. VI, Sittings 45 to 51, Strasbourg: Council of Europe, 1380–1412.

—— (1997), Parliamentary Assembly, Resolution 1123 on the honouring of obligations and commitments by Romania.

Csergo, Z. (2002) 'Beyond Ethnic Division: Majority-Minority Debate about the Postcommunist State in Romania and Slovakia', *East European Politics and Societies*, 16 (1): 1–29.

Decker, D.C. (2007) 'The Use of Cultural Autonomy to Prevent Conflict and Meet the Copenhagen Criteria: The Case of Romania,' *Ethnopolitics*, 6 (3): 437–450.

Divers (2007a) 'Hungarian "Radicals" Claim EU, UN's Territorial Autonomy', *Divers Bulletin*, 13 (256), 9 April.

—— (2007b) 'UDMR to Joint [sic] with Tokes Laszlo at EP Elections,' *Divers Bulletin*, 28 (271), 23 July.

—— (2008a) 'EU-Deputy Tőkés to Have Lobby Office for Ethnic Hungarians Everywhere', *Divers Bulletin*, 49 (292), 28 January.

—— (2008b) 'Two UDMR Deputies "Teach" Autonomy Classes', *Divers Bulletin*, 52 (295), 18 February.

Duminica, G. (2004) 1 June, Executive Director of Agency for Community Development 'Impreuna', Bucharest, interview by author.

EU (1993) *Presidency Conclusions, Copenhagen European Council – 21–22 June 1993*, Brussels: European Union.

European Commission (1997) *Agenda 2000 – Commission Opinion on Romania's Appli-*

cation for Membership of the European Union, Brussels: European Commission. Online, available at: http://ec.europa.eu/enlargement/archives/pdf/ dwn/opinions/ romania/ro-op_en.pdf (accessed 12 September 2007).

—— (1998) *1998 Regular Report from the Commission on Romania's Progress Towards Accession*, Brussels: European Commission. Online, available at: http:// ec.europa.eu/ enlargement/archives/pdf/key_documents/1998/romania_en.pdf (accessed 12 September 2007).

—— (2003a) *Equality, Diversity and Enlargement Report on measures to combat discrimination in acceding and candidate countries*, Luxembourg: Office for Official Publications of the European Communities. Online, available at: http:// ec.europa.eu/ employment_social/fundamental_rights/pdf/pubst/equaldivenlarge_en.pdf (accessed 7 September 2007).

—— (2003b) *2003 Regular Report on Romania's Progress Towards Accession*, Brussels: European Commission. Online, available at: http://ec.europa.eu/ enlargement/archives/ pdf/key_documents/2003/rr_ro_final_en.pdf (accessed 12 September 2007).

—— (2004) *2004 Regular Report on Romania's Progress Towards Accession*, Brussels: European Commission. Online, available at: http://ec.europa.eu/ enlargement/archives/ pdf/key_documents/2004/rr_ro_2004_en.pdf (accessed 12 September 2007).

—— (2006a) *Communication from the Commission: Monitoring report on the state of preparedness for EU membership of Bulgaria and Romania*, Brussels: European Commission. Online, available at: http://ec.europa.eu/enlargement/pdf/key_ documents/2006/sept/report_bg_ro_2006_en.pdf (accessed 15 September 2007).

—— (2006b) *Commission Staff Working Document Romania: May 2006 Monitoring Report*, Brussels: European Commission. Online, available at: http://ec.europa.eu/ enlargement/pdf/key_documents/2006/monitoring_report_ro_en.pdf (accessed 15 September 2007).

Freedom House (2007) *Freedom in the World: Romania*. Online, available at: www. freedomhouse.org/template.cfm?page=22&country=7257&year=2007 (accessed 15 September 2007).

Gallagher, T. (1995) *Romania after Ceauşescu: The Politics of Intolerance*, Edinburgh: Edinburgh University Press.

Ganga, D. and Zoltan, P. (2007) 'The First Romani Mayor', *Transitions Online*, 4 July.

Government Office for Hungarian Minorities Abroad (2006). *Reports on the Situation of Hungarians: The Situation of Hungarians in Romania in 2006*. Online, available at: www.hhrf.org/htmh/en/?menuid=0404 (accessed 24 August 2007).

Grigore, D. (2004) 4 June, Executive President of *Aven Amentza*, Bucharest, interview by author.

Hungarian Human Rights Foundation (2006) *EU Enlargement Watch Romania*, 2, 13 November. Online, available at: www.hhrf.org/newsletter/02/ (accessed 19 October 2007).

Iliescu, I. (1995) 'Declaraţia domnului Ion Iliescu, Preşedintele Romaniei, cu prilejul intrarii in vigoare a Acordului de asociere a Romaniei la Uniunea Europeană: 1 Feb. 1995, Bucuresti' [Statement of Mr. Ion Iliescu, President of Romania, on the occasion of the entry into force of the Association Agreement of Romania to the European Union], in *De la Essen la Cannes: Itinerarul Strategiei Romanesti de Integrare Europeană* [From Essen to Cannes: The Route of the Romanian Strategy of European Integration], Bucharest: Editura Academiei Romane.

Institutul National de Statistica (2002) 'Recensământ 2002 [2002 Census]'. Online, available at: www.recensamant.ro/ (accessed 24 August 2007).

Kovács, M. (2005) 'The Politics of Non-Resident Dual Citizenship in Hungary', *Regio*, 8: 50–72.

Magyar Hirlap (2001) 'Romanian President Views Hungarian–Romanian Relations', 20 February, p. 8, FBIS-EEU-2001–0220.

Mato, Z. (2000) 'Romania's Hungarian Democratic Federation Experiences Turmoil Again', *RFE/RL Newsline*, 11 July.

Nicoara, M. (ed.) (2007) *DecadeWatch: Roma Activists Assess the Progress of the Decade of Roma Inclusion 2005–2006*, Hungary: Open Society Institute. Online, available at: www.romadecade.org/index.php?content=6 (accessed 18 July 2007).

Niculescu, T. (2004) 7 June, Executive Vice President of the Department for European Integration of DAHR, Bucharest, interview by author.

Open Society Foundation, Center for Legal Resources, Resource Center for Roma Communities (2006) *Brief Assessment on Romania's Compliance with Some Critical EU Requirements: Accomplishments and Weaknesses*, Bucharest: Soros Foundation. Online, available at: www.osf.ro/en/pulicatii.php?id_cat=10 (accessed 7 September 2007).

Open Society Institute (2002) *Monitoring the EU Accession Process: Minority Protection Volume I: An Assessment of Selected Policies in Candidate States*, Budapest: Open Society Institute.

—— (2007) *Equal Access to Quality Education for Roma* (Summary 1), Budapest: Open Society Institute.

Radio Romania Network (1994) 'PUNR Leader Urges Outlawing, Isolating UDMR', 5 August, FBIS-EEU-94–174.

Ram, M.H. (2001) 'Minority Relations in Multiethnic Societies: Assessing the European Union Factor in Romania,' *Romanian Journal of Society and Politics*, 1 (2): 63–90.

—— (2003) 'Democratization through European integration: The case of minority rights in the Czech Republic and Romania', *Studies in Comparative International Development*, 38 (2): 28–56.

—— (2004) 'Lobbying the European Union from Afar: NGO Advocacy on Minority Rights in Candidate States', paper presented at the conference on 'Organized Civil Society and European Governance: Training, Recruitment and Practices of Interest Group Representatives in the European Union', Institut d'Etudes Politiques, Strasbourg, 21–23 June.

Roma Virtual Network (2007) 'Romania's Romany Representatives Gather in Single Organization', MINELRES listserv message (13 September 2007).

S.P.A. (1998) 'Belá Markó Answers President Constantinescu – UDMR is Not a Show Piece', *Adevarul* (Bucharest), 30 October 1998, p. 3, FBIS-EEU-98–303.

Szakáts, R. (2004) 15 June, Ethnocultural Diversity Resource Center (EDRC), Cluj, interview by author.

UNICEF (2007) TransMONEE database.

Voicu, M. (2007) 'Toleranţă şi discriminare percepută [Tolerance and perceived discrimination]' in Open Society Foundation (ed.) *Barometrul Incluziunii Romilor* [Roma Inclusion Barometer], Bucharest: Open Society Foundation.

Vollebaek, K. (2008) 'Education for Democracy, Pluralism and Citizenship', address to the Babeş-Bolyai University, Cluj-Napoca, Romania, 13 February. Online, available at: www.osce.org/documents/hcnm/2008/02/29969_en.pdf (accessed 16 April 2008).

World Bank (2007) World Development Indicators database.

14 Slovakia

From marginalization of ethnic minorities to political participation (and back?)

Stefan Auer

Introduction

Slovakia likes to present itself as 'a young state, but an old nation'. The notion is based on the idea that the origins of Slovakia can be traced back to the eighth century Great Moravian Empire. The seemingly indispensable corollary of this ethnocentric view of history is the myth of 1,000 years of Slovak oppression by the Hungarians (Findor 2005). In line with this, the creation of the independent Slovak Republic on 1 January 1993 is presented as the culmination of a centuries-long struggle for independence, directed first against the Hungarians, and later against the Czechs.

Yet, it may well be argued that the creation of Slovakia was rather the result of a historical contingency: the failure of Czech and Slovak elites after the 1989 collapse of communism to find a new constitutional order that would satisfy the legitimate demands of Slovaks alongside other ethnic groups, without undermining the unity of the Czechoslovak state. It is worthwhile recalling that the leading Slovak politician who is often credited with the accomplishment of Slovak statehood, Vladimír Mečiar, won the elections in 1992 promising his electorate to

Map 14.1 Slovakia (source: http://maps.mygeo.info/maps_eu_sk.html – accessed 2 November, 2007).

Table 14.1 Key indicators for Slovakia

Total population (millions)[a]	5.4 (2006)
Urban population (% of total)[a]	56.3 (2006)
GDP per capita, PPP (US$)[a]	17,827 (2006)
Unemployment rate (%)[b]	10.4 (2006)
Ethnic composition (2001 census)[c]	Slovak: 85.8%
	Hungarian: 9.7%
	Roma: 1.7%
	Czech: 0.8%
	Ruthenian/Ukrainian: 0.7%
	Other:: 1.3%

Sources: a World Bank 2007; b Economist Intelligence Unit 2007; c Institute for Public Affairs 2007.

Notes
PPP: purchasing power parity; unemployment rate is an Economist Intelligence Unit estimate; GDP per capita is given in current international US$.

fight for the preservation of Czechoslovakia as a federative or confederative state (Leško 1996: 47–89). Neither Czech nor Slovak politicians in 1991–92 had a popular mandate for the policies that led to the disintegration of Czechoslovakia (Bútorová 1997: 152).

The political constellation that shaped the newly created nation-state boded ill for the position of ethnic minorities. Slovak independence was not just reinterpreted as Mečiar's greatest personal achievement, it was also hailed as a victory by the more extreme nationalist forces, including radical elements from within the Slovak National Party (Slovenská národná strana, SNS), which gained almost 14 per cent of the vote in the first free elections in 1990. Hungarians, the largest ethnic minority in Slovakia constituting about 10 per cent of the population (see Table 14.1), had very few reasons to welcome the move towards Slovak independence (Gyárfášová 2001: 262), while the position of the Roma minority (which is generally assumed to be much larger than indicated in the census results) was also bound to deteriorate if the newly created state was to be driven by extreme nationalist agendas.

The aim of this chapter is to show what impact, if any, the European Union (EU) had on minority policies in Slovakia. To deal with this question, I will focus primarily on the Hungarian minority. As Melanie H. Ram and Peter Vermeersch demonstrate (see Chapter 5), the Roma have attracted the attention of the EU and other international organizations, but their impact on domestic policies in the new EU member states was somewhat mixed. To the extent that the EU relied on domestic actors for its influence, the lack of a coherent political body representing the Roma proved a major hindrance in achieving much progress. The Hungarian minority in Slovakia, by contrast, successfully mobilized political support and strengthened its position in the ongoing domestic political contest by enlisting the support of European partners. This leads to the working hypothesis that animates this chapter: Europe is as powerful as domestic actors make it.

Slovakia as ethnic democracy?

One of the decisive factors for the post-communist democratization of Slovakia was whether the new republic was going to be based on ethnocentric or civic principles. The conflicting conceptions of the Slovak state were anticipated in the preamble of the constitution adopted in September 1992:

> *We, the Slovak nation*, bearing in mind the political and cultural heritage of our predecessors [. . .] together with members of national minorities and ethnic groups living on the territory of the Slovak Republic, in the interest of continuous peaceful cooperation with other democratic countries [. . .] *thus we, the citizens of the Slovak Republic*, have, herewith and through our representatives, adopted this Constitution.
>
> (Constitution, emphasis added)

The opening statement implies that the Slovak nation is defined along ethnic lines, with explicit references to national historical legacies. However, the concluding phrase seems to come closer to a civic conception of the nation. This ambiguity is symptomatic of one of the key challenges for liberal democracy in Slovakia: the question of an appropriate conception of the *demos* (people). The constitutional preamble foreshadowed political divisions within the country: the ongoing contest between the pro-Western, liberal-minded political elites, who tended to be open to the legitimate demands of ethnic minorities, against the more populist and ethnocentric elites, who often pursued policies hostile to minorities and who were less concerned about their isolation from Europe. As a number of attitudinal surveys demonstrate, this elite division reflects a deep-seated divide in Slovak society (Krivý 2005).

This political division allows for a periodization of the post-communist history of Slovakia. The first two government coalitions in 1992–98 (apart from a short intermezzo in March–December 1994; Mečiar's rule was suspended in this period due to a split in his party and Slovakia was ruled by a broad, pro-Western coalition) were characterized by the authoritarian rule of Vladimír Mečiar, who 'has in several years changed from a charismatic, commonly liked populist to a nationalist populist with dictatorial ambitions' (Krivý 1998: 37). The ensuing two government coalitions in 1998–2006 were characterized by a markedly stronger commitment to liberal values and included the Hungarian Coalition Party (*Strana maďarskej koalície*, SMK). The most recent elections in June 2006 marked a setback for democracy in Slovakia, empowering the populist leader of '*Smer* (Direction) – Social Democracy', Robert Fico, to lead a government coalition that brought back to power the extremist Slovak Nationalist Party alongside Mečiar's 'People's Party – Movement for a Democratic Slovakia' (*Ľudová strana – Hnutie za demokratické Slovensko*, ĽS-HZDS).

Failure or success of EU conditionality?

Depending largely on the point in time in its turbulent post-1989 development and differing perspectives of commentators, Slovakia has been used either as an example of a country that successfully defied the pressure of the EU, or as an example of a country that succumbed to this pressure. For Geoffrey Pridham, for example, Slovakia was 'a clear-cut instance of failed response to democratic conditionality' (Pridham 1999: 1223). Three years later, however, the same author argued that 'it was clear [. . .] that Brussels' demands of democratic conditionality have had a direct and not inconsiderable impact' on Slovakia (Pridham 2002b: 964; similarly in Pridham 2002a: 222). Even more confident about a successful outcome of conditionality were many scholars writing after the 2002 elections, which returned to power another anti-Mečiar, pro-European coalition led by Mikuláš Dzurinda (Glenn 2003; Harris 2004: 190; Fisher 2006: 13). However, a number of commentators remained skeptical both about the prospects for democracy in Slovakia and about the impact that the EU might have had on Slovak politics (Duin and Poláčková 2000: 335; Strážay 2005; Haughton 2007: 236). These skeptical voices seem to have been vindicated by the 2006 elections that brought to power a new populist leader, Robert Fico.

How was it possible for one country to be used as both an example of the EU's power over potential member states, or conversely as an example showing the limitations of this power? One of the reasons for this confusion is the contested nature of the very concept of conditionality. Whenever scholars focused on the role that Brussels played in relation to the Slovak government, they were bound to conclude that the period between 1992 and 1998 demonstrated the failure of conditionality. It seemed obvious that the EU was going to have very little impact when the government of the day was not concerned about possible penalties, judging the price for compliance to be higher than possible costs. But the EU cannot be reduced to Brussels, just as national polities cannot be judged solely by the erratic behaviour of their governing elites.

1992–98: the rise and fall of 'Mečiarism'

A perspective that reduces the EU to its institutions and focuses on their formalized behaviour, such as accession negotiations, ignores other important dimensions of this unique polity. The EU is more than just a supranational regulatory framework embodied in the *acquis communautaire*. The EU is often more powerful when its power is less visible. This phenomenon is usually described as 'soft power Europe': a process in which European norms – such as the commitment to liberal democracy, respect for fundamental human rights and the state of law – are diffused not by imposition, but rather through domestic actors. In this account, the EU can have a transformative effect on potential as well as existing member states by radically changing the context within which political contests take place. That is how Europe is domesticated by nation-states, empowering domestic actors who follow their specific political agendas. This approach better illuminates the dynamics of power that led to the eventual demise of 'Mečiarism' in Slovakia, opening new possibilities for the political participation of ethnic Hungarians.

The EU has also been very successful in capitalizing on the influence and expertise of other international organizations, such as the Council of Europe, and the Office of the OSCE (Organisation for Security and Co-operation in Europe, until 1994 named Conference for Security and Co-operation in Europe, CSCE) High Commissioner on National Minorities (HCNM). The recommendations of these organizations gained much more impact, once the EU started using them as a point of reference in the process of accession negotiations (Skovgaard 2007; Schimmelfennig 2007: 128).

Mečiar's 'argumentative self-entrapment'

It is useful to recall that even Mečiar liked to present himself as a politician committed to Europe. This is not to ignore his violations of basic democratic rules, or the populist posturing at the expense of the Hungarian minority, but rather to stress the pervasive nature of the process of Europeanization. Even nationalist leaders felt compelled to make at least rhetorical gestures towards Europe and to engage with European institutions. Mečiar's policies in the second half of the 1990s present a classic case of 'argumentative self-entrapment' (Risse 1999). The populist leader was unwittingly caught in a trap, as he found himself increasingly isolated from both the EU and the United States, while attempting to retain his rhetorical commitment to the aims of European integration and the Western alliance. The repeated official protests issued by the EU and US diplomats seemed to have had no immediate impact in the mid 1990s. However, over time they eroded Mečiar's credibility with the electorate that was concerned about Slovakia's international isolation. This became particularly apparent after the decision at the Luxembourg European Council in 1997 to open accession negotiations with five potential member states, including the neighbouring Czech Republic, Hungary and Poland, while deferring the negotiations with Slovakia.

The 1998 elections in Slovakia were to a large extent shaped by European agendas (Bútora and Bútorová 1999). While Mečiar's party tried to avoid direct references to European integration, even their posters included slogans like 'Slovakia – the free heart of Europe' (Fisher 2006: 158). In contrast, the leaders of the opposition were in a far stronger position to stress their European credentials. This strategy resonated with a large proportion of the population. The opposition election campaign also benefited from support by a number of non-governmental organizations (Bútora and Demeš 1999), which were partly funded by international donors, including the EU and its member states (Deegan-Krause 2003: 80).

The power that the EU exercised in the 1998 elections in Slovakia was predicated to a large extent on the dynamics of the accession process: the EU's influence was at its height, while it was still possible to issue credible threats to withdraw the offer of membership. After the 2006 elections that returned to power the xenophobic Slovak Nationalist Party, alongside Mečiar's People's Party – Movement for a Democratic Slovakia, Slovakia is once again seen as an exemplary case that appears to demonstrate how little impact the EU has on the political developments in its member states (Pop-Eleches 2007: 151). Robert Fico, the leader of the strongest party in the 2006 elections, *Smer* – Social Democracy, disappointed his European partners by entering into coalition with the internationally discredited People's Party – Movement for a Democratic Slovakia, and the extremist and openly anti-Hungarian Slovak Nationalist Party. In response to this controversial decision, *Smer*, which always prided itself on its European connections, had its membership in the Socialist Group of the European Parliament suspended. However, the new government declared that it will uphold existing standards of minority protection and oppose extremism.

Symbolic politics – history wars

The position of ethnic minorities in Slovakia has been negatively affected by the ethnocentric historiography that has been imposed, with various degrees of success, on the Slovak educational system and symbols of the state. This did not remain unchallenged. Critical arguments against the narrow-minded, nationalistic vision of Slovak history have been effectively voiced with reference to lessons of European history and European values. A number of Slovak intellectuals have critically engaged with their nation's history to advance arguments in favour of 'liberal nationalism', which is characterized by a strong commitment to universal liberal values, embedded in particular national specificities (Auer 2004). The EU has influenced these 'history wars' by altering the parameters of the debate and by empowering the more liberal-minded domestic actors.

The EU was directly involved in a controversy triggered by the publication of a supplementary textbook for primary and secondary schools, *Dejiny Slovenska a Slovákov* (A History of Slovakia and the Slovaks), by Milan S. Ďurica in 1995. The textbook glorified the legacy of the first Slovak Republic (1939–45), and played down the responsibility of its leader, Jozef Tiso, for the deportation of the Slovak Jews. The publication was widely criticized by the Slovak media, as well as by representatives of the European Commission, which unwittingly co-funded it. While the Mečiar-led governing coalition initially ignored all objections to the project, in the summer of 1997 it succumbed to increased domestic and European pressure and withdrew the book from Slovakia's schools. A new textbook was then produced which critically engages with the darker aspects of Slovak history, without mystifying or glorifying the first Slovak state (Niznanský 2007). However, the contest for the appropriate version of Slovak history continues. The leader of the Slovak National Party, Ján Slota, recently reiterated his dissatisfaction with current history textbooks and announced plans for their revision (*Sme* 2007).

Another divisive issue is the expulsion of ethnic Hungarians after the Second World War, which was formally legalized in the post-war Czechoslovak Republic by the Beneš decrees. In contrast to Czech and Slovak political elites who have defended the decrees as being instrumental in ensuring peace and stability in post-war Europe, their critics in Austria, Germany and Hungary (alongside a handful of critics in the Czech Republic and Slovakia) argue that the decrees are incompatible with European values and contravene basic legal principles. The controversial post-war policies of retribution were based on the assumption of collective guilt, stripping ethnic Germans and Hungarians of their fundamental rights, confiscating their property and forcing them out of the country (Deák 2002).

Representatives of both sides of the argument tried to use European institutions to pursue their agendas, particularly before Slovakia's EU accession. The Hungarian prime minister in 1998–2002, Victor Orban, for example demanded the repeal of the decrees when addressing the European Parliament in 2002. While the European Parliament eventually adopted a resolution that stated that the Beneš decrees did 'not constitute an insurmountable obstacle to accession', the resolution also voiced its disapproval with specific provisions of the decrees (European Parliament 2002). Interestingly, the Beneš decrees were only mentioned in relation to the Czech Republic, not Slovakia.

The controversy was reignited when a number of ethnic Hungarian members of the Slovak parliament called for compensation or at least a symbolic apology to the victims of the forced post-war expulsion (Lesná 2007). In response, the Slovak parliament adopted a resolution in September 2007 proclaiming the inalterability of the Beneš decrees. The resolution was initiated by the extremist Slovak Nationalist Party, but only the ethnic Hungarian members of parliament (MPs) voted against it. The move exacerbated tense Slovak-Hungarian relations, with representatives of both sides of the argument accusing each other of violating European principles. When the issue was raised in the European Parliament, a Slovak member of the European Parliament (MEP) for *Smer*, Monika Beňová-Flašíková, accused the ethnic Hungarian politicians of pursuing revanchist policies that could destabilize Europe (Beňová 2007). Domestically, the proponents of the Beneš decrees, including prime minister Robert Fico, were able to exploit the ambiguity of the earlier resolution of the European Parliament by stressing its finding that the decrees were not incompatible with European legislation, while ignoring its more critical content. In this way, the conflict was almost immediately 'Europeanized'.

The fact that the resolution in favour of the Beneš decrees received such strong support in the Slovak parliament demonstrates that even the pro-Western opposition was not immune to populist anti-Hungarian gestures. This suggests that Dzurinda-led coalition governments might not have made as many concessions to their Hungarian coalition partner, was it not for the external pressure from the EU. The position of ethnic Hungarian politicians and other critics of the decrees was further weakened by the absence of a clearly articulated stance of the European Parliament. It seems that 'soft power Europe' is undermined when there is no sufficient unity within the EU. Moreover, EU pressure can ironically strengthen the populist and illiberal tendencies of political elites afraid of the backlash from the electorate on issues, on which there is a strong national consensus.

However, value preferences can and do change over time. The focus on 'soft power Europe' should not obscure the importance of EU legislative instruments, which directly impact on national legislation as well as on political culture. The transposition of EU anti-discrimination directives into Slovak legislation, for example, triggered intensive political debate that significantly influenced public perceptions of the position of ethnic and other minorities. According to a survey of the Institute for Public Affairs, 85 per cent of Slovaks were in support of the EU-inspired anti-discrimination law by the end of a lengthy process of public debate (*The Slovak Spectator* 2004).

The legislative measures required by EU directives – the Council Directive 2000/43/EC that prohibits discrimination on the basis of ethnic and racial origin and the Council Directive 2000/78/EC for equal treatment in employment – met with strong resistance particularly with respect to positive discrimination and the protection of minorities with different sexual orientations. The process of transposition was delayed. In early 2002 the Slovak parliament adopted a declaration sponsored by the Christian Democratic Party that called on the EU to respect the sovereignty of member states in 'cultural-ethical questions' (Dimitrova and Rhinard 2005: 25). It took another two years of political wrangling for the anti-discrimination law to be passed by the Slovak parliament on 20 May 2004. The anti-discrimination legislation significantly enhanced the role of the Slovak National Human Rights Centre. Although the centre had been established already in 1993, very few citizens and potential victims of discrimination have been aware of its activities (Guráň and Poláková 2007: 161). However, the political dispute over the anti-discrimination law continued after its adoption when the justice minister, Daniel Lipšic, argued that the provisions for positive discrimination entailed in the law violated the Slovak constitution. In October 2005 the Constitutional Court ruled that these provisions were indeed unconstitutional.

Language rights

The Slovak constitution from 1992 entails explicit provisions for ethnic minorities, including language rights. These provisions were reinforced in 2001 by a constitutional amendment adopted in anticipation of EU membership. Law No. 90/2001 aimed to ease the transposition of EU legislation by explicitly stipulating that 'legally binding acts of the European Communities and of the European Union shall have precedence over laws of the Slovak Republic'. More generally, the amendment provided for international treaties (especially regarding human rights and fundamental freedoms) to have precedence over Slovak law (Procházka *et al.* 2002: 95). These include the Council of Europe Framework Convention for the Protection of National Minorities (ratified by Slovakia in 1995), the European Charter for Regional or Minority Languages (ratified by Slovakia in 2001), and bilateral treaties, such as the 1995 Treaty on Good Neighbourly Relations and Friendly Cooperation between the Slovak Republic and the Hungarian Republic or the Agreement between the Slovak Government and the Hungarian Government on Mutual Support for Ethnic Minorities in the Field of Education and Culture (ratified in 1996).

Article 34 of the 1992 Slovak constitution states that citizens of ethnic minorities have the right to be educated in their language, the right to use it in dealings with authorities, and the 'right to participate in the solution of affairs concerning national minorities and ethnic groups'. These provisions afford a relatively high standard of protection in comparison with other countries in Europe (Šutaj 2004). Still, as an influential constitutional expert commented, these legislative instruments do not warrant the implementation of the postulated rights (Orosz 2004, 2007). This is particularly the case, when there is insufficient political will to turn the constitutional provisions into law, as was clearly the case under the Mečiar-led coalitions between 1992 and 1998. With regard to legislative amendments, the position of the Hungarian minority in Slovakia in fact deteriorated in the mid 1990s, when the impact of international players, including the EU, in the legislative sphere proved extremely limited. While Slovakia, alongside with Hungary and Romania, was amongst the first countries to sign and ratify the Framework Convention for the Protection of National Minorities in 1995 (see Chapters 9 and 13 in this volume), in the same year it adopted a piece of domestic legislation that clearly undermined the provisions of the convention – the 1995 State Language Act.

This act curtailed the language rights of ethnic Hungarians and reinforced the dominance of the Slovak language. Particularly offensive to ethnic minorities was the requirement to 'Slovakize' female personal names in official documents by attaching the Slovak feminine suffix '-ová'. Furthermore, members of ethnic minorities were restricted in their choice of given (first) names, as registry offices were instructed to accept only names from a limited list (Csergo 2007). After more than ten years of political wrangling, the second Dzurinda-led administration adopted an amendment that significantly eased these restrictions by allowing 'the registration of feminine surnames of people of other than Slovak ethnicity without the Slovak suffix' (Dostál 2007: 171).

Even more divisive proved names for geographical locations. The historical Hungarian term *Felvidék*, which is still widely used in Hungary to describe the territory of contemporary Slovakia, is derogatory in the Slovak context (Kollai 2006: 31). Hence, when Miklós Duray, a member of the Slovak parliament for the Hungarian Coalition Party voiced his support to the FIDESZ party in Hungary and its nationalist leader, Viktor Orbán, in the 2002 elections, saying that '*Felvidék* is with you, *Felvidék* supports you, Viktor', his comments caused outrage on the Slovak political scene (Strážay 2005: 55). Duray was criticized even by colleagues from his own party, while one of the most outspoken attacks came from Robert Fico. This pattern of Hungarian nationalist arguments feeding into Slovak nationalist agendas has been intensified since the change of government in 2006.

As Zsuzsa Csergo extensively documented, all post-1992 Slovak governments aimed to protect the dominance of the Slovak language in public discourse and official communication. Even the pro-Western coalition governments in

1998–2006 led by Mikuláš Dzurinda had to be pressurized to make concessions to their Hungarian coalition partner. The excessive measures of the nationalist coalition governments led by Mečiar included a fine imposed on the Hungarian language newspaper *Komáromi Lapok* 'for using the city's Hungarian name, *Komárom*, in its title, instead of the Slovak *Komárno*' (Csergo 2007: 126, original emphasis). In contrast, the 1999 minority language law 'permitted the display of minority language names of streets and other geographical names' (Csergo 2007: 137). This legislation marked a turning point also by enabling the Hungarians living in communities in which they constituted more than 20 per cent of the population to address their local officials in their native language. While the moderate Slovak elites were reluctant to adopt even this law, their Hungarian partners demanded a significantly lower threshold, at 10 per cent. 'The government had produced a minimal minority language law, which could just about meet with the approval of the EU and the OSCE' (Duin and Poláčková 2000: 353), but fell short of the expectations of ethnic Hungarian MPs. Yet, even this modest improvement might never have occurred, was it not for the leverage that the ethnic Hungarian party gained within the government coalition thanks to the EU (Bugár 2007).

Another significant institutional innovation of the second Dzurinda government was the establishment of the János Selye University in Komárno in 2004. The representatives of the Slovak Nationalist Party originally protested against its establishment. Once they returned to power in 2006, however, they were forced to accept it. Despite the fact that the present government led by the populist politician Fico is composed of parties that were openly xenophobic and extremist in the past, it has not significantly altered the policies that affect national minorities. In other words, the coalition has so far not behaved as an extremist, xenophobic government. This is not to ignore a number of controversial steps in the realm of symbolic politics, including the endorsement of the Beneš decrees mentioned above. But it is worth noting that no significant practical measures have been introduced that would fundamentally undermine the position of minorities.

Political representation of the Hungarian minority

In contrast, previous Mečiar-led government coalitions repeatedly distorted political processes in a way that clearly disadvantaged their political opponents, including ethnic Hungarians. One of the most significant steps in this direction was the change to the electoral system introduced shortly before the 1998 elections. It prevented political parties from entering into governing coalitions, if they failed to secure less than 5 per cent of the vote (Mesežnikov 1999: 22–23). This change of the electoral system eventually forced smaller parties into amalgamation, resulting for example in the creation of the Hungarian Coalition Party, which merged three smaller ethnic Hungarian parties with a clearer left/right divide: the Hungarian Christian Democratic Movement, the Coexistence Movement, and the Hungarian Civic Party. The long-term consequence of this development is that ethnic Hungarian politicians now depend almost exclusively on the 'ethnic vote', as they have reduced opportunities to develop a more clearly defined ideological profile. This is not to downplay the accomplishments of the Hungarian Coalition Party, particularly during its participation in the coalition governments between 1998 and 2006. The fact that ethnic Hungarian politicians were able to earn respect from the Slovak electorate, owing to their constructive contribution to political issues far beyond their concerns for ethnic Hungarians, has had a lasting impact on Slovak political culture. To the extent that their coalition government sought to advance the interests of all citizens of Slovakia, regardless of their ethnicity, the credibility of extreme nationalist arguments about Hungarians presenting an ongoing threat to the very existence of the Slovak nation has been considerably undermined. Béla Bugár, the former leader of the Hungarian Coalition Party believes that 'this experience cannot be undone' (Bugár 2007). He predicts that the position of ethnic minorities 'will never again be threatened to the extent experienced under Beneš's nationalistic policies, or Gottwald-Husák's [communist] party-state apparatus, or the more subdued repressive machinery of Mečiar's despotism' (Bugár 2004: 47).

The crucial question is to what extent the position of ethnic minorities such as the Hungarians is safeguarded through Slovak membership in the EU. Bugár is skeptical about the role that the EU can play in protecting ethnic minorities in Slovakia, due to the lack of a clearly developed legislative framework. Yet, he acknowledges that his party skillfully used Europe in pressurizing coalition partners in the pursuit of their policies.

Conclusions: from Mečiar to Fico (and Mečiar) – vicious or virtuous circle?

The position of ethnic minorities in Slovakia has been repeatedly threatened by the rise of nationalist and populist tendencies. Will the process of European integration strengthen or weaken these tendencies? Will the interaction between the EU and domestic players lead to a further improvement or a deterioration of the position of minorities?

Once Slovakia became a full member of the EU in 2004, the EU had very little means to prevent extremist elements to enter Slovakia's government. The EU has virtually no capacity to alter the ideological orientation of domestic political actors, such as the Slovak Nationalist Party, especially when they command considerable public support. Yet, the EU can influence their behaviour. To the extent that all political actors are forced to operate within the EU system of governance, their space for manoeuvre is somewhat constrained. As these actors become increasingly enmeshed within European debates on how to deal appropriately with the challenges of ethnic diversity, they forfeit the possibility to adopt more radical 'solutions'. The Slovak government manifesto from August 2006, endorsed by all governing parties including the Slovak National Party, made a commitment to a number of current EU agendas, such as the common currency and Schengen. It stressed that the EU is primarily 'a union of values [. . .] respecting human rights, including the rights of individuals belonging to minorities' and promised compliance with the European Charter of Regional or Minority Languages.

It appears that the current government is entangled in a number of fundamental contradictions. It seeks to gain political capital through economic nationalism, repeatedly attacking foreign investors and the alleged 'sell-out' of the country's assets by previous governments. Yet, the same government is also 'totally committed' to the introduction of the common European currency, the euro. Similarly, Fico's government relies on symbolic nationalism. It defends the Beneš decrees and incites fear from 'Hungarian revisionists' who purportedly want to change the post-war settlement and threaten Slovak territorial integrity. Yet, the same government is also committed to the introduction of the Schengen agreement that makes boundaries irrelevant and the notion of territorial integrity a thing of the past – if only between member states. The puzzle of contemporary Slovak politics is: how can a populist, nationalist government be committed to defining agendas of European integration?

At the time of the writing, it became clear that the temporary exclusion of *Smer* – Social Democracy from the Socialist Group of the European Parliament had little impact on its popularity (*Smer* was re-admitted into the group in February 2008). A vast majority of *Smer*'s supporters rejected this action from the outset as 'unacceptable meddling with Slovakia's internal affairs' (Bútorová and Gyárfášová 2007). Will the current government end up replicating Mečiar's experience of 'argumentative self-entrapment'? Slovak voters may have ignored the action of the Socialist Group of the European Parliament, but they are likely to be concerned about further alienation from the EU in general.

The seemingly haphazard development of minority policies in post-communist Slovakia and their relation to the EU shows a pattern. Whenever the salience of the EU on the governing political parties and their electorate was high, the EU and its institutions proved reasonably influential, as was the case in 1998–2006. When the salience of the EU appeared lower or non-existent, its impact was limited too, particularly in 1992–98. However, Mečiar's defiance of the EU eventually contributed to his demise. As long as the Slovak population remains staunchly pro-European, with 85 per cent in favour of membership in November 2006 (Bútorová and Gyárfášová 2007: 240), it is difficult to imagine a Slovak government that can successfully defy Europe and its values, at least in the long run. Whether the balancing act of the current government between a strong rhetorical commitment to Europe and the populist gesturing at the expense of ethnic minorities can be maintained, might prove decisive for the future of minority policies in Slovakia.

References

Auer, S. (2004) *Liberal Nationalism in Central Europe*, London: Routledge.
Beňová, M. (2007) 'Dekréty prezidenta republiky Beneša – návšteva u prezidenta EP [Beneš' presidential decrees – a visit to the President of the European Parliament]'.

Online, available at: http://blog.aktualne.centrum.sk/blogy/monika-benovaphp?itemid =123 (accessed 5 January 2008).

Bugár, B. (2004) *Žijem v takej krajine [I live in such a country]*, Bratislava: Kalligram.

—— (2007) Interview with the author, Bratislava, 4 September 2007.

Bútora, M. and Bútorová, Z. (1999) 'Slovakia's Democratic Awakening', *Journal of Democracy*, 10: 80–95.

Bútora, M. and Demeš, P. (1999) 'Občianske organizácie vo voľbách 1998 [Civic organizations in the 1998 elections]', in M. Bútora, G. Mesežnikov and Z. Bútorová (eds) *Kto? Prečo? Ako? [Who? Why? How?]*, Bratislava: Inštitút pre verejné otázky: 129–40.

Bútorová, Z. (1997) 'Public Opinion in Slovakia: Continuity and Change', in S. Szomolányi and J.A. Gould (eds) *Slovakia: Problems of Democratic Consolidation*, Bratislava: Slovak Political Science Association: 129–155.

Bútorová, Z. and Gyárfášová, O. (2007) 'Public opinion', in M. Bútora, G. Mesežnikov and M. Kollár (eds) *Slovakia 2006: A Global Report on the State of Society*, Bratislava: Institute for Public Affairs: 221–246.

Constitution of the Slovak Republic, Online, available at: www.legislationline.org/ upload/legislations/0f/f8/3d4977d97d4d8fe818a162fe2c0e.htm (accessed 20 January 2008).

Csergo, Z. (2007) *Talk of the nation: language and conflict in Romania and Slovakia*, Ithaca: Cornell University Press.

Deák, I. (2002) 'Die Vergessenen: Die Vertreibung der Ungarn aus der Slowakei [Those who had been forgotten: the expulsion of Hungarians from Slovakia]', in B. Coundehove-Kalergi and O. Rathkolb (eds) *Die Beneš-Dekrete [The Beneš decrees]*, Wien: Czernin Verlag: 107–117.

Deegan-Krause, K. (2003) 'The ambivalent influence of the European Union on democratization in Slovakia', in P.J. Kubicek (ed.) *The European Union and Democratization*, London: Routledge: 56–86.

Dimitrova, A. and Rhinard, M. (2005) 'The Power of Norms in the Transposition of EU Directives', *European Integration Online Papers* (16). Online, available at: http:// eiop.or.at/eiop/texte/2005–016a.htm (accessed 10 January 2008).

Dostál, O. (2007) 'Ethnic minorities', in M. Bútora, G. Mesežnikov and M. Kollár (eds) *Slovakia 2006: A Global Report on the State of Society*, Bratislava: Institute for Public Affairs: 169–186.

Duin, P. and Poláčková, Z. (2000) 'Democratic Renewal and the Hungarian Minority Question in Slovakia', *European Societies*, 2: 335–360.

EIU (2007) *Economist Intelligence Unit Country Report, Slovakia*, June.

European Parliament (2002) *European Parliament resolution on the progress made by each of the candidate countries towards accession, adopted in plenary 20 November 2002*, Strasbourg: European Parliament. Online, available at: www.europarl.europa.eu/ sides/getDoc.do?pubRef=-//EP//TEXT+TA+P5-TA-2002-0536+0+DOC+XML+V0// EN&language=EN (accessed 5 January 2008).

Findor, A. (2005) 'Tisícročná poroba?' [A thousand years of servitude?], in E. Krekovič, E. Mannová and E. Krekovičová (eds) *Mýty naše slovenské [Our Slovak myths]*, Bratislava: Academic Electronic Press: 71–76.

Fisher, S. (2006) *Political change in post-Communist Slovakia and Croatia: from nationalist to Europeanist*, New York: Palgrave Macmillan.

Glenn, J.K. (2003) 'EU Enlargement', in Michelle Cini (ed.) *European Union Politics*, Oxford: Oxford University Press: 211–228.

Guráň, P. and Poláková, A. (2007) 'Human Rights', in M. Bútora, G. Mesežnikov and M. Kollár (eds) *Slovakia 2006: A Global Report on the State of Society*, Bratislava: Institute for Public Affairs: 150–167.

Gyárfášová, O. (2001) 'Individuálna historická pamät [Individual historical memory]', in O. Gyárfášová, V. Krivý and M. Velšic (eds) *Krajina v pohybe: Správa o politických názoroch a hodnotách ľudí na Slovensku [A country on the move: report about people's political views and values in Slovakia]*, Bratislava: Inštitút pre verejné otázky: 251–264.

Harris, E. (2004) 'Europeanization of Slovakia', *Comparative European Politics*, 2: 185–211.

Haughton, T. (2007) 'When Does the EU Make a Difference? Conditionality and the Accession Process in Central and Eastern Europe', *Political Studies Review*, 5: 233–46.

Institute for Public Affairs (2007) 'Basic Statistics Regarding the Slovak Republic', in M. Bútora, G. Mesežnikov and M. Kollár (eds) *Slovakia 2006: A Global Report on the State of Society*, Bratislava: Institute for Public Affairs: 17–20.

Kollai, I. (2006) 'Shattered Past. Socio-Psychological Aspects of Slovak–Hungarian Relations', *International Issues & Slovak Policy Affairs*, 15: 27–43.

Krivý, V. (1998) 'Citizens' value orientations', in Z. Bútorová (ed.) *Democracy and Discontent in Slovakia: A Public Opinion Profile of a Country in Transition*, Bratislava: Institute for Public Affairs.

—— (2005) 'Hodnotové orientácie, kolektívne identity a hodnotové štiepenia v Slovenskej spoločnosti [Value orientations, collective identity and value divisions in Slovak society]', *Slovenský národopis [Slovak ethnography]*, 53: 262–284.

Leško, M. (1996) *Mečiar a mečiarizmus: Politik bez škrupúľ, politika bez zábran [Mečiar and Mečiarism: A politician without qualms, politics without constraints]*, Bratislava: VMV.

Lesná, Ľ. (2007) 'Duray re-opens debate over Beneš decrees', *The Slovak Spectator*, 23 April, 2007.

Mesežnikov, G. (1999) 'Vnútropolitický vývoj a systém politických strán [Domestic politics and the system of political parties]', in G. Mesežnikov and M. Ivantyšyn (eds) *Slovensko 1998–1999: Súhrnná správa o stave spoločnosti [Slovakia 1998–1999: A global report on the state of society]*, Bratislava: Inštitút pre Verejné Otázky: 17–114.

Niznanský, E. (2007) 'Short Analysis of the Representation of the Second World War and the Holocaust in Slovakian History Textbooks for Schools'. Online, available at: www.holocaust-education.de/?site=pp.20051021195136 (accessed 15 November 2007).

Orosz, L. (2004) 'Ústavná úprava práv osôb patriacich k národnostným menšinám a etnickým skupinám v Slovenskej republike a jej komparatívna analýza [Constitutional amendments of minority rights in Slovakia and their comparative analysis]', in Š. Šutaj (ed.) *Národ a národnosti [Nation and nationalities]*, Prešov: Univerzum: 44–55.

—— (2007) 'Politická reprezentácia maďarskej menšiny a jej postoj k formovaniu ústavného systému Slovenskej republiky [Political representation of the Hungarian minority and its attitude towards the constitutional system of the Slovak Republic]', *Človek a spoločnosť [Man and society]*, 10.

Pop-Eleches, G. (2007) 'Between Historical Legacies and the Promise of Western Integration: Democratic Conditionality after Communism', *East European Politics and Societies*, 21: 142–161.

Pridham, G. (1999) 'Complying with the European Union's Democratic Conditionality: Transnational Party Linkages and Regime Change in Slovakia, 1993–1998', *Europe-Asia Studies*, 51: 1221–1244.

—— (2002a) 'EU Enlargement and Consolidating Democracy in Post-Communist States – Formality and Reality', *Journal of Common Market Studies*, 40: 953–973.

—— (2002b) 'The European Union's Democratic Conditionality and Domestic Politics in Slovakia: the Mečiar and Dzurinda Governments Compared', *Europe-Asia Studies*, 54: 203–227.

Procházka, R., Hrubala J., Mathernová, K. and Pirošík, V. (2002) 'Rule of Law, Legislation and Law Application', in G. Mesežnikov, M. Kollár and T. Nicholson (eds.) *Slovakia 2001: A Global Report on the State of Society*, Bratislava: Institute for Public Affairs: 93–111.

Risse, T. (1999) 'International Norms and Domestic Change: Arguing and Communicative Behavior in the Human Rights Area', *Politics & Society*, 27: 529–559.

Schimmelfennig, F. (2007) 'European Regional Organizations, Political Conditionality, and Democratic Transformation in Eastern Europe', *East European Politics and Societies*, 21: 126–141.

Skovgaard, J. (2007) *Towards a European Norm? The framing of the Hungarian Minorities in Romania and Slovakia by the Council of Europe, the EU and the OCSE*, Florence: European University Institute Working Paper.

Sme (2007) 'Slota: Súčasné učebnice nie sú objektívne [Slota: current textbooks are not objective]', *Sme*, 11 October 2007.

Strážay, T. (2005) 'Nationalist Populism and Foreign Policy: Focus on Slovak-Hungarian Relations', *Slovak Foreign Policy Affairs*, 1: 47–59.

Šutaj, Š. (ed.) (2004) *Národ a národnosti na Slovensku: Stav výskumu po roku 1989 a jeho perspektívy [Nation and nationalities in Slovakia: the state of research after 1989 and its prospects]*, Prešov: Univerzum.

The Slovak Spectator (2004), 'Poll: 85 Percent of Slovaks favour anti-discrimination bill', *The Slovak Spectator*, 8 October 2004.

World Bank (2007) *World Development Indicators*, Online database.

15 Slovenia

Ethnic exclusion in a model accession state

Jelka Zorn

Introduction[1]

Slovenia seceded from Yugoslavia and became an independent state on 25 June 1991. According to the census taken that year, 1,689,657 (88.3 per cent) people identified themselves as Slovenes, 2,959 as Italians (0.2 per cent), 8,000 as Hungarians (0.4 per cent), and 2,259 (0.1 per cent) as members of the Roma community (Statistical Office of the Republic of Slovenia 2007). The number of Roma, however, is significantly higher than that shown in the census. According to the Government Office for National Minorities (2007) there are 7,000–10,000 Roma living in Slovenia, which is approximately 0.5 per cent of the population.

Italians and Hungarians constitute Slovenia's officially recognized 'national minorities', whereas Roma are defined as an 'ethnic community'. Collective rights of all three groups are mentioned in the 1991 constitution. The rights of the Italian and Hungarian minorities are clearly defined by the constitution and over 70 individual laws (Komac 2002). With regard to the Roma community, Article 65 of the constitution stipulates that '[t]he status and special rights of the

Map 15.1 Slovenia (source: http://maps.mygeo.info/maps_eu_si.html – accessed 6 December, 2007).

Table 15.1 Key indicators for Slovenia

Total population (millions)[a]	2.0 (2006)
Urban population (% of total)[a]	51.2 (2006)
GDP per capita, PPP (US$)[a]	24,169 (2006)
Unemployment rate (%)[b]	5.8 (2005)
Ethnic composition[c]	Slovenes: 83.1%
	Unknown: 6.4%
	Not declared: 2.5%
	Serbs: 2.0%
	Croats: 1.8%
	Bosniacs: 1.1%
	Muslims: 0.5%
	Bosnians: 0.4%
	Hungarians: 0.3%
	Albanians: 0.3%
	Macedonians: 0.2%
	Roma: 0.2%
	Italians: 0.1%
	Other: 1.1%

Sources: a World Bank 2007; b UNICEF 2007; c Statistical Office of the Republic of Slovenia 2007.

Notes
PPP: purchasing power parity; unemployment rate is based on registered unemployment as a percentage of 15–59 year olds; GDP per capita is given in current international US$.

Roma community living in Slovenia shall be regulated by law' (Republic of Slovenia 1991a). However, it took 16 years before a specific law on the rights of the Roma was adopted: the 2007 Roma Community Act (Republic of Slovenia 2007a). Until then, the rights of the Roma were mainly defined in sector-specific laws which were adopted sporadically in the areas of local elections and voting, culture, education and kindergarten, media, public libraries, and regional development (Government Office for National Minorities 2007). The Roma community is granted a significantly lower level of protection than the Italian and Hungarian minorities, a fact that is reflected in government spending. In 2004, Slovenia allocated €11,250,000 for the protection of the Italian and Hungarian minorities, but only €550,000 for the protection of the Roma community (National Assembly of the Republic of Slovenia 2005).

When Slovenia seceded from Yugoslavia in 1991, the issues of citizenship and minority protection surfaced. The protection of the Italian and Hungarian minorities was a legacy of the minority protection afforded in the Socialist Federal Republic of Yugoslavia and in the newly established state of Slovenia these groups were recognized as 'national minorities', while the Roma minority gained recognition as an 'ethnic minority'. Internal immigrants from other Yugoslav republics and their offspring, who once shared Yugoslav citizenship, however, were not recognized as ethnic or national minorities. According to the 1991 census, these included 52,876 Croats (2.8 per cent of the population), 26,577 Muslims (1.4 per cent), and 47,401 Serbs (2.5 per cent). Furthermore, 12,075 (0.6 per cent) individuals identified themselves as Yugoslavs (perceived as a transnational category), 8,716 (0.5 per cent) did not wish to declare their ethnicity, 42,355 persons (2.2 per cent) were of unknown ethnicity, and 5,178 person (0.3 per cent) defined themselves through their regional belonging (such as Bosnians or Istrians) (Statistical Office of the Republic of Slovenia 2007).

European Union (EU) accession reports, the Council of Europe European Commission against Racism and Intolerance, the Advisory Committee on the Framework Convention for the Protection of National Minorities, and the national Ombudsman have expressed their concern about discrimination against these new minorities and lacking institutional frameworks for their protection. At the governmental level, only the Ministry of Culture supports all ethnic and national minorities. It not only funds organizations of the Italian, Hungarian and Roma communities, but also provides financial support to non-recognized ethnic minorities: Albanians, Croats, Bosniacs, Bosnians, Muslims, Germans, Macedonians, Montenegrins, and Serbs (Ministry of Culture 2007).

Furthermore, some immigrants from other republics of the former multinational state, who had been permanent residents for many years or were even born in Slovenia, did not acquire Slovene citizenship, but instead fell victim to an extreme act of discrimination: they were unlawfully omitted from the Register of Permanent Residents of the Republic of Slovenia. This 'erasure' of 18,305 persons (0.9 per cent of the population) will be discussed in detail below.

As the treatment of immigrants from other former Yugoslav republics illustrates, Slovenia has not applied a uniform approach towards its minorities. Minority policies have been shaped by both the minority protection legacies of the Yugoslav federation and distinct policies of the new Slovene state. The new policies after secession developed in the context of nationalism in the form of anti-Balkanism (discrimination against and marginalization of individuals from the former Yugoslavia) and accession to the EU (and the 'European' values of democracy and protection of human rights). This chapter focuses on the two groups that have faced the greatest challenges in terms of human and minority rights: the 'Erased' and the Roma.

Secession, citizenship and ethnic discrimination

Slovenia's secession from Yugoslavia was not only justified through ethno-nationalist demands. The independence movement initially began as a movement for democratization, respect for human rights, and economic transition. Almost simultaneously with Slovenia's secession, the country's political elite initiated the process of acquiring EU membership, claiming that Slovenia had always belonged to 'Europe' and does not belong to 'the Balkans'.

Respect for human rights and the rights of minorities – principles widely promoted before and during the independence process (see Government of the Republic of Slovenia 1991) – have undergone a metamorphosis, when implemented in practice after secession. An examination of the state's juridical foundation reveals both the protection of the rights of immigrants and the nationalizing character of the new state. The protection of immigrants prevailed before and during the plebiscite on independence, which was held on 23 December 1990. All permanent residents of Slovenia were eligible to vote, regardless of their national or ethnic belonging. Yet, the nationalizing character of the state became evident partly in the Slovene constitution and overwhelmingly in the 1991 Citizenship Act (Republic of Slovenia 1991b).

The initial citizenship policy was based on a combination of the residence principle (*ius domicili*) and the blood relation principle (*ius sanguinis*), and recognized two methods for obtaining citizenship. The *ius sanguinis* principle ensured that ethnic Slovenes automatically became Slovene citizens in 1991. It derived from the Citizenship Act of the Socialist Republic of Slovenia of 1976, which introduced republican citizenship, a kind of sub-citizenship which had no meaning at the time and went unnoticed by the vast majority of Yugoslav citizens. In 1991, however, this citizenship became relevant. Persons who had been registered in the Republican Book of Citizens of the Socialist Republic of Slovenia automatically became citizens of the newly independent state. A vast majority of Slovenia's residents were eligible for this automatic transformation of their citizenship status.

The second method for obtaining citizenship was based on the *ius domicili* principle. Permanent residents of Slovenia who had immigrated from other republics of Yugoslavia and their children born in Slovenia could apply and in most cases received citizenship in the new state. This applied to approximately 171,000 persons, or 8.5 per cent of the total population. However, they were required to obtain citizenship in a manner that differed from the procedure for ethnic Slovenes. National belonging in ethnic terms became decisive in the process of the formation of the new state and its initial citizenship rules (Zorn 2007b).

The independence process was a period of strong anti-immigration sentiment. At the time, approximately 10,000 persons left the country and the 'erasure' left 18,305 persons without citizenship. They either did not apply for citizenship or their applications had been rejected. The reasons for not applying for Slovene citizenship were diverse: some did not apply as a personal protest against assimilatory pressures, while others were not properly informed about the procedure. It was generally believed that they would be entitled to the rights of legal aliens on the basis of their permanent residency in Slovenia, their marital relations to Slovenes, and/or their full integration into Slovene society. Their subsequent erasure from the Register of Permanent Residents was impossible to predict, despite the presence of strong anti-immigrant sentiment (Beznec 2007). The erasure occurred on 26 February 1992 as a secret measure of the Ministry of Interior (Dedić *et al.* 2003). The enforcement of the Aliens Act annulled all the rights these residents once possessed; in the eyes of the law they were equated with illegal immigrants. Persons erased from the Registry were stripped of the right to reside in Slovenia, the right to cross state borders, the right to employment, and all other economic, social, and political rights. Some were even detained and deported. Some Roma, one of the most oppressed minorities in Slovenia, were also among the Erased. In effect, the state produced illegality, depriving thousands of their legal status and preventing many from obtaining a new one (Zorn 2005).

The process of EU accession

Membership in the EU was one of the new state's primary foreign policy objectives. Consensus on the issue was broad; the EU membership objective was supported by all parliamentary parties and monthly opinion polls showed that public support rarely fell below 50 per cent (Government Communication Office 2007). A Europe Agreement was signed on 10 June 1996 and entered into force on 1 December 1999. In a referendum in March 2003, 89.6 per cent of the Slovene electorate voted in favour of EU membership, and in May 2004 the country joined the EU (Government Communication Office 2007). In January 2007, Slovenia became the first new EU member state from Central and Eastern Europe to adopt the euro as its currency.

In the context of EU accession, Slovenia ratified the European Convention for the Protection of Human Rights in 1993, the Framework Convention for the Protection of National Minorities in 1998, and the European Charter for Regional or Minority Languages in 2000. Both, the Framework Convention and the European Charter, however, are only applied to the Italian and Hungarian minorities and, to some degree, to the Roma community, and their protection is not afforded to Slovenia's other ethnic minorities.

An important legislative element of the EU accession process was the adoption of the 2007 Implementation of the Principle of Equal Treatment Act (Republic of Slovenia 2007c). This law transposes EU anti-discrimination directives and bans direct and indirect discrimination, victimization, and harassment. The law provides for the establishment of two bodies: the Council for Fulfilling the Principle of Equal Treatment and the Advocate of the Principle of Equality, which is competent to hear and process individual complaints.

> There are no major problems regarding the observance of fundamental rights in the country. The rights of minorities are guaranteed and protected. [. . .] Slovenia is a democracy with stable institutions which guarantee the rule of law, human rights, and respect for, and the protection of, minorities.
>
> (European Commission 1997: 21)

This optimistic quote from the European Commission was published in 1997, in its Opinion on Slovenia's application for membership. Later Commission and Council of Europe reports, however, were increasingly sensitive and more critical. They noticed that the adoption of minority rights was not necessarily followed by positive developments in practice. For example, persons erased from the Register of Permanent Residents and Roma facing government ill-treatment and persecution have not been protected by the new anti-discrimination framework.

The Italian and Hungarian minorities were positively mentioned in the EU monitoring reports. Their protection is based on the designation of 'nationally mixed territories' (Advisory Committee 2005a, 2005b; Komac 2002). These territories are mainly borderland areas towards Italy and Hungary where, in addition to Slovenian, Italian or Hungarian are used as official languages. This means that all public institutions operate bilingually. Schools at the primary and secondary level are organized in both languages and Slovene children are obliged to learn the language of the national minority as part of intercultural education for tolerance. Furthermore, participation in decision-making processes is guaranteed at the local and national level. Both the Italians and the Hungarians have a guaranteed seat in parliament. These and other rights, such as the right to economic development, including positive discrimination, are well documented (see Advisory Committee 2005a, 2005b; Komac 2002).

Apart from the question of the Erased, three main issues of concern were mentioned in the EU accession reports with regard to minority protection: the Roma, the lacking protection of minorities from the former Yugoslavia, and the status of refugees from Bosnia and Herzegovina. The Roma community faces obstacles in all aspects of life. One of the obstacles to addressing the situation of the Roma has been a division into 'autochthonous' and 'non-autochthonous' Roma. This division has been unclear and without any legal justification (Advisory Committee 2005a). Since all measures to improve the situation of the Roma community have been applied to Roma designated as 'autochthonous', this division has discriminated against 'non-autochthonous' Roma. Despite the fact that the Roma Community Act broke away with this pattern and refers to the Roma community in general, discrimination against 'non-autochthonous' Roma has not yet been overridden in practice (Meden 2007).

A second issue of concern mentioned in the EU monitoring reports was the absence of intercultural dialogue and the lacking protection of unrecognized minorities from the former Yugoslavia. Although not considered national minorities in a legal sense, they constitute the largest ethnic minority population in Slovenia (see Table 15.1). Furthermore, most of the 174,913 (8.9 per cent of the population) persons, who did not wish to declare their ethnic identity in the 2002 census or were classified as of unknown ethnicity, have ties with former Yugoslav nationalities. However, none of these groups enjoys the status of a national minority, although they clearly outnumber Italians, Hungarians, and Roma.

Efforts of public authorities to obstruct the building of a mosque in the capital of Slovenia, Ljubljana, can be seen as a result of the general lack of intercultural dialogue and protection of minorities from the former Yugoslavia. In its Opinion on Slovenia, adopted in September 2002, the Advisory Committee on the Framework Convention for the Protection of National Minorities (2005a) noted that there were repeated, but unsuccessful, requests from the Muslim community for the construction of a mosque in Slovenia and recommended that the authorities address this issue. In 2003, the Slovene Environmental Agency did in fact issue a permit for the construction of a mosque at a designated location in the outskirts of Ljubljana. This decision, however, prompted a pervasive anti-mosque campaign led by a member of the city council. The campaigners demanded that a referendum on the construction of a mosque be held in Ljubljana city. Although they collected a sufficient number of signatures to start the referendum procedure (5 per cent of the electorate of Ljubljana city), the mayor and the mufti argued that demanding a referendum was unacceptable and asked the Constitutional Court to rule on the subject. The Court eventually dismissed the proposed referendum, which weakened the anti-mosque campaign (Constitutional Court 2004). However, by the end of 2007, a mosque had still not been built.

A third issue of concern identified in the accession reports was the status of refugees from Bosnia and Herzegovina. To regularize their situation and to define their rights, the Temporary Asylum Act (Republic of Slovenia 1997) was introduced in 1997. Compared to refugees according to the Geneva Convention, and foreigners with permanent residence permits, the rights of refugees from Bosnia and Herzegovina were defined in a much narrower sense, especially in the area of employment. In 2002, after a policy of 'voluntary' return expired, the Temporary Asylum Act was amended, so that persons subject to this law could acquire permanent resident status. With this, they were able to claim rights on a more equal footing with the majority population.

In general, the protection of minorities depends on functioning institutions that translate legal standards into practice. The following two sections, concerned with the Roma and the Erased, illustrate the weakness of institutions charged with the protection of human and minority rights in Slovenia.

The Roma minority

One issue that was mentioned in all reports of the European Commission and the Council of Europe is the discrimination faced by Roma, their significantly lower socio-economic status, and their non-participation in decision-making processes. Already before the Europe Agreement was signed in 1996, the government adopted the Programme of Measures for Assisting the Roma in 1995. This programme focuses on living standards, education and employment and is still valid today (Government Office for National Minorities 2007). Despite the fact that the government allocated funds in all these areas, progress towards achieving equal opportunities for the Roma has been slow (Urh 2006).

At the primary school level, the practice of segregating Roma children into 'special schools' (originally created for children with learning difficulties) persists, forcing Roma children into an unequal position. 'Many of these children are being placed in these institutions because they are less familiar with the Slovene language when they enter school or because of real or perceived cultural differences' (Advisory Committee 2005a: 17). In 2004, the government adopted the 'Strategy for Education of Roma in the Republic of Slovenia' (Ministry of Education and Sport 2004) which envisages the pre-school enrolment of Roma children in order to improve their language skills, both in Slovenian and Romany. The strategy further envisages additional support to classes with Roma children, the introduction of Roma assistants, the introduction of Roma language classes as an optional subject, and the inclusion of Roma culture and history in the curriculum and in educational programmes for teachers (Commissioner for Human Rights 2006).

Since the 2003/04 school year, the creation of separate classes for Roma children has been prohibited (Commissioner for Human Rights 2006). However, this led to reaction from non-Roma parents. In April 2005, parents of some non-Roma children at Bršljin elementary school organized a school boycott, arguing that the educational level of Roma pupils is lower. They requested that the 86 Roma pupils of the elementary school should be dispersed evenly across the schools of the municipality (*Novo mesto*). In response, the Ministry of Education and Sport proposed that subjects such as Slovenian or mathematics should be taught in different groups, taking account the performance of pupils. This 'solution' is in violation of the Elementary School Act and legitimated the segregation of Roma pupils (Krek 2005: 13).

However, there are also some positive developments in the area of education. In 2007, 11 primary schools had appointed Roma assistants to help the children in school and to support their full attendance, out of a total of 60 schools that would need such assistants (Zorko 2007). In 2006, 30 Roma coordinators successfully finished their training. Their task is to act locally among the Roma community and to facilitate interaction between Roma and state institutions (Žagar 2006: 277).

The political representation of Roma at the local and national level has been another problem area. While no progress has been made concerning the appointment of a Roma representative at the national level, significant progress has been achieved at the local level. On the basis of a 2001 decision of the Constitutional Court and the Local Self-Government Act, 20 municipalities were designated in which the Roma community is guaranteed representation in local councils (Constitutional Court 2001, Republic of Slovenia 2007b). Nineteen of these municipalities have implemented the provision, but, as of 2007, the Grosuplje municipality refused to include a Roma representative in the local council (Urh and Žnidarec Demšar 2007).

Due to low levels of education, and anti-Roma discrimination, unemployment among Roma is very high. It has been estimated that 80–90 per cent of working-age Roma are unemployed, which is far above the national average (Urh 2006). The government has already acknowledged this problem in its 1995 Programme of Measures for Assisting the Roma, but either envisaged measures were never implemented (such as Roma cooperatives) or public employment was provided on a short-term basis and with minimal payment (Open Society Institute 2002).

Another important challenge is housing. This problem is partly a result of the restitution process which followed Slovenia's secession. Prior to independence, many Roma lived on state-owned land. When the land was returned to its pre-nationalization owners, Roma in many places became illegal inhabitants (Advisory Committee 2005a). Most Roma still reside in isolated settlements or on the borders of settled areas, often in appalling conditions (such as in caravans or housing containers lacking water and electricity supply). Public tenders for municipalities to obtain resources for constructing basic public utility infrastructure in Roma settlements were issued in 2002, 2004 and 2005 (Government Office for National Minorities 2007: 3). Municipalities with Roma populations were also able to apply to the national Housing Fund to acquire up to 75 per cent of funds for providing rental, non-profit apartments (Government Office for National Minorities 2007: 4). However, some municipalities lacked information on these public tenders, while the refusal of Grosuplje municipality to admit a Roma representative into the city council renders it ineligible to apply for these public tenders (Urh 2007).

Another problem related to housing is the fact that Roma are generally unwelcome as neighbours. In 2002, the Advisory Committee observed

> the persistence of attitudes of rejection and hostility towards the Roma on the part of the majority population, especially in Dolenjska region [. . .]. It appears that on several occasions residents have organized petitions against the presence of Roma families or petitions requesting their departure, sometimes without the local authorities having sufficiently reacted to reduce tensions. In some cases, Roma families have had no option but to leave as a result of neighborhood pressure.
>
> (Advisory Committee 2005a: 13)

The problems Roma continue to face in Slovenia can be illustrated by the case of the Strojan family. Hostility towards this Roma family, who used to live in the village of Ambrus, escalated in November 2006 when a mob attacked the approximately 30 members of the family, after one member of the Roma household had been involved in a criminal incident. The mob shouted death threats and demanded that the family should leave the village. With 200 policemen, the police and the Ministry of Interior protected the Roma family from physical harm and attempted to reach some sort of agreement. On the spot, the Minister of Interior persuaded the members of the Strojan family to leave the village temporarily. The Minister, however, then took the megaphone and told the mob that the family would never return again (Peace Institute and Legal Information Centre for NGOs 2007a). The family was placed in a refugee camp in another part of the country. Meanwhile, their modest dwellings were destroyed by the authorities, which argued that the Strojan family did not have a building permit. The family was later resettled to an isolated area owned by the Ministry of Defence. One year after their expulsion, they were still without a proper home.

Which institutions guaranteed the 'rule of law, human rights, and the protection of minorities' in this case? Matjaž Hanžek, the Slovene Ombudsman (whose mandate came to an end in February 2007, shortly after the events in the village of Ambrus) characterized the events as a result of racial hatred. He wrote a letter to the Commissioner for Human Rights of the Council of Europe, Thomas Hammarberg, who immediately came to Slovenia to meet with the Minister of Interior, the Minister for Education, the Minister of Environment, and non-governmental organizations (RTV Slovenia 2006, Peace Institute 2007). In his letter to the Slovene prime minister, Hammarberg urged the government to respect the European Convention on Human Rights and warned that this case could set a bad example and encourage xenophobic tendencies (Hammarberg

2006). The Ombudsman who followed Matjaž Hanžek, however, abstained from making critical statements about the events.

Another institution which could have been expected to condemn the events and to initiate appropriate proceedings is the Office for Equal Opportunities, together with its two relevant institutions: the Council for Fulfilling the Principle of Equal Treatment and the Advocate for the Principle of Equality. Ironically, the head of the Council at the time of the incident was Milan Zver, the Minister for Education and one of the persons responsible for preventing the return of the Strojan family to their home village. Although the Council condemned the actions of the government, this critique was neither publicly visible nor effective.

The Advocate of the Principle of Equality, on the other hand, did not even mention the Strojan family in her annual report on 2006 (Advocate of the Principle of Equality 2007). Moreover, when in January 2007 the Peace Institute and the Legal Information Centre for NGOs demanded that she initiate proceedings in line with the Implementation of the Principle of Equal Treatment Act, the Advocate replied that the complainant should provide the names of persons responsible for discrimination (although these were generally known) and evidence of discrimination by pointing out similar cases of Slovene families who were treated differently (although the Implementation of the Principle of Equal Treatment Act provides for the reversal of the burden of proof) (Peace Institute and Legal Information Centre for NGOs 2007b).

The Peace Institute and the Legal Information Centre for NGOs also filed a complaint with the public prosecutor, and the Peace Institute complained to the Council of National Television about a TV show which allegedly spread racial hatred against the Strojan family. These two complaints have not yet been met with formal replies (Kogovšek 2007a).

The case of the Strojan family indicates that, despite the introduction of a relevant legal and institutional framework for combating discrimination, the institutions in question (the Advocate for the Principle of Equality and the Council for Fulfilling the Principle of Equal Treatment) have so far been rather passive and uncritical of government actions. It seems that not only the Office for Equal Opportunities, but also the Office for National Minorities supported the government's decision to resettle the Strojan family, as the Office for National Minorities has not made any critical public statements on this issue (see Hanžek 2006).

The Erased and the 2004 referendum

The Erased and their lacking legal status figured in all reports of the Council of Europe and all accession reports of the European Commission, even as early as 1997. The Slovene Constitutional Court demanded, both in 1999 and 2003, that the legal void contained in Article 81 of the Aliens Act be remedied through the re-registration of persons erased from the Register of Permanent Residents on 26 February 1992. The Act Regulating the Legal Status of Citizens of the Former Yugoslavia Living in the Republic of Slovenia (Republic of Slovenia 1999), which came into effect in 1999, partly solved the problem of long-term residents without status. This law was adopted both as a result of European Commission accession reports and the 1999 decision of the Constitutional Court. The majority of the Erased (approximately 12,000 of the 18,305 persons without citizenship) were able to obtain permanent residence permits under this law. Nonetheless, the law proved to be unsatisfactory in certain aspects: it was not retroactive, it excluded those who were removed from Slovenia or prevented from returning, and it provided only a three-month window for application (Kogovšek 2007b; Zorn 2007a). Overall, it was not in compliance with the decision of the Constitutional Court. A few years later, the Association of the Erased Residents was established and filed a complaint with the Constitutional Court. In April 2003, the Court ruled in favour of the Erased.

However, the Slovene government has been reluctant to respect this ruling. On the contrary, public discourse and government actions have taken a more restrictive course. In 2004, the erasure became one of the topics of the campaign for parliamentary elections (see ECRI 2007). Campaigners, led by some members of the opposition, openly said that the decision of the Consitutional Court should not be respected. They spread ethnic hatred and mistrust by claiming that the Erased were non-Slovenes who did not want Slovene citizenship and by justifying the erasure with alleged 'disloyality' to the Slovene nation. The campaigners proposed a referendum on the so-called Technical Act which had been drawn up by the Ministry of Interior to redress the erasure. The election campaign against the Erased contributed to the victory of the centre-right Slovenian Democratic Party (*Slovenska demokratska stranka* – SDS) whose leader Janez Janša became the new prime minister. Following the 2004 elections, the government of the Slovenian Democratic Party has continued to use hate speech against the Roma and the Erased.

A paradox of the referendum on the Technical Act was that a majority voted on an issue concerning a minority which was ineligible to vote. As a referendum was held on an issue already decided on by the highest juridical authority, there were persistent public protests and calls for a boycott of the referendum. Nevertheless, the referendum was held on 4 April 2004 and 94.7 per cent voted against the law, with a voter turnout of 31.1 per cent (Šeruga 2004). It was a symbolic vote against the Erased.

Given the context of the referendum, it is not surprising that the current government did not attempt to respect the 2003 decision of the Constitutional Court and respective recommendations of the Council of Europe. On the contrary, in 2006 the government issued a draft Constitutional Law, aiming to bypass the decision of the Constitutional Court (Kogovšek 2007b). The proposal, however, could also serve to maintain the status quo, as, requiring a two-third majority, it does not stand a chance of being passed in parliament.

Conclusions

The exclusion of the Roma, the lacking protection of minorities from the former Yugoslavia, and the case of the Erased have all been criticized by the EU and the

Council of Europe. The case of the Erased is particularly instructive. They have not only attempted to inform European organizations, but have also used the EU as a broader point of reference, positing that with Slovenia's accession they have become 'the Erased of the EU'. Where the permanent resident status of the Erased has been restored, they are considered as third country nationals without European citizenship. Where their status has still not been restored, they are comparable to persons without papers (*sans-papiers*) throughout Europe. The peculiar situation of the Erased highlights the shortcomings of the EU's rhetoric on human rights, the protection of minorities, and the rule of law (Zorn 2007a).

As the European Commission's accession reports have shown, the Commission has been well informed about the erasure, ever since it issued its Opinion on Slovenia's application for membership in 1997. Prior to 2002, when the erasure became an issue of public debate in Slovenia, the Commission seems to have been better informed about this issue than many Erased themselves and the Slovene public in general. Despite the violation of basic human rights and the non-compliance with the 2003 decision of the Slovene Constitutional Court, Slovenia was considered to fulfil the criteria of membership and joined the EU in 2004. With the issue of the Erased still not resolved, discrimination against the Roma unabated, and without a single mosque in a state with an established Muslim community, Slovenia held the presidency of the EU in 2008.

Note

1 I am grateful to Darja Zaviršek for constructive discussions and valuable comments on earlier versions of this chapter. I am also grateful to Bernd Rechel, not only for his constructive comments and questions with regard to the content of this chapter, but also for his valuable work on stylistic matters.

References

Advisory Committee (2005a) *Opinion on Slovenia, adopted on 12 September 2002, published on 14 March 2005*, Strasbourg: Advisory Committee on the Framework Convention for the Protection of National Minorities. Online, available at: www.coe.int/t/e/ human_rights/minorities/2._framework_convention_(monitoring)/2._monitoring_ mechanism/4._opinions_of_the_advisory_committee/1._country_specific_opinions/1._ first_cycle/PDF_1st_OP_Slovenia.pdf (accessed 9 December 2007).

Advisory Committee (2005b) *Opinion on Slovenia, adopted on 26 May 2005, published on 1 December 2005*, Strasbourg: Advisory Committee on the Framework Convention for the Protection of National Minorities. Online, available at: www.coe.int/t/e/human_ rights/minorities/2._framework_convention_(monitoring)/2._monitoring_mecha-nism/4._opinions_of_the_advisory_committee/1._country_specific_opinions/2._ second_cycle/PDF_2nd_OP_Slovenia_eng.pdf (accessed 10 December 2007).

Advocate of the Principle of Equality (2007) *Poročilo o delu zagovornice za leto 2006 [Annual report of the advocate for 2006]*. Online, available at: www.uem.gov.si/ fileadmin/uem.gov.si/pageuploads/PorociloZagovornica2006.pdf (accessed 9 September 2007).

Beznec, B. (2007): 'Nemogoče je mogoče, Intervju z Aleksandrom Todorovićem [The impossible is possible: an interview with Aleksander Todorović]', *Časopis za kritiko znanosti [Journal for the Critique of Science, Imagination, and New Anthropology]*, 35 (228): 34–45.

Commissioner for Human Rights (2006) *Follow-up Report on Slovenia (2003–2005) Assessment of the progress made in implementing the recommendations of the Council of Europe Commissioner for Human Rights*. Strasbourg: Council of Europe. Online, available at: https://wcd.coe.int/ViewDoc.jsp?id=984025&Site= CommDH&BackColo rInternet=FEC65B&BackColorIntranet=FEC65B&BackColorLogged=FFC679# P104_10139 (accessed 21 December 2007).

Constitutional Court (2001) *Odločba [Decision] No. U-I-416/98–38*, Official Gazette of the Republic of Slovenia, No. 28/01. Online, available at: www.uradni-list.si/1/objava. jsp?urlid=200128&stevilka=1694 (accessed 9 December 2007).

—— (2004) *Odločba [Decision] No. U-I-111/04–21, 8 July 2004*. Online, available at: www.us-rs.si/media/ui-111–04.pdf (accessed 9 December 2007).

Dedić, J., Jalušič, V. and Zorn, J. (2003): *The Erased. Organised Innocence and the Politics of Exclusion*, Ljubljana: Peace Institute.

ECRI (2007) *Third Report on Slovenia, adopted on 30 June 2006, made public on 13 February 2007*, Strasbourg: European Commission against Racism and Intolerance. Online, available at: www.coe.int/t/e/human_rights/ecri/1-ecri/2-country-by-country_ approach/Slovenia/Slovenia_CBC_3.asp#TopOfPage (accessed 9 December 2007).

European Commission (1997) Agenda 2000 – Commission Opinion on Slovenia's Application for Membership of the European Union, Brussels: European Commission. Online, available at: http://ec.europa.eu/enlargement/archives/pdf/ dwn/opinions/slove-nia/sn-op_en.pdf (accessed 6 December 2007).

Government Communication Office (2007) *Accession of Slovenia*. Online, available at: http://evropa.gov.si/en/accession (accessed 28 August 2007).

Government Office for National Minorities (2007) *Roma Ethnic Community*. Online, available at: www.uvn.gov.si/en/minorities_national_communities/roma_ethnic_ com-munity/ (accessed 9 December 2007).

Government of the Republic of Slovenia (1991) *Statement of Good Intent*. Online, available at: www.ukom.gov.si/10years/path/documents/good-intent/ (accessed 9 December 2007).

Hammarberg, T. (2006) *The situation of the Roma community in Ambrus, Letter addressed to Mr. Janez Janša, Prime Minister of the Republic of Slovenia by Mr Thomas Hammarberg, Council of Europe Commissioner for Human Rights, following his visit to Slovenia (Ljubljana, 15-16 November 2006)*. Online, available at: https:// wcd.coe.int/ViewDoc.jsp?id=1100865&BackColorInternet =FEC65B&BackColorIntra net=FEC65B&BackColorLogged=FFC679 (accessed 11 September 2007).

Hanžek, M. (2006) 'Leva politična opcija ti vsaj prizna, da imaš drugačno mišljenje, in se šele nato požvizga nata. Ta oblast pa drugačnega mišljenja sploh ne dovoli. V trenutku postanejo histerični! [Left wing political parties at least acknowledge that your opinion is different, and only then they ignore you. This government does not allow even different opinions. In a moment they become hysteric!]', interview with Ombudsman Matjaž Hanžek by Vanja Pirc, Mladina, 22 December 2006. Online, available at: www. mladina.si/tednik/200652/clanek/slo-intervju–vanja_ pirc/ index.print.html-l2 (accessed 18 August 2007).

Kogovšek, N. (2007a) 'Strojanovi [The Strojan family]' E-mail correspondence of the author with Neža Kogovšek from the Peace Institute, 7 September 2007.

—— (2007b) 'The erased: the proposal of a constitutional law as the negation of the rule of law', *Časopis za kritiko znanosti [Journal for the Critique of Science, Imagination, and New Anthropology]*, 35 (228): 177–193.

Komac, M. (2002) 'Varstvo narodnih skupnosti v Sloveniji [Protection of National Minorities in Slovenia]', in M. Polzer, L. Kalčina and M. Žagar (eds) *Slovenija in evropski standardi varstva narodnih manjšin [Slovenia and European Standards of Protection of National Minorities]*, Ljubljana: Informacijsko dokumentacijski center Sveta Evrope pri NUK, Inštitut za narodnostna vprašanja, and Avstrijski inštitut za vzhodno in jugovzhodno Evropo. Online, available at: www.coe.si/ sl/dokumenti_in_ publikacije/dokumenti_v_slovenscini/#1306 (accessed 10 December 2007).

Krek, J. (2005) 'Izvedbeni model izobraževanja romskih učencev za OŠ Bršljin [Implementation Model of Education for Roma Pupils at the Primary School Bršljin]', in S. Autor and R. Kuhar (eds) *Poročilo skupne za spremljanje nestrpnosti Nr. 4 [Intolerance Monitoring Group Report]*, Ljubljana: Peace Institute.

Meden, K. (2007) Interview of author with Ms Katarina Meden, Ljubljana, 6 December 2007.

Ministry of Culture (2007) *Kulturne pravice manjšin in razvoj kulturne raznolikosti [Minority Cultural Rights and Development of Cultural Diversity]*. Online, available at: www.mk.gov.si/en/working_areas/minority_cultural_rights_and_the _development_of_cultural_diversity/ (accessed 17 September 2007).

Ministry of Education and Sport (2004) *Strategija vzgoje in izobraževanja Romov v Sloveniji [Strategy of Education of Roma in Slovenia]*. Online, available at: www.mss.gov. si/si/delovna_podrocja/razvoj_solstva/projekti/enake_moznosti/#c842 (accessed 20 December 2007).

National Assembly of the Republic of Slovenia (2005) Poslanska vprašanja in pobude [Deputies' questions and requests] Online, available at: www.dz-rs.si/index.php? id=94 &type=98&sb=2&o=1290&unid=VPP%7C445DC732E01BEDE4C1256FEB005068A E&showdoc=1 (accessed 19 December 2007).

Open Society Institute (2002) *Monitoring the EU Accession Process: Minority Protection, Volume 1*, Budapest: Open Society Institute.

Peace Institute (2007) *Annual report of the Peace Institute 2006*. Online, available at: www.mirovni-institut.si/ (accessed 26 August 2007).

Peace Institute and Legal Information Centre for NGOs (2007a) 'Pobuda po 12. členu Zakona o uresničevanju načela enakega obravnavanja in prošnja za prednostno obravnavo [Request with regard to the Article 12 of the Implementation of the Principle of Equal Treatment Act and request to consider it a priority]', letter to the Advocate for the Principle of Equality on 29 January 2007. Online, available at: www.mirovni-institut.si/slo_html/novosti/pobuda_zagovornica.pdf (accessed 28 August 2007).

—— (2007b) 'Dopolnitev pobude po 12. členu Zakona o uresničevanju načela enakega obravnavanja in prošnja za prednostno obravnavo [Supplementation on the request with regard to the Article 12 of the Implementation of the Principle of Equal Treatment Act and request to consider it a priority]', letter to the Advocate for the Principle of Equality on 2 March 2007, personal e-mail to author by Neža Kogovšek, 7 September 2007.

Republic of Slovenia (1991a) *Constitution of the Republic of Slovenia*, Official Gazette of the Republic of Slovenia, No. 1–4/91-I and 19/91.

—— (1991b) *Citizenship of the Republic of Slovenia Act*, Official Gazette of the Republic of Slovenia, No. 1I-1991-I.

—— (1997) *Temporary Asylum Act*, Official Gazette of the Republic of Slovenia, No. 20/1997. Online, available at: www.uradni-list.si/1/objava.jsp?urlid=199720& stevilka=1139 (accessed 9 December 2007).

—— (1999) *Act Regulating the Legal Status of Citizens of the Former Yugoslavia Living in the Republic of Slovenia*, Official Gazette of the Republic of Slovenia, No 61/99. Online, available at: www.uradni-list.si/1/objava.jsp?urlid=199961& stevilka=2913 (accessed 10 December 2007).

—— (2007a) *Roma Community Act*, Official Gazette of the Republic of Slovenia, No. 33/2007. Online, available at: www.uradni-list.si/1/objava.jsp?urlid=200733 &stevilka=1762 (accessed 9 December 2007).

—— (2007b) *Local Self-Government Act*, Official Gazette of the Republic of Slovenia, No. 94/2007. Online, available at: www.uradni-list.si/1/objava.jsp?urlid=200794 &stevilka=4692 (accessed 9 December 2007).

—— (2007c) *Implementation of the Principle of Equal Treatment Act*, Official Gazette of the Republic of Slovenia, No. 93/2007. Online, available at: www.uradni-list.si/1/objava.jsp?urlid=200793&stevilka=4600 (accessed 9 November 2007).

RTV Slovenia (2006) 'Upor občine in krajanov proti Strojanovim [Struggle of the Municipality and Locals against the Strojan family]', News on RTV Slovenia, 14 November 2006. Online, available at: www.rtvslo.si/modload.php?&c_mod=rnews&op=sections &func=read&c_menu=1&c_id=125642&tokens=strojan (accessed 28 August 2007).

Šeruga, K. (2004) 'Ljudska volja povozila tehnični zakon [Peoples' Will Overridden Technical Law]', *Večer*, 5 April 2004. Online, available at: www.vecer.com/ arhiv/default.asp?jezik=SLO&kako=0&od=6 (accessed 7 September 2007).

Statistical Office of the Republic of Slovenia (2007) *Population census results*. Online, available at: www.stat.si/popis2002/en/rezultati/rezultati_red.asp?ter=SLO&st=7 (accessed 6 December 2007).

UNICEF (2007) *TransMONEE database*, 2007 version.

Urh, Š. (2006) 'Socialna izključenost Romov v Beli Krajini [Social Exclusion of Roma in Bela Krajina]', *Socialno delo [Social Work]*, 45 (1/2): 41–49.

—— (2007) Interview of author with Špela Urh, Ljubljana, 20 December 2007.

Urh, Š. and Žnidarec Demšar, S. (2007) 'Ethnically Sensitive Social Work with Roma', in D. Zaviršek, J. Zorn, L. Rihter and S. Ž. Demšar (eds) *Ethnicity in Eastern Europe. A Challenge for Social Work Education*, Ljubljana: Faculty of Social Work.

World Bank (2007) World Development Indicators, Online database.

Žagar, N. (2006) 'Program usposabljanja romskih koordinatorjev [Training Programme for the Roma Coordinatiors]', in N. Žagar and V. Klopčič (eds) *Poklicno informiranje in svetovanje za Rome – PISR [Vocational information and guidance for Roma]*, Črnomelj: Zavod za izobraževanje in kulturo.

Zorko, M. (2007) 'Po letu dni mandata romski svetniki nemočni [Powerless situation of Roma members of city council]', *Dnevnik*, 10 December 2007. Online, available at: www.dnevnik.si/tiskane_izdaje/dnevnik/286242/ (accessed 21 December 2007).

Zorn, J. (2005) 'Ethnic Citizenship in the Slovenian State', *Citizenship Studies*, 9 (2): 135–152.

—— (2007a) 'New Borders, New Exclusions', in D. Zaviršek, J. Zorn, L. Rihter and S. Ž. Demšar (eds.) *Ethnicity in Eastern Europe. A Challenge for Social Work Education*, Ljubljana: Faculty of Social Work.

—— (2007b) ' "Mi, etno-državljani etno-demokracije" – nastajanje slovenskega državljanstva ["We, the ethno-citizens of ethno-democracy" – the formation of Slovene citizenship]', *Časopis za kritiko znanosti [Journal for the Critique of Science, Imagination, and New Anthropology]*, 35 (228): 17–33.

Part III

Conclusions

16 The way forward

Bernd Rechel

Have minority rights in Central and Eastern Europe been a success or a failure of EU conditionality? The answer to this question, which has important policy implications, is far from straightforward. It depends on an assessment of the current state of minority rights in the region and of the role the EU has played in influencing the course of developments. As many of the preceding chapters have shown, both of these aspects are subject to conflicting interpretations.

What can be stated with certainty is that since the end of communism, there has been a large range of activities with regard to minorities in Central and Eastern Europe. Some of these aimed to set up a system of minority protection, others were connected to socio-economic integration, and still others aimed at administrative exclusion and encouraging emigration of members of minorities. While all ten countries under discussion have departed from communism and are now EU members, there is a perplexing variation of minority rights, both within countries and across them. What is surprising, is that there might not be a clear-cut and consistent trend towards improved systems of minority protection. Much depended on the point of departure at the end of communism, the ethnic make-up of the country, historical legacies, and whether the country experienced territorial changes or not.

The contributions to this volume identify three important aspects of minority rights: protection from discrimination, positive minority rights (such as those related to language or culture), and citizenship. The importance of anti-discrimination legislation was largely ignored by the countries of the region until 2000, when the EU Race Equality Directive was adopted. In the following years, all countries moved towards transposition of the EU's anti-discrimination directives. Although they did so with varying speed and comprehensiveness, the improvement of anti-discrimination legislation is clearly a converging trend among the ten countries under discussion. The imposition of anti-discrimination legislation through the *acquis* is also the clearest case of the EU's impact on minority rights in the region. Much of the accession process was driven by the transposition of the *acquis* and extending it to cover some aspects of minority protection resulted in clearly attributable legislative changes, although some question marks remain with regard to the actual implementation of the new anti-discrimination legislation.

The second aspect of minority protection – positive minority rights – received clearly less attention from the EU or was ignored entirely. While accession to the Council of Europe's Framework Convention, which was expected from all EU candidate states, provided some impetus for extending the rights of minorities, there continues to be considerable variation across the region, as well as across minorities, with Roma typically enjoying fewer rights than other traditional minorities, such as Hungarians. Furthermore, some countries, such as Bulgaria and Latvia, do not seem to have amended any legislation as a result of acceding to the Framework Convention. While most countries of the region now grant traditional minorities cultural and language rights, several had already embarked on such minority rights regimes at the beginning of the 1990s (such as Lithuania in 1989–92 or Hungary in 1993), so that these cannot be attributed to EU expectations.

The third aspect of minority protection – citizenship – emerged as a crucial factor in some of the six states that were newly established or restored in 1989–93 (Czech Republic, Estonia, Latvia, Lithuania, Slovakia, Slovenia). With the new statehood, these countries had to decide whom to grant citizenship and several countries (Czech Republic, Estonia, Latvia, and Slovenia) used the instrument of citizenship legislation to exclude unwanted minorities, even if those had been long-term residents of the country. In all four countries, an implicit aim of the new legislation was to encourage emigration of members of minorities. Excluded from the basic human rights associated with citizenship, specific minority rights remained even more elusive.

In the sphere of citizenship, EU conditionality has been only partially applied. The EU accepted the restorationist argument of Estonia and Latvia, according to which the Russian-speaking immigrants in these countries were illegal settler populations. The EU subsequently pressed for some liberalizing changes of citizenship and language laws and for the integration of stateless residents, but the basic parameters of minority policies remained unchanged. In Slovenia, EU expectations contributed to the adoption of the 1999 Aliens Act, which partly solved the problem of long-term residents without residency or citizenship status. However, a 2003 Constitutional Court decision that the law does not fully resolve the 1992 erasure of persons from the Register of Permanent Residents was ignored by the government. Finally, international pressure, including from the EU, resulted in amendments to the 1992 Czech Citizenship Law, although this law was only partially amended and the final amendment took place as late as 1999.

The Roma minority deserves special mention. Not only is it the largest ethnic minority in the enlarged EU, it is also the most marginalized one and Roma face substantial obstacles to realizing their human rights. The problems are of great magnitude, and it is not always clear what the solutions are. Simultaneous efforts need to be undertaken in all social areas, including education, employment, health care, and housing. Often, however, the precarious present situation is a result of lacking minority protection in the past. Roma have been exposed to centuries of exclusion and discrimination and this is why anti-discrimination measures and positive minority rights (such as mother tongue education or support of Roma culture) are relevant to improving the situation of the Roma.

While the EU has largely ignored the question of positive minority rights for the Roma, it has justifiably brought attention to the need for integrating the Roma minority in Central and Eastern Europe, although it has partly done so for the wrong reason of being driven by the desire of avoiding large-scale migration to the West. EU expectations were instrumental in putting Roma issues on government agendas and Roma integration programmes have been initiated in all countries with substantial Roma populations. Despite these initiatives, however, few real changes on the ground can be detected. Furthermore, now that the pressure of conditionality has gone, there is a real danger that often unpopular policies in support of Roma will slip down on the list of priorities.

The record of EU conditionality with regard to the Roma is somewhat mixed. On the one hand, it inspired numerous policy initiatives and Roma integration programmes. On the other hand, however, these initiatives were often of a token nature and the EU paid insufficient attention to actual implementation. The apparent imposition of Roma programmes from outside, often without any domestic political debate on the need for such programmes, had contradictory effects. The governments could point to the EU when initiating unpopular policies, but they did so without challenging public attitudes. This undermined both the development of such policies and their actual implementation. Several of the contributions to this volume identify public attitudes as a major impediment to minority protection. Overall, the EU seems to have paid insufficient attention to challenging public attitudes, in particular with regard to anti-Roma racism. The Council and the European Parliament have declared the year 2007 as the Year of Equal Opportunities for All, and the year 2008 as the European Year of Intercultural Dialogue, but more needs to be done at EU level to raise awareness of the new anti-discrimination framework and demonstrate the benefits of ethnic diversity.

With regard to the Russian-speaking populations in Estonia and Latvia, considerable challenges of integration remain. In May 2006, 9 per cent of the population in Latvia remained non-citizens (Naturalization Board of the Republic of Latvia 2008), and the proportion, at 17 per cent in April 2007 (Estonian Ministry of Foreign Affairs 2008), was even higher in Estonia. There is a danger that this ethnic exclusion will remain entrenched for years to come.

What measures can be taken by the EU to make sure that there is no backtracking on commitments for the integration of minorities? One possible approach is concerned with the security aspect of ethnic conflicts. With the Eastern enlargement of the EU, it has become increasingly involved in dealing with ethnic conflicts at its Southern and Eastern peripheries, such as in Cyprus, Serbia and Montenegro, Moldova, and Georgia (Coppieters *et al.* 2004). This case-based approach is likely to be a prominent area for future EU involvement with regard to minority protection at the European periphery. Considerations for regional security were paramount in putting minority protection on the agenda of Western governments in the early 1990s and the 'security track' of minority rights, particularly pursued by the OSCE, remained an approach to minority protection in Central and Eastern Europe that was always more important than the 'legal rights track' in determining actual interventions (Kymlicka 2006: 52–53, 2007: 233). However, this approach sends problematic messages to both states and minorities, as it tends to reward 'state intransigence and minority belligerence' (Kymlicka 2007: 236). It is also worth noting that in some cases, such as in Cyprus, EU diplomacy increased rather than decreased tensions (McGarry *et al.* 2006: 19–20).

A much more ambitious option would be to extend the codification of minority rights at the level of the EU. The transposition of the EU's anti-discrimination directives into the domestic legislation of member states and the public debate around anti-discrimination this has triggered show the singular power of the EU to affect minority protection in member states when adopted as part of the *acquis*. This provides a powerful case for expanding the *acquis* to cover other aspects of minority protection. However, any such attempt will face major political obstacles. As Melanie H. Ram and Peter Vermeersch note in their contribution to this volume, even new anti-discrimination legislation might not be easily adopted in the current political circumstances. There has also been a broader move away from the codification of minority rights at the European level (Kymlicka 2006: 45). Furthermore, there is the problem of defining EU minorities (Toggenburg 2004: 10–16) and the major challenge of identifying minority rights that would be agreeable for all EU member states (Kymlicka 2007).

While the establishment of a full supranational minority protection regime at the level of the EU may not be feasible (Toggenburg 2004: 31), there is scope for expanding the *acquis* to benefit the Roma in the enlarged EU. One way of doing so would be the adoption of a Roma Integration Directive which would oblige states to promote equal opportunities for Roma and undertake special measures for their integration (European Commission 2004; European Union Network of Experts in Fundamental Rights 2004). Another possibility is the adoption of a Desegregation Directive that explicitly prohibits ethnic and racial segregation. The EU could establish a coordination structure on Roma issues that could be linked to the promotion and implementation of these directives. Furthermore, the EU could develop a Framework Strategy for Roma which would allow the coordination of all activities of the European Commission (Hollo 2006).

The EU structural funds provide another opportunity for addressing the integration of minorities and several countries of the region have started to make use of this source of funding. It will be important to align this funding instrument with the aims of minority integration programmes and to ensure the participation of minority representatives in the development, implementation, and monitoring and evaluation of relevant structural fund programmes (Rorke and Wilkens 2006). More generally, the impact of the assessment process could be extended to make sure that EU programmes do not indirectly discriminate against minorities (Hollo 2006). Increased opportunities for cross-border and inter-state cooperation can also benefit minorities (McGarry *et al.* 2006: 13–16).

Post-accession monitoring of EU member states is another area which could be further developed. Apart from the Race Equality Directive, post-accession monitoring of the new member states in the sphere of minority rights and racism on behalf of the EU seems to be almost entirely missing, with the exception of the reports of the EU Agency for Fundamental Rights (formerly the European Monitoring Centre on Racism and Xenophobia) (see: European Union Agency for Fundamental Rights 2007).

What lessons can be learnt from the enlargements in 2004 and 2007 for future enlargements of the EU? The contributions to this volume illustrate that the EU can bring extraordinary weight to bear on candidate countries to improve particular minority policies, far outweighing other international actors or human rights treaty obligations. The timing of EU demands seems to be of particular importance. Successful outcomes of conditionality in the sphere of minority rights have been linked to a credible threat of withdrawing the offer of membership. The power of EU conditionality would increase enormously, if the question of compliance with the political criteria was left open, rather than being closed in the very beginning of the monitoring procedure. In the case of the ten countries under discussion here, compliance with the political criteria was declared too early and this has dramatically decreased the EU's leverage in this policy area.

Finally, with regard to positive minority rights and citizenship regulations, the EU has failed to pursue a coherent and consistent approach towards the accession countries from Central and Eastern Europe. This seems to have been partly due to a lack of capacity on the part of the EU. It may therefore be helpful if the EU makes more concerted efforts of drawing on the expertise of other relevant European institutions, such as the Council of Europe and the OSCE, and if it expands its own expertise on minority protection. There is clearly a need for lesson-learning from past rounds of EU enlargement that could inform the evaluation of current and future candidate countries.

Minority rights are certainly no panacea for all problems faced by members of ethnic minorities in Europe. However, there is an increasing global recognition that minority rights are an essential part of human rights. In this sense, the state of minority rights in the countries of Central and Eastern Europe is an indicator of democratic consolidation. The experience of the new EU member states shows that the accession process provides a unique opportunity of pushing the agenda of minority protection forward. This opportunity has been used in a number of ways, but it could have been used better. The challenge for the future will be to keep the spotlight on the state of minority rights in Central and Eastern Europe. This book is a first modest step in this direction.

References

Coppieters, B., Emerson, M., Huysseune, M., Kovziridze, T., Noutcheva, G., Tocci, N. and Vahl, M. (2004) *Europeanization and Conflict Resolution: Case Studies from the European Periphery*, Gent: Academia Press.

Estonian Ministry of Foreign Affairs (2008) *Population by Nationality*. Online, available at: www.vm.ee/estonia/kat_399/pea_172/4305.html%20-%20Estonia% 20in%202006 (accessed 23 February 2008).

European Commission (2004) *The Situation of Roma in an enlarged European Union*, Brussels: European Commission.

European Union Agency for Fundamental Rights (2007) *Report on Racism and Xenophobia in the Member States of the EU*, Vienna: European Union Agency for Fundamental Rights.

European Union Network of Experts in Fundamental Rights (2004) Report on the Situation of Fundamental Rights in the European Union for 2003, Brussels: European Union Network of Experts in Fundamental Rights.

Hollo, L. (2006) *Equality for Roma in Europe. A Roadmap for Action*, New York: Open Society Institute.

Kymlicka, W. (2006) 'The evolving basis of European norms of minority rights: Rights to culture, participation and autonomy', in J. McGarry and M. Keating (eds) *European Integration and the Nationalities Question*, London and New York: Routledge, 35–63.

—— (2007) *Multicultural Odysseys: Navigating the New International Politics of Diversity*, Oxford: Oxford University Press.

McGarry, J., Keating, M., Moore, M. (2006) 'Introduction: European integration and the nationalities question', in J. McGarry and M. Keating (eds) *European Integration and the Nationalities Question*, London and New York: Routledge, 1–20.

Naturalization Board of the Republic of Latvia (2008) *Facts and statistics on residents*. Online, available at: www.np.gov.lv/index.php?en=fakti_en&saite=residents.htm (accessed 23 February 2008).

Rorke, B. and Wilkens, A. (eds) (2006) *Roma Inclusion: Lessons Learned from OSI's Roma Programming*, New York: Open Society Institute.

Toggenburg, G.N. (2004) 'Minority Protection in a Supranational Context: Limits and Opportunities', in G.N. Toggenburg (ed.) *Minority Protection and the Enlarged European Union: The Way Forward*, Budapest: Open Society Institute, 1–36.

Index

For Product Safety Concerns and Information please contact our EU
representative GPSR@taylorandfrancis.com
Taylor & Francis Verlag GmbH, Kaufingerstraße 24, 80331 München, Germany